Let's START *with the* Children

Journey to St. Ann's

7/13

Let's
START
with the
Children

Journey to St. Ann's

Al Colella

with

STEVEN
LIPPINCOTT

WESTBOW
PRESS
A DIVISION OF THOMAS NELSON

WestBow Press books may be ordered through booksellers or by contacting:

WestBow Press
A Division of Thomas Nelson
1663 Liberty Drive
Bloomington, IN 47403
www.westbowpress.com
1-(866) 928-1240

ISBN: 978-1-4497-7891-0 (sc)
ISBN: 978-1-4497-7892-7 (hc)
ISBN: 978-1-4497-7890-3 (e)

Library of Congress Control Number: 2012923709

Printed in the United States of America

WestBow Press rev. date: 1/9/2013

"<u>ALL</u> CHILDREN ARE IMPORTANT – NO EXCEPTIONS!"

Dedication

This book, our prayers, our efforts are faithfully and most respectfully dedicated to Mother Martha, the disadvantaged children, the children who overcome their disadvantages, the children who are rising above their disadvantages and especially those children who 'never' have a chance. An equal measure of acknowledgement is due to all those 'voices' for humanity- past, present and future-and their listeners who readily 'stepped up to the-plate'.

In his own words.... :

"It has been my pleasure to read a draft of Al Colella's book, *Let's Start With The Children,* which is an inspiring account of the efforts of many members of St. John's Episcopal Church of Barrington, Rhode Island. Joining with the parishioners of St. Ann's Church in the South Bronx, they have worked for many years to help African-American and Hispanic children of that parish. Colella's writing, which ranges widely, makes clear the genesis and development of their efforts in response to the long-standing disadvantages of the inner city.

The book is smoothly written and covers a great deal of ground from the slave trade years until today. I was taken most by the stories and reflections by and about the inner city children particularly those that reveal how very unaware they are of the larger world and the opportunities there. Reflections by both parishioners as well as by the children themselves from both communities are especially interesting and moving, revealing the many beneficial results of these efforts.

The premise of the book-and its title-is that the young children are [1] least defined, relatively, by the inner city environment and [2] are, probably, the most receptive candidates for a change in the direction of their lives.

The author also addresses the subject of the 'costs' of inner city residency both in human and dollar terms; specifically, the 'costs' of 'doing business as usual' far exceed those of a sustained and meaningful solution imbedded within a national, political and social will and commitment."

James T. Patterson, professor of history, emeritus, Brown University

Author of *Freedom Is Not Enough*-THE MOYNIHAN REPORT and AMERICA'S STRUGGLE over BLACK FAMILY LIFE from LBJ to OBAMA [Basic Books, New York, 2010]

Table of Contents

CHAPTER 17

Chapter 18

Chapter 19

Chapter 20

Prologue

The story to follow is a living fabric that has its genesis in the abundance of available literature addressing the innate damages to the humanity of inner city residents. This array of writings, commentary and books addressed the needs of both adults and especially children who are disadvantaged for life because of their birthplace and their younger years in a segregated environment that also earned the infamous label of 'third world equivalence' and all of its innate disadvantages. One would think that, in the current year of 2012, decades after the civil rights movement of the 1960s and more than nearly a century and a half after the *Emancipation Proclamation*, some significant measure of progress would have been made to alleviate these disadvantages that have a life-long impact upon the lives and wholeness of the children. However, history and experience has depicted not only little improvement but, perhaps, a worsening situation. One reference-one of many-that, in the opinion of this author, that certainly stands out from the *very representative* reservoir of relevant literature is Patterson's *Freedom Is Not Enough-The Moynihan Report and America's Struggle Over Black Family Life from LBJ To* Obama. The story within - this special fabric - is also made up of the threads of human kindness and goodness, individual and collective spiritual journeys, the belief that life itself is a unique gift, a sharing of a myriad gifts of this life with those in need, a collateral passion [aka 'the fire in one's belly'], thanksgiving, a perseverance of character that overcomes these unsought and undeserved disadvantages, faith in a greater power,........, a societal mandate as well as a moral and spiritual mandate. This story certainly provides an answer to that age-old question: "What is the real meaning of life?" It is a story of inspiration, making a difference, mutual enrichment of those in need and those who choose to serve. It is history. More importantly, it is a story of humanity and human goodness. It is a love story. It can also serve as a moral compass. *It is a spiritual journey for all involved!*

This book embraces a continuing journey that was and remains characterized by so many unexpected but wonderful outcomes. When the road had became so challenging and even threatening, something totally unexpected would take place that made the road smooth and clear again. More than several times one could hear the expression "Isn't that amazing?" Of course, more than several times many others were all thinking "Hmmmm! It's really the power of the spirit of *Amazing Grace!*".

Every story throughout the ages starts with a 'philosophy': a setting of the stage, some necessary background, a relevant context et al that seems to transition the story from one of interest to a unique and enduring meaningfulness. Parents, grandparents, teachers, professors, mentors, advocates and others have always employed, often very creatively, a 'philosophy' as a launching pad for their respective stories. For example, there was a brilliant university professor that always opened his lectures and seminars with a 'philosophy' that, for most listeners, seemed to be abstract, unrelated and irrelevant to the expected specific lecture or seminar topic. Of course, an individual would have had to experience this strategy once, several or even more times before recognizing the linkage between the professor's 'philosophy' and its enabling power for the full meaning, depth and impact of a specific topic or 'story' that would soon follow. This acknowledgement, this appreciation, this recognition was never an *a priori* experience. Rather it was always a retroactive process and could be better characterized as 'lessons learned'. Simply put, the depth, comprehension and insight into the story realities could never be fully realized without the 'philosophy' provided by the professor as a requisite foundation. His 'philosophy' was sort of a roadmap or GPS system into that learning process and moral compass embedded in the story. Most novitiates might think or say "Why is he telling us this?" or "Why don't we just move right to the story itself?" in much the same fashion that the readers of this story may do quite soon.

Chapter 1

Introduction: Historical Context & Background

One of the historical and always continuing proud legacies of America is its prompt and compassionate response to those in need; as a starting point there is the inscription at the base of the Statue of Liberty:

"Not like the brazen giant of Greek fame.
With conquering limbs astride from land to land.
Here at our sea-washed, sunset gates shall stand
A mighty woman with a torch, whose flame
Is the imprisoned lightning, and her name
Mother of Exiles. From her beacon-hand
Glows world-wide welcome; her mild eyes command
The air-bridged harbor that twin cities frame.
"Keep ancient lands, your storied pomp!" cries she
With silent lips. "Give me your tired, your poor,
Your huddled masses yearning to breathe free,
The wretched refuse of your teeming shore.
Send these, the homeless, tempest-tossed to me,
I lift my lamp beside the golden door!"

[Emma Lazarus, early 1900s]

The essence of this inscription has transcended into compassionate activities on the national level but so many, many more at the local and community levels. Compassion and a willing and generous service have earned their rightful place in the American legacy and landscape. This great country takes its place in history via the simply outstanding and unique resources of a diverse population brought about by the waves of immigrants first from Europe and, then, from all corners of the world. The remarkable success of these equally remarkable immigrants had many contributing factors, e.g., the Constitution [a document, incidentally, that recognizes the ***humanity*** of every individual-no exceptions], personal initiatives and ambitions, family and community advocacy, etc. Each entering population was armed with not only a self-advocacy but also an environmental advocacy; in short, it had a 'voice': sometimes its own and usually from their respective family, local and national resources but, always, a 'voice'. This concept of having a 'voice' was, is and always will be an enabling factor for meaningful success in America. As time marched on over the last several centuries, the plight and 'voice' of some African-Americans for whom America's promise of opportunity for every individual has fallen by the wayside-even pushed to the wayside.

One very relevant example of some added clarity and understanding of a 'voice' was eloquently provided by the author John Grisham's 2010 commencement address, ***Find a Voice***, at the University of North Carolina at Chapel Hill. Grisham referred to "The most difficult task facing a writer is to find a voice in which to tell the story." He also talks about "The voice of change, the voice of compassion, the voice of the future, the voice of his generation, the voice of her people. We hear this all the time. Voices, not words." Grisham then encourages those 2010 graduates to find a voice. This is certainly true and appropriate for themselves so that they may be heard. But what of those who don't have a 'voice' and, therefore are not heard. Their situation is aggravated significantly when one considers that for what little voice they have, there are no listeners. Fortunately, there have been some 'voices' throughout history that have risen above the noise and deafening silence of those who chose to remain silent. This unique principle of [1] speaking out for those who cannot and [2] for giving voice to those who simply do not have a 'voice' has become a valued earmark of the American landscape. Today, America is rich with those 'voices' of compassion and awareness for disenfranchised groups and populations, e.g., the disabled, the elderly, veterans, the physical and mentally ill, the disadvantaged, the abused et al but, today, especially the children of the inner-cities of America. The immeasurable value of these 'voices' is firmly imbedded in that closely-linked societal triad of awareness, compassion and, inevitably, action to right the wrong, to correct the injustice and to recognize the rights of every human being. However, in those dark days for those four centuries of slave trade, there was almost a total absence of 'voices' for the victims of the slave-based economies of the Atlantic. Fortunately, then and now, there are shining exceptions to this particularly sad situation. One of the earlier 'voices' was that of President Theodore Roosevelt on October 16, 1901 when the President heard that Booker T. Washington would be in Washington, DC. The President had some initial but very short-lived reluctance to issuing a dinner invitation to a black man. President Roosevelt did not really accept the common belief that blacks were innately inferior to 'whites'. His beliefs were in direct contrast to the lingering societal attitudes toward blacks. An excerpt from *Theodore Rex* [Edmund Morris, 2001, Random House] offers the following: 'The President felt entirely at ease "so natural and proper" to have Washington wield his silver. Here, dark and dignified among the paler company, was living proof of what he had always preached: that Negroes could rise to the social heights, at least on an individual basis. Collective equality was clearly out of the question, given their perceived "natural limitations" to the evolutionary scheme of things.' However, Morris's book addresses the reaction of the Negro community, e.g., "Greatest step for the race in a generation." and favorable reactions from that very limited population of whites with a tendency toward liberal instincts. However, the cruel, racist and inhuman reaction that rolled like thunder across America made the most noise! This thunderstorm would continue to show its ugly face throughout most of the twentieth century. However, most Americans can readily cite Abraham Lincoln and his Executive Order of January 1, 1863, known as the ***Emancipation Proclamation,*** which was the initial step in America toward 'freeing the slaves'. Actually, though, only some of the slaves but additional federal and state actions subsequently made it the law of this land for all its citizens. This law was certainly a necessary one in terms of 'talking the talk' but the nation has always struggled and delayed itself with 'walking the walk'. It is interesting to note that an important 'piece' of the American heritage of 'freedom for all' had its genesis years before the Emancipation Proclamation of 1863. Ironically enough, it was in England, one of the major players in the slave trade. It came in the person of William Wilberforce [1759-1833]. He was a British politician, a philanthropist and leader of the movement to address and abolish England's role in the slave-based economy. He became an evangelical Christian and made lifestyle changes including concern for social reform. He became the spokesman for a group of anti-slave-trade activists who, individually and collectively, were really the 'voice' of the slaves. It was this band of activists that enabled and encouraged William Wilberforce to take up the flag and cause of freedom for the slaves and, in doing so, a strong 'voice' and an advocate for abolition were born. He became one of the leading English abolitionists and fueled the parliamentary efforts to abolition slavery within the English empire. His efforts consumed 26 years of his life until the Slave Trade Act of 1807 was finally passed. This incredible 26 year delay was a direct result of Parliamentary unwillingness to react to what should have been an obvious social and very inhumane disease. His efforts still continued beyond 1807 and eventually led to the total abolition of slavery and the Slavery Abolition Act of 1833 which became effective days before his death. Appendix A offers a very poignant biography of William Wilberforce. His life also brings to the forefront the contemporary term *political will*: its meaning, value and relevance! In retrospect, the actions of those abolition activists in 18th and 19th century England gives a crystal clear definition to the term of *political will.*

Conversely, the lack of a political will not only by activist groups but also by those who have political position, influence and power inevitably delays progress on most quite obvious societal issues, problems and concerns. One can ask: "What is it that makes the lack of political will so prevalent in the face of those obvious inhumanities imposed upon any group or population?" The answer, perhaps, is that other concerns, issues and matters are so willingly given a significantly higher-indeed, a much higher-priority. Concerns, issues and matters such as greed, profit, power, position, comfort and so on come to mind but the most dominant factor is the inability and/or unwillingness to see the humanity of those on the lower end of the ladder of priority. Some call this a form of denial. Call it *denial and a blindness of personal, social and human responsibility!*

Of course, the population of concern, at that time and for the decades to follow, was most of the African-American population. This particular population is also imbedded within the story of this book. Despite those legal actions for the freedom of all slaves-essentially, this African-American population, true freedom was not forthcoming

4

for a "long, long time" [as another 'voice', Dr. Martin Luther King, Jr. told the nation-100 years after *the Emancipation Proclamation*- at the Washington Monument].

One of the impacts of the *Emancipation Proclamation* is offered from a Library of Congress Resource Guide for the Study of Black History & Culture; specifically, the migration of the African-American population is summarized with the following excerpt:

'When the Emancipation Proclamation was signed less than 8 percent of the African-American population lived in the Northeast and Midwest. Even by 1900, approximately 90 percent of all African-Americans still resided in the South. However, migration from the South has long been a significant feature of black history. An early exodus from the South occurred between 1879 and 1881, when about 60,000 African-Americans moved into Kansas and others settled in the Oklahoma Indian Territories in search of social and economic freedom.

In the early decades of the twentieth century, movement of blacks to the North increased tremendously. The reasons for this "Great Migration", as it came to be called, are complex. Thousands of African-Americans left the South to escape sharecropping, worsening economic conditions and the lynch mob. They sought higher wages, better homes, and political rights. Between 1940 and 1970 continued migration transformed the country's African-American population from a predominantly southern rural group to a northern urban one.

The movement of African-Americans within the United States continues today. Further research in the Library's general and special collections could help assess how migration affected social and economic changes in individual cities, towns, neighborhoods, and even families.'

A more detailed and personalized view of this "Great Migration" is offered in *The Warmth of Other Suns* [Isabel Wilkerson]; a recent review by Adam Bradley follows:

'They came from Natchez and Eustis and Port Arthur and Selma. They rode the rails, drove new Buicks and old Packard's, whatever it took to cover those hundreds of miles. Their journeys ended in New York and Chicago and Detroit and Los Angeles. This great migration, as historians would come to call it, saw millions of Black Americans relocate from the rural South to the Urban North and West between 1910 and 1970, reshaping the nation's cultural, political and social landscape in the span of a lifetime.

In *The Warmth of Other Suns,* Isabel Wilkerson has rendered the most sweeping, most moving record of the great migration to date. It is at once history told on a grand scale-like Taylor Branch's civil rights era trilogy-and biography written with a quality perhaps only available to a child of the Migration itself. Wilkerson, a Pulitzer Prize-winning journalist, now professor of Journalism and Director of Narrative Nonfiction at Boston University has synthesized a staggering amount of material, comprising 1,200 interviews with migrants conducted over ten years as well as countless archival documents and newspaper reports. She argues that the great migration is "the most underreported story of the twentieth century," an historical turning point that would "transform urban America and recast the social and political order of every city it touched."

The roots of 21st century racial inequality, Wilkerson argues, pass directly through the Great migration. New arrivals from the South faced lower wages and higher rents, economic exploitation and continued segregation, setting up a cycle of inequality that became a birthright to their children and their children's children. "Multiplied over the generations," Wilkerson writes, "it would seem a wealth deficit between the races that would require a miracle windfall or near asceticism on the part of [black] families if they were to have any chance of catching up or amassing anything of value."

The Warmth of Other Suns, however, is more narrative than polemic. Wilkerson grounds her book in the life stories of three migrants-Ida Mae Glade, Robert Foster, and George Starling-each of whom, she explains "left different parts of the South during different decades for different reasons and with different outcomes." She takes us into places that few writers have gone: the sharecropper's day of reckoning with the white planter; the Pullman porter's deft handling of a potentially incendiary racial confrontation; the citrus picker's last minute escape from the lyncher's rope.

In her loving projections of the internal lives of her subjects, Wilkerson takes us beyond the shock of racism to a kind of nostalgia for a type of black experience that may have only existed under segregation. This experience is, of course, shot through with peril-the arbitrary horror of racial violence, the everyday privation of life under Jim Crow-but nonetheless suffused with richness: the warmth of close communities, the sweet pleasures of companionship and music and laughter. Finally, Wilkerson's narrative is not a tale of loss but a life-affirming portrait of endurance and transcendence of simple acts done with deliberate intent.

One hesitates to describe a book that stretches beyond 700 pages as vigorously paced, but that is precisely what Wilkerson has achieved. Short sections comprised of shorter chapters that alternate among her three subjects generate and sustain a crisp narrative momentum. This patchwork structure, however, occasionally comes at a cost. In particular, the numerous epigraphs that introduce both the book's parts and its chapters [there are a staggering forty-seven epigraphs in all] soon come off more like impediments than insights. Nonetheless, such minor narrative detours finally serve to remind us that only a chorus of voices could make such a book possible.

The Warmth of Other Suns is an impassioned history, by turns sweeping and specific, celebratory and shocking. Like a literary companion to the artist Jacob Lawrence's Migration series, it tells the story of the Great Migration in terms both vibrant and bold. It is a history not of power barons and political leaders, but of everyday people whose individual acts of bravery and self-assertion combined to reshape a nation. Wilkerson has done an invaluable service to all those who would resist the slow creep of historical amnesia, particularly when it comes to the most painful details of our national life. This is a book that enacts the very thing it describes; like the brave lives of the people she writes about, it is a testimony, a challenge, and a time reminder of our still unfulfilled promise of a more perfect union.'

Summarily, then, it became quite clear that [1] Wilkerson wrote her book through the lens of humanity and [2] there exists a strong resonance between the humanity, spirit,' voice', intent and meaning of her book and this one as well as those other 'voices' of the past and present.

For a number of formidable reasons, this African-American population remained in a virtual prison of poverty, racism, plight and lack of that opportunity available to other ethnic populations. In his article, ***The Caging of America***, in The New Yorker, [January 31, 2012] Adam Gopnik addresses some aspects of real incarceration in America and reminds the readers that 'More than half of all black men without a high-school diploma go to prison at some time in their lives.' It is so ironic that the lack of an education is linked to another type of education that one receives in prison. Of course, there are those who still maintain that the

African-Americans [largely direct descendants of the 19th century slave population] could, after all, simply 'pick themselves up by their bootstraps' as other ethnic groups did?.......and why don't they? Without exception, other ethnic groups had several common threads that were positively and rigorously sewn into their fabric of success; amongst these threads were family wholeness and its support, guidance and advocacy for the importance and criticality of 'an education' that simply wasn't available to America's first-generation immigrants but they clearly understood its intrinsic value. This knowledge was entered into the family hierarchy and was passed on to the children of immigrants [non-slaves] by their parents and grandparents. This family advocacy was and still is a key ingredient for personal progress in America including a relatively small number of African-Americans. Indeed, these successful exceptions stand as a model for the intelligence, creativity and upward mobility innate to the overall African-American population; indeed, to all ethnic populations without exception. Also, it is interesting to note that Harlem was and is again becoming a community of stability, culture, upward mobility and opportunity for its residents. It is a more comprehensive model for those resources available in any community-regardless of ethnic orientation. However, this advocacy and enabling environment simply were not present in most of the African-American population and, when it tried to take root and develop there, it was usually discouraged both in subtle and often brutal fashions. One could ask "Where were the African-American families in this scenario?" The simple answer is that the African-American family structure was essentially obliterated in the period from the 15th century to the 19th century due to the enormously popular and profitable *slave trade* that was used to fuel the economies of the Atlantic Ocean communities. The *Slave Ship: A Human History* by Marcus Rediker [2007] is representative of the documentation that addresses the tragedy and horror of slaves for those four centuries; the author makes a strong case that the violence of this trade was no accident but was central to the rise of global capitalization. The truth is overwhelming: families were taken from Africa, separated there and throughout the passage to and their social imprisonment in America; millions died and were cast into the sea; family structures, essentially, became non-existent! This absence of traditional family structures has had a debilitating social, economic and educational impact that continues today. The plight of the African-American and the African-American family is unique. In this context, then, there was *an absence of the ability to see and understand the humanity of the African-American slaves. Simply put, they were a depersonalized 'commodity' in the growing agricultural and industrial economies of the Atlantic neighborhood.*

History-then and now-has abundantly demonstrated that this strange malady of blindness to the humanity of an individual has inevitably led to racism, ethnic abuse and cleansing, human trafficking, oppression, physical and virtual imprisonment et al. This malady of blindness inevitably leads to the degradation of the human spirit and the intrinsic value of the human being. The plight of the African-American community is powerfully symbolic of the linkage of this blindness [aka total insensitivity] to the humanity of the individual and their populations and the consequential and simply enormous and immeasurable human cost and its longevity! An example of this 'blindness/insensitivity' can be found in ***The Forgotten Man: A New History of the Great Depression*** by Amity Shlaes [2008]. Although this book addresses so many who were so tragically affected by the great depression and the resultant hardships of life in America in the 1930s, one of the most significantly forgotten individuals is the African-American. Shlaes writes about these years as the years of Franklin Delano Roosevelt's New Deal and its linkage to the chaos of the depression. However, imbedded within this book, is a powerful reminder of the 'failure to see the humanity' [aka ***the lack of political will***] of the American Negro [a term used in that era]; as the Congress struggled with the economic and political issues of those years, it also failed *repeatedly* to pass legislation that would have outlawed, forbidden and illegalized the act of lynching a Negro. Again, what is now viewed as what could and should have been an obvious social and humanitarian step forward for America, it was 'taken off the table' for issues and actions more important than humanity of an entire ethnic population. Once again, the malady of social blindness, i.e., the sheer inability to see the humanity of another human being, raised its ugly head. History is a wonderful and rich-in-information arena; history provides the answers to those questions that address the reasons and rationale for a particular social situation. Simply put "How did this come about?", "What caused this to happen?" or "Who is responsible for this mess?" are questions common throughout history. An additional reference point, for those who are doubtful and/or dismissive about 'this mess', that provides some insight into the plight of the American Negro as recent as the 1950s and 1960s can be found in ***Black Like Me*** [Howard

Griffin, 1959].Decades more would pass before the nation's social sight would be more significantly restored in the late 1950s and more robustly in the 1960s. A more balanced and hopeful view of the Congress is found throughout its years of existence but the one source that I have commonly cited for those politicians who have demonstrated a need for social sight improvement is ***Profiles in Courage*** by John F. Kennedy [1955]. It is a prize-winning biography describing acts of principle, bravery and integrity by eight United States senators who risked their political lives in doing so.

The references being cited certainly do not constitute a comprehensive list but they are of the utmost relevance; they collectively and accurately represent a meaningful historical perspective and an appropriate background and context for this book. As the country was developing and enacting the civil-rights legislation of the 1960s, another 'voice' stepped forth. It was the voice of Daniel Patrick Moynihan who was President Johnson's Assistant Secretary of Labor. In 1965, Daniel Patrick Moynihan released a government report [from the Office of Policy Planning and Research of the United States Department of Labor] addressing the plight of lower-class black life in America. This report was entitled ***The Negro Family: The Case for National Action*** [1965]. Being a relatively 'new voice', there were the usual controversial overtones ranging from 'a new refreshing look at the devastated and still declining African-American family situation' to 'those who considered the report to be a very negative-even racist-report on the black family'. The positive essence of this report was readily cited by President Johnson at the commencement exercise at Howard University on June 4, 1965. The President indicated that despite the passage of the Civil Rights Act of 1964, it simply wasn't enough. Years-even decades and centuries-of injustice, racism, personal degradation, economic deprivation and a host of foregone opportunities and resultant immeasurable human cost could not simply be erased with the stroke of a pen-***but it was a starting point!*** In retrospect one does not need to be a social scientist or a proverbial rocket scientist to recognize and understand that what took years, decades and centuries to create would most certainly take a significantly long time to resolve. This perception, this belief is directly and emphatically not consistent with America's love affair with 'quick solutions'. A reference to these times of creation and solution was made by Dr. Martin Luther King, Jr. in his address at the Annie Merner Pfeiffer Chapel at Bennett College in Greensboro, North Carolina on February

11, 1958. The violence, threats and intimidations of those times gave rise to a hesitancy by many to have Dr. King as a speaker. However, Dr. Wlla Player, then the President of Bennett College, said "This is a liberal arts school where freedom rings. So Martin Luther King, Jr. can speak here." ***Dr. King's pointed reference was "We have come a long, long way but we have a long, long, l-o-n-g way to go!"*** Moynihan's report, however, fueled hope anew that this nation could and would do something. Expectations for forward social action and progress then reached new heights in the 1960s but would wither with time and the advent of other national and global events and, of course, that nemesis of a renewed blindness to the human conditions of most African-Americans in America. Then forty years later, some writings, commentary and books reminded the nation that the overall situation for most inner-city African-Americans was not getting better but was actually worsening. Then, a few years later James T. Patterson, an acclaimed historian and a professor emeritus at Brown University, took a reflective look at Moynihan's report in his book ***Freedom Is Not Enough***. Initially, Moynihan's report was considered controversial for shedding light upon an area that that most avoided, i.e., the plight of African-Americans in the inner-cities of America. However, Patterson commended Moynihan not so much for providing a solution but for raising the issue. Patterson said as he referenced Moynihan not for saying "This is what we must do!" but rather advocating that something needs to be done. An article in the Providence Journal [June 27, 2010] reviews Patterson's book [Appendix B].

Patterson's book, *Freedom Is Not Enough, "The Moynihan Report and America's Struggle over Black Family Life from LBJ to Obama"*, makes reference to the fact that the principal ethnic groups of New York City maintained a time-varying 'identity' based on values, faith, family structure et al. However, this 'identity' for most inner-city African-Americans was and remains poverty-driven and lacking in an integral family structure enjoyed by other ethnic populations. Patterson also references "the condition of the Negro family where the cycle of poverty is transferred from one generation to the next." This author respectfully adds that the developed poverty-driven culture of inner-city life was also passed on from one generation to another. There exists a spectrum of factors that imprison the inner-city families in this cycle of poverty and persistent disenabling culture. Moynihan has emphatically put forth both historical and now contemporary barometers that characterize and even quantify the disadvantages of much of the African-American population. Even in contemporary times there are indicators that reflect a continuing disadvantage to some upward mobile African-Americans. For example, Sandra Block's article *Pulling Funds From 401[k] May Hurt Later,* in USA Today {April 3, 2012], shows that 401[k] loans, in general have increased from 2007 to 2010. However, the increase for 'whites' and 'Asians' has been 26% and 22%, respectively, while the increase for African-Americans and Hispanics has been 49% and 40%, respectively. Hardly indicating a level playing field! A relevant question, then, may be "Why is the journey of inner-city African-Americans and Hispanics so much more difficult for them compared to other ethnic populations?"

The Providence Journal review was followed by another on July 18, 2010 by Kevin Boyle in the Washington Post. Boyle's review clearly reminds us of the facts of the disintegration of traditional family life of blacks. For example, Boyle reports that "the conflict so scarred liberals that for almost 20 years they refused to acknowledge the crisis in inner-city life." Only in the mid-1980s did they begin to change their minds; a transformation led by social scientists like William Julius Wilson, who wrote in his brilliant 1987 book, that Moynihan's analysis had been "prophetic." In addition to the historical perspective and background presented to this point, there is one other 'piece' or 'thread' that contributes to the completeness, understanding and meaningfulness of this story. It is yet another 'voice'! Appendix A certainly offers a more detailed account of and abundant relevant references to the years surrounding the turn of the 18th century into the 19th century and England's role in the abolition of slavery. The missing 'piece' refers to the hymn, *Amazing Grace*, one of a number of hymns contributed by John Newton at that time. Ironically, Newton was an active player in the slave trade but his growing belief in a greater power- in God- moved him to rethink his earlier views of his role in the slave trade. Simply put, he acquired a new vision for the humanity of slaves; he saw them as more than economical commodities to fuel a global economy. This vision and his compassion were translated into his orders to treat the slaves under his care in a more humane manner. John Newton, slave-trader, writer of hymns, became an advisor and mentor to William Wilberforce and his parliamentary efforts to abolish slavery. Could this relationship have been a mere coincidence? The tune of the hymn, *Amazing Grace*, some say, can be so appropriately traced back to a Negro spiritual; this hymn has become enormously prevalent and popular in faith communities. It has become an iconic symbol for faith in a greater power, in God, especially in difficult, challenging and hopeless times and situations. There is a movie [2007] also entitled ***Amazing Grace*** that received nothing less than national acclaim and outstanding reviews for its historical and factual content; it is emotional, inspirational, historical and a story of 'making a difference-a huge difference'. The hymn is really about the presence of a greater power, God, and this theme is reflected within the movie. It is the theme that took on an increasingly greater omnipresence, realization and meaning in the journey to St. Ann's Episcopal Church in the South Bronx'.

The context for this story is nearly complete! The initial impetus for embarking on this journey was twofold: [1] the belief within the St. John's body of parishioners [in Barrington, RI] that service to others is not a convenience-driven option but it is a societal, moral and spiritual mandate and [2] an awareness of the needs of the children-indeed, the entire St. Ann's community-within the poverty-driven and disheartening environment of the South Bronx. The journey then became a willing, enthusiastic and natural response to and union of these two factors. There will be the inevitable questions by some of the readers, as it has been for some of those observers of the journeys to the South Bronx, e.g., "Why the South Bronx?" The answer to this particular question will manifest itself throughout the book but, at this point, the short answer is "Why not!" As a sort of compass for the reader, one must remember that the situation for the inner-city African-Americans-indeed for all those slaves and most of their descendants-really took centuries to develop; the 'solution', if you will, will take a long, long, l-o-n-g time! The development of the inner-city situations throughout America is really a complex and complicated historical mosaic. There are a multitude of factors involved, e.g., the construction of parkways, expressways and highways served to isolate segments of a community. One only has to read ***The Power Broker: Robert Moses and the Fall of New York City*** [Robert Caro, 1974, Knopf] to [1] gain an appreciation that the parkways, boulevards and expressways in New York City were intended to provide direct access to the greater New York City but also had the collateral impact of isolation for some communities. It is true that Robert Moses was creative and innovative with a 'systems' [aka 'big picture'] mindset. However, his consideration of the inner-city poor, especially Negroes, raises the possibility of incompetence, insensitivity to their human condition and/or racism. Consider his planning for parks:

amongst his many interests and ambitions was his goal of a network of state parks. From Caro's book: "Moses had been uninterested in building for the 'lower classes.' He was still uninterested-although he was building parks in the city, where those classes lived." His inner-city 'park program' was a huge failure because parks were not being provided for the inner-city dwellers that had the greatest need for them. Again, from Caro's book on page 490: "The protests about this policy from the slums themselves were faint and few: slum dwellers-particularly slum dwellers with black skins-weren't making many protests in the 1930s. But some reformers raised their voices on their behalf." Another factor is that the populations of these physically 'isolated' areas found themselves on the 'forgotten' list of services and the 'remembered' list of neglects. I have heard the term *'the political construction of the inner-cities'* more than several times; I also believe that it has both relevance and credibility. This mosaic is certainly more than that 'straight-line-model' relating slavery to the inner-city morass. However, this somewhat simplistic model is not intended to deny or to minimize history but it does have relevance and significance. The cause-and-effect between slavery and the inner-city situation of so many African-Americans cannot be denied or minimized either. The 'solution' will require the efforts of many throughout an equally l-o-n-g duration of time. One of the more profound realizations that surfaced during this journey to the St. Ann's community in the South Bronx is that 'we must start with the children there'. If those with a faith and a [political] will sustain their collective efforts, then these children and their children and, then, their children in the South Bronx [and, of course, elsewhere] will also move beyond all those economic, health, educational and environmental walls of the inner-city. The spirit of *Amazing Grace* has made some progress in this direction possible and, perhaps, just perhaps, that ripple of progress can grow and continue into the future generations of children. As the third stanza in the hymn reminds us: It's Grace that brought me safe thus far and Grace will lead me home'.

Although this background, this context was written earlier in 2011, there is an even more recent [Providence Journal, 3/26/11] reference to the slave trade and its long-term impact upon the integrity and wholeness of African-Americans. Ruth Simmons, President of Brown University provided some powerful insight and comment at a recent [3/25/11] United Nations event. Specifically, she mentioned the following: [1] "nations permitted the systematic destruction" of not just lands and families but languages, religions and histories; [2] those efforts that are a "constant reminder" of the slave trade will give 'voices' and faces to those who suffered and help world leaders deal with other forms of contemporary slavery. Also, she said "We feel that the stories need to be told because the lessons from our past inform the present, and will most certainly influence the future." The latter factor is a statement by Jamaica's U.N. ambassador, Raymond O. Wolfe. This Providence Journal article is included in its entirety in Appendix E.

Chapter 2
Author's Perspective

Having provided somewhat of a historical context and foundation for this book, it only seems appropriate to provide a collateral context for the mindset of the author. What follows is drawn from the article, ***What Feeds My Soul?,*** from the annual Lenten Reflection series of documented thoughts and experiences of some of the parishioners of St. John's Episcopal Church in Barrington, RI. In the spring of 2003, I wrote the following which includes some [minor] reflective editing:

"My shared ministry really began as a child although, at that time, I simply did not have the proverbial clue as to the reason or rationale for the full meaning of 'service to others'. However, via the advantage of hindsight and reflection, I do recall that there were feelings of pride, goodness and accomplishment whenever I was able to participate in those community and sharing efforts and events of our family and friends; particularly, when those efforts were a direct response to the needs of others. My ministry in later years included working with young adults [ages 13-16] who were preparing for confirmation in the Roman Catholic Church in our ethnically Italian community. It should not come as a surprise that these Sunday morning confirmation classes were not exactly the high point of students' weekends. Of course there was a prescribed and approved 'curriculum' but it did not provide a bridge to the real-life and spiritual needs of these young adults. I recall that my students and I entered into a contract, so to speak, that we would use the first 45 minutes to cover the approved curriculum but we would use the final 45 minutes to address, discuss and explore those topics that these young adults considered of interest and relevance to their lives at that time. Topics like relationships, issues and problems of their family members, their likes and dislikes, their perceived 'unfairness' of life [which was an opportunity to talk about 'fairness'], their fears and worries and so on were put forth and embraced with careful thought, realism and a passion; all these topics simply that didn't exist in the approved curriculum. Our shared discussions emphasized the 'gifts' and 'needs' of all people-through all time and the world and, most importantly, in each of their lives. And what a wonderful world it would be should each of us, all of us simply share our 'gifts' with those in need! This concept of having the ability, the power to help others-*as we would like to be helped* -to make a difference in the lives of others as others have made difference in ours. These discussions inevitably brought a deeper meaning to the familiar words of the golden rule.

During those years with the direction-seeking younger set [which included four daughters of my own], a simple but two very empowering paradigms emerged. Given all the rules of society, community, school, family and church et al, an individual could simply "Love God" and "Love your neighbor!" [Matthew 22:37-40, New Oxford Bible, 1991]; the linkage between these two commandments is "Whatever you do for the least of your brethren, you do for Me!" [Matthew 25:45, New Oxford Bible, 1991]. Hmmmm! What a simple but absolutely profound concept that is available to all and so easily realized-anytime, anywhere!

Additional reinforcement for this concept and spiritual tool was provided by my steadily-increasing awareness through the years and continuing today-that many individuals-some unknown to me-have shared their gifts with me in my times of need. I now understand that phrase heard so many times in so many places, i.e., "Each of us stands on the shoulders of those who came before us." I also became equally aware that 'coincidences' don't always just happen; they are a direct result of the sharing of gifts [including prayer] by others.

My awareness of the direct-and possibly rich and meaningful-relationship between 'gifts' and 'needs' is, indeed, a gift in of itself. The daily opportunities for breathing life into this relationship became more obvious with the passing years. My compassion and action radars became larger in scope and clarity! The feelings of pride, goodness and accomplishment of my early years transitioned into increased commitment, spiritual excitement and growth and life-meaningfulness as years passed. The experiences of being a community and inner-city tutor, mentor, and advocate, a Big Brother, a member of the meal-site team at the Cathedral of St. John in

Providence, RI, a volunteer at St. Paul's Chapel at Ground Zero after the 9/11 attack there, etc., etc., etc. but especially the ministry at St. Ann's in the South Bronx-*these experiences and feelings are really what feeds my soul!* It is somewhat difficult to express these feelings with words but let me try: not only do I consider the sharing of one's gifts as a Christian obligation-indeed, a moral obligation- as opposed to being an option or something to be done when it is personally convenient, I feel blessed, privileged and honored to have had the many opportunities to serve others, to "love my neighbor" and "to do for the least of my brethren". It may be helpful to note that the 'least of my brethren' does not compromise the principle that each individual was, is and will always be as important as the next. The word 'least' is not intended to detract from the humanity of the individual but rather refers to those in a state of need-indeed, a far greater state of need and, at times, those marginalized as human beings.

It is important to remember that this Lenten Reflection was written in the spring of 2003. At that time, the ministry efforts of more and more St. John's parishioners with the children and parishioners of St. Ann's Church in the South Bronx had stirred a growing interest and participation in even more St. John's parishioners of all ages. I was often asked: "What is it really like in the South Bronx?" *Let's Start With the Children* and other parallel efforts certainly provide a clear and abundant answer to that question.

However, another response-as many have experienced-is to simply say "Come and see!"[John 1:29-42] Yes, "Come and see!"[John 1:35-42, New Oxford Bible, 1991] the extraordinary goodness of others as they share their myriad gifts with their neighbors and those in a far greater need. Come, partake of the spiritual food. Come and experience the wonderful events of a ministry of your choice. Come and hear person after person after person comment "Isn't that amazing!" and then listen to those soft whispers and acknowledgements say "It's more than amazing, it's *Amazing Grace.*"

This is an additional author's note [2011]. In response to a user-interactive website that invites users' responses to a variety of posted questions. One question: *Do you sometimes have the feeling that you are part of something bigger.....greater....some big plan?* prompted a number of very interesting answers. One particular answer offers some food for thought. This answer follows: "I have these feelings very often..... everything makes sense, some mechanism, the mechanism of life, our purpose as human beings, higher consciousness....I feel it....I think we are part of something bigger, we have to travel the road here, to do as much as possible and probably advance to next levels.....when I'm connected with the higher consciousness [GOD], everything makes sense and you feel united with the universe, everything is one. What do you think about that?

Chapter 3

Some Background on St. Ann's Episcopal Church

The ***Introduction*** mentions children who are inherently disadvantaged for life by virtue of their place of birth and residence. Many authors have addressed those children within the inner cities of America, e.g., the South Bronx area of New York City, who are so disadvantaged for life because of health, economic, family, educational and high-risk environment reasons. Those children have been identified as equally disadvantaged as those children living in third world countries. There are individuals who have referred to St. Ann's Episcopal Church as 'a candle in the darkness' within this environment. The Rector, the Reverend Martha Overall, the teachers, the staff and the community volunteers have been committed for more than 16 years to providing an alternative path for the lives of those children inherently disadvantaged ***for life*** by nature of their South Bronx birthplace and its environment. For example, the percentage of children who make it to high-school and graduate with meaningful diplomas [as opposed to 'certificates of attendance' or joining the drop-out ranks] is shamefully low-very low! There have been some very modest and scattered improvements over the years but, on balance, the educational situation is still segregated, still risky and still invoking an unnecessary cost to humanity. Not only can one ask: "What will life be like for those who are ill-prepared for life rather than well-prepared as most children are but, clearly, as ***all*** American children should be?" but also "What happens to those many children who have fallen through the cracks in the floors of education and humanity?"

"What happens to those children whose only known legacy is continue to do what those children who came before them did?"

For a variety of reasons, the children of the South Bronx are especially vulnerable during the after-school and early evening hours and during the long days of the summer months. This vulnerability only serves to compound the inherent disadvantages of residency in the South Bronx. St. Ann's not only provides a safe haven during these times of high risk but also provides a supportive and constructive environment as well as an educational arena to minimize the effect of the educational disadvantages of South Bronx residency. This arena is the St. Ann's after-school program and the summer's Freedom School.

During the days and years of segregation in the South, black children went to churches after 'school' so that they could get a real education. The churches conducted what they called 'Freedom Schools' where young children were taught reading, writing and arithmetic and civics by loving members of the black community. The days of segregation-however they may have evolved in today's society-are not totally extinct. The 1990s were a decade of educational resegregation; this process still exists today. A study by the Harvard Civil Rights Projects has shown that schools in New York State [and in inner-cities elsewhere] are the most segregated in the United States. A map of the schools attended by the average black and Hispanic students would almost match perfectly a map of high poverty schools.

"The Freedom Schools were the model for the educational input St. Ann's added to its after-school and summer camp programs. So, when I learned about the Children's Defense Fund Freedom School program, it was a natural, " explained the Reverend Martha Overall, Rector at St. Ann's but aka **Mother Martha** to the entire St. Ann's community and beyond. "The Freedom School program gives our teachers the training they need, and they have a superb curriculum based on books about people our children can easily identify with." Weekly parent seminars are an integral part of the Freedom School program in order to foster the concept that education is a continuing process and that time-proven efforts of family support, participation and encouragement are such important ingredients for a meaningful and successful education. [Author's note: much like those students in middle-class and the more privileged communities of America]. As incredulous as it may seem or sound, the children do not have books of their own or ready access to them-so very different from other community environments. As a result, another priority at the Freedom

School is to establish and maintain a library for ready access and ownership of books of relevance. One of the many 'pieces' of the St. John's/St. Ann's collaboration is to provide support for and the continuing donation of literally hundreds and thousands of books; more details of this ministry component is provided in the section on *Mission Trips*.

An excerpt from the ***St. Ann's Covenant*** [Volume 16, Number 1, December 2010] provides some relevant insight into the Freedom School operations:

The summer of 2010 was St. Ann's 10th Freedom School and its best ever. Our staff was outstanding, led by Veora Layton, who teaches during the school year and hopes one day to be a minister. "The keys to our success," Veora believes, "are organization and team work, plus we added some new components for the children with music and entrepreneurship." Another staff member thought that "the children felt a new sense of responsibility and leadership this year." Yet another added, "The parents were much more involved this summer. They really appreciate the program. You can tell, because whenever feedback time comes, they always say, 'Just keep doing what you're doing.' "

Freedom School is an all day, six week summer program which teaches the children to love to read with a curriculum based on the theme "I can make a difference in myself, my family, my community, my country and my world." The program is free for the students, but attendance at a weekly parent seminar is mandatory.

A special feature of St. Ann's Freedom School is trips. We try to get the children out of the South Bronx at least once a week. This year we even took some of them to see King Tutankhamun. The cost of Freedom School to St. Ann's is over $1,600 per child for each of 100 children, but the benefits are far greater. Time Magazine recently quoted a Johns Hopkins study concluding that "...while students made similar progress during the school year regardless of economic status, the better off kids held steady or continued to make progress during the summer---but the disadvantaged kids fell back. By the end of grammar school, low income kids had fallen nearly three grade levels behind, and summer was the biggest culprit. By ninth grade, summer learning loss could be blamed for roughly two-thirds of the achievement gap separating income groups." A forthcoming section in *Potpourri* together with supportive text in Appendix D address the question: *Why 'start with the children'?*

Without question the most important goal of the ministry efforts

of St. John's is to directly support the St. Ann's goal, i.e., the practical and educational welfare of the children! It is all about:

[1]   Erasing the inherent disadvantages of birth/residency in the South Bronx.

[2]   Raising the visions, hopes, abilities and self-expectations of each child.

[3]   Equipping each child with those skills and self-confidence so necessary for success in the arena of education but also in the arena of life.

There are a number of continuing efforts at St. Ann's that enable/support this most important goal. There are significant facility maintenance and upgrading requirements in order to sustain this 'safe place, family and community outreach efforts, continuing budget challenges, training, acquisition of basic school supplies, meeting the very basic clothing requirements of the children, individuals and families within the St. Ann's circle of life.......the list is practically endless. [Author's note: the wide spectrum of efforts at St. Ann's by the St. John's community are described elsewhere in this book] ; each of these efforts has been specifically shaped to fit the needs of the St. Ann's community within the excellent and incisive guidance of Mother Martha. It is so relevant and important to acknowledge the truly remarkable leadership of Mother Martha. More will be said about Mother Martha in the next section.

Let the reader remember those words found in the *Prologue*, i.e., 'we must start with the children there.' Having said that, the very different communities of St. Ann's [inner-city] and St. John's [suburbia] have enjoyed a collaboration for more than 15 years; this team effort has resulted in a variety of special and enduring relationships with the children of St. Ann's and, in many cases, their families. As Martha Mother remarked to me in response to my comment that "It takes an entire village to raise a child!": "No, Al, it really takes two villages!" During these years, more than two hundred parishioners and friends of St. John's have made the trek to the South Bronx-some have been there once, many have been there several times or more and more-than-a-few have been there dozens of times. A related topic to be addressed elsewhere in this book is that each summer since 2002 many children from the South Bronx have made the trek to summer camps and home visits in Rhode Island. All have been there in the South Bronx and here in Rhode Island because of the shared belief in and the commitment to the children of St. Ann's. A common thread amongst these many ministry efforts is the building of relationships with the children, the mentoring of these children and the extraordinary efforts addressed to lifting their self-esteem as well as their hopes, visions, self-expectations and life skills level. ***Perhaps, it can be better said in another way with fewer words: we do what we do in order to validate the children and their humanity.*** One of the 'engines' driving this ministry is the commitment to 'making a difference' but there was, as the readers shall see in ***reflections*** from both communities, an unexpected outcome. Simply put, the members of each community, i.e., the two 'villages', have indeed made a difference in the lives of the other! Each of these two communities has lifted the other up to a much better place.

Chapter 4
Some Background on 'Mother Martha'

The Reverend Martha Overall was an outstanding student and leader at the Garrison Forest School and received her baccalaureate degree there in 1965. She is also a 2011 inductee into the Garrison Forest [GFS] School Hall of Excellence; The GFS Hall of Excellence was established by the parents and grandparents of the Class of 2000 to honor extraordinary members of the GFS community across a wide array of fields.

Martha Overall attended Radcliffe College and the New York University Law School before embarking on a thirteen year career in corporate law for major New York law firms. After caring for her dying brother, she enrolled in the Union Theological Seminary. In 1991, she entered the Episcopal priesthood. As an ordained priest, she sought the Bishop's approval for an assignment to St. Ann's Episcopal Church in the South Bronx. At that time, St. Ann's was struggling to survive as a parish and was in dire need of both practical and spiritual leadership as well as effective management. Her request was not initially approved due to the Bishop's situational perception that such an assignment was just too challenging. Following a path of persistence, self-confidence and sheer determination, The Reverend Martha Overall was appointed as Rector at St. Ann's in 1993. She is nationally recognized amongst the nation's best-known urban priests; this recognition assumes a greater significance when one considers the inner-city environment of the South Bronx in the early 1990s. 'Mother Martha' as she is known throughout the community she serves and beyond, has been the Rector of St. Ann's Episcopal Church, a historic church on St. Ann's Avenue in the South Bronx since 1993. Although her initial assignment was expected to be a year or, perhaps, several, she has been the Rector there for nearly two decades. There is no doubt that the duration of her assignment was predicated upon her sustained performance of spiritual and managerial expertise and her ability to resolve a myriad issues and community conflicts.

The *Today Show* has hailed her as 'the only light of hope the children have in the South Bronx.' She is the recipient of an honorary degree, Doctor of Divinity, from Ursinus College [2000]. The Reverend Martha Overall also received an honorary degree from Yale University's Berkeley Divinity School. She was also the recipient in 2009 of the Bishop's Cross by the Bishop of New York.

Chapter 5
Overview: 'One Ministry Begets Another'

The necessary blocks of the foundation are in place, i.e., the historical context, the author's perspective, that 'candle' called St. Ann's Episcopal Church, the willingness of the parishioners of St. John's to 'step up to the plate' and, most importantly, that spiritual mandate [1] found in those 'voices' of awareness advocacy and action that seem to surface and even rise to a level above and beyond the material and eventually meaningless values of life and [2] the innate ability and passion of the Reverend Martha Overall to give life and meaning to this spiritual mandate.

The condensed version of this book, i.e., a 'snapshot' of the earlier years of this ministry that built upon these foundational blocks follows:

'One Ministry Begets Another' [2004]

Throughout the years since the civil rights movement of the 1960s, a number of authors have focused a revealing light upon the plight of disadvantaged children throughout the world via a series of absolutely compelling books about these children some of whom have residence in the United States of America. They can be found in so many of the inner-cities of America. Barbara Ehrenreich, in one of her book reviews, comments that "one author reminds us that, with each casualty, part of the beauty of the world is extinguished, because these are children of intelligence and humor, of poetic insight and luminous faith. This particular review addresses a book that is written in a gentle and measured tone, but you will wonder at the end why the God of love does not return to earth with his avenging sword in hand."

This extremely challenging ministry at St. Ann's-but an absolutely wonderful and rich ministry-offers a safe place, a respectful place, a haven amongst the chaos and risks associated with an inner-city, third world equivalent ghetto. These multiple disadvantages are economic, health, educational, quality of life,....and, in aggregate form, a loss of their sense of wholeness, hope and humanity. All of the children at St. Ann's are Hispanic or African-American. Mother Martha's ministry is performed with minimum resources that are hardly ever sufficient to cope with the daily demands and needs of more than 100 children [and often their families] as well as members of the greater St. Ann's community. This ministry was brought to the attention of the St. John's community by The Reverend Shirley Andrews, Associate Rector there. The Outreach Team of St. John's Church in Barrington, RI has been proactively and passionately involved in the development and practice of its commitment to 'making a difference' for those who are less blessed and less fortunate in their arena of life. The ministry of the Reverend Martha Overall has served as the 'fuel' and motivation for the engine of the St. John's Outreach Team. The genesis of this effort lies in their commitment to 'making a difference' *and* putting their faith into action. The resultant synergism of led to some initial and modest efforts for the donation of goods, services [aka ***time, treasure and talents***]. However, this supportive outreach ministry grew in commitment and intensity during 1999 and 2000, accelerated and, then, simply shifted into a higher gear following the events of September 11, 2001. The months that followed the events of this day were serendipitous in nature; the efforts continue and grow with time due to this initial joint involvement in volunteer efforts at Ground Zero in lower Manhattan ***and*** at St. Ann's in the South Bronx.

Chapter 6
The Birth Of A Ministry

In the closing paragraphs of **Introduction: Historical Context & Background** but prior to the **Author's Perspective**, there was offered a very brief response, "Why not?" to the question, "Why go to the South Bronx?" Of course, it was also pointed out that this response receives abundant amplification, validation and meaning as the story of this book unfolds. This very brief response also has partners that provide the answers to the questions "Why do *you* go to the South Bronx?" and "Why do *you* go now?" The obvious answers are "If not *us* then who?" and "If not *now*, when?" Maybe, just maybe "It's the right thing to do!"

As a systems analyst in the professional arena, I came to understand, develop and appreciate a skill for 'connecting the dots' in order to see the relevance and full meaning of a scenario of dots, i.e. to 'see' the bigger picture, rather than to view each dot as disjointed from the others. In 2007 at commencement exercises at Stanford University, Steve Jobs, Apple CEO, mentioned that one cannot connect 'dots' forward but only backward. In similar fashion the birth of this wonderful and rich ministry-and its continuing growth and development-has its genesis and path imbedded in a number of 'dots' or events that led the parishioners of St. John's Episcopal Church to take US 95 South to St. Ann's Episcopal Church in the South Bronx. Clearly, the first 'dot' is the interest stirred up by the then-Associate Rector at St. John's, the Reverend Shirley Andrews, aka the second 'dot', had read about the conditions in the South Bronx-especially within the St. Ann's community-and brought it to the attention of the parishioners. Although it may sound somewhat unexpected at this point, the next 'dot' is that entity entitled human goodness. Some explanation is in order but we shall return to additional 'dots'. It is relevant to note that the reading of books that address the many dimensions of an individual's and their community's spirituality is an on-going process incorporating a search for the 'truth' and meaning of life, spiritual guidance, a moral compass and generous doses of personal 'reflections'. This process is a common thread through most faith communities. For example, a most meaningful example, "The word *Mitzvah* has many different meanings. It could refer to the commandments of the Torah, along with the seven rabbinic commandments." In modern society, though, Mitzvah is most often used as a term to refer *an act of kindness.* A Mitzvah is an important part of Jewish society, just as it is important with other religions and [faiths] as well. When Mitzvah is considered to be an act of human kindness, *it transcends all religions [and faiths].* While historically, Mitzvah is considered to be a term related to Judaism, anyone in any religion [or faith] can perform a Mitzvah. While they may not refer to it by that name, they can still perform an act of kindness for another person. As that familiar-to-all term expresses so very well: "It is what it is!"

In order to successfully fulfill a Mitzvah, you have to perform an act of kindness that is above and beyond the normal act of kindness. {Author's note: In vernacular terms, this is the equivalence of 'stepping up to the plate' even though it isn't the most convenient thing-and, more than likely, it's challenging and most inconvenient.] Still further from the same reference: 'A Mitzvah is really what religion should be about. Random [and intended] acts of kindness will always have a place in religion, and they help society every time they are performed. Mitzvahs are necessary in order to remain powerful in the world today. They get to the heart of religion and remind people what faith is all about. Goodness has a place in every religion. Performing a Mitzvah is one of the most important things anyone can do in a religion. When people perform acts of kindness, they remember why they believe in their religion. They believe because of the goodness, and that goodness allows them to help others. The Christian equivalent of Mitzvah has previously been set forth in just two commandments [Matthew 22:37-40], i.e., "Love God!" and "Love your neighbor!" [Matthew 22: 37-40, New Oxford Bible, 1991]; the linkage between these two commandments [Matthew 25:40] is: "Whatsoever you do for the least of your brethren, you do for Me!" [Matthew 25:45, New Oxford Bible] These two commandments are fully reinforced by the words of the Bible and other religious teachings and writings, e.g., Episcopal Book of Common Prayer. In this Book, one can read on page 365: [Episcopal Book of Common Prayer, 1979] "Send us now into the world in peace, and grant us strength and courage to love and serve you with gladness and singleness of heart." or on page 366: [Episcopal Book of Common Prayer, 1979] "And now, Father, send us out to do the work you have given us to do......". It has been pointed out earlier that blindness to one's humanity-or a community's humanity or even an entire population-inevitably leads to a devaluing and abuse of that individual or that entire population. My goodness! One can even find in Charles Dickens' **Christmas Carol** that powerful reminder that "Mankind *[aka 'humankind']* **is** your business!"

It is this intrinsic goodness that is the foundation for that service provided to others without question, reluctance or doubt that gives rise to the 'goodness model'. This model was developed during the years of ministry at St. Ann's but is hardly unique to St. Ann's. President George Bush once referred to **1000 points of light in America** and frequently acknowledged and honored some of them publicly. It would not come as a surprise that there must exist at any given time thousands of points of light-even tens of thousands or millions of points of light that penetrate the darkness of need and inhumanity! This model embraces the belief that there is goodness in every individual that is all too often an untapped reservoir. There are countless individual and groups that draw upon their individual and collective reservoirs and do 'step up to the plate' in time of need. Conversely, there are so many others that need some encouragement, motivation and, in some cases, some gentle and persuasive 'shoving' to 'step up to the plate'. One of the dynamics of this goodness model is that you can offer a private or public seminar on 'service to others' with myriad words. The words will be most certainly be heard but not quite fully understood in most cases. An example that I have used more than a few times 'vanilla ice cream' as an analogy to service. It goes something like this: when talking with an individual or addressing a group advocating for outreach or community I ask them to use their imagination to visualize that they have never had vanilla ice cream or any other flavor. I can enumerate and describe the many wonders of vanilla ice cream but, for those who have never had tasted vanilla ice cream, they do hear my words but simply do not fully appreciate the wonders of vanilla ice cream. An alternative strategy would be to actually offer each listener a dish of vanilla ice cream: the outcome would surely be a full understanding of those wonders. Service to others is sort of like vanilla ice cream: one can talk about it, encourage it et al but, once you have done some measure of service to others, you gain a full understanding of all the miracles and goodness associated with service to others, with the real meaning of Mitzvah! [Author's note: this analogy is valid for all flavors of ice cream; I chose vanilla because-as a young boy-it was one of the more memorable events of my young life and remains so to this day]. This phenomenon of enrichment via a service-to-others experience is too often an untapped resource for those for whom 'service to others' is not a priority; conversely, there are a myriad community service ministries that have enriched the lives of all who choose to participate. For example, the 'Journey to St. Ann's' on April 30th and May 1st of 2011 provides an ample demonstration of the impact of 'mitzvah', of 'community service', of 'being your brother's keeper',........, of 'loving your neighbor'. The reader will soon discover some very moving 'reflections' not only from this particular journey but also from personal 'reflections' from both the St. Ann's and St. John's communities that span more than a decade.

The relevance of the goodness model to ministry is that it is this reservoir of goodness-when tapped-becomes the sustaining force during the life of any particular ministry. Additionally, in the same sense that *one ministry begets another* so does *goodness beget goodness.* It is both of these two dynamic phenomena that literally release the waters of goodness from the myriad individual and community reservoirs into the arena of need. I believe that there resides an innate goodness in each and every individual but it is often a dormant goodness simply waiting for the opportunity to come to life. An invitation to a specific ministry effort no matter the size from one individual to another is so often the key to life for the awakening of this dormant goodness. This goodness model has received abundant validation at that special candle of light in the South Bronx: St. Ann's. The St. Ann's-St. John's joint effort began in 1996 and remains 'alive and well' at this writing! This ministry of goodness-like so many others-has given birth and impetus to additional ministries of goodness.

Another version of this 'goodness' model' is the Outreach Model of St. John's [Appendix H] which evolved during its journeys to St. Ann's and continues to grow in maturity and meaning with the passage of time.

Returning to the story of the 'dots' which, in time, formed-and continues to shape- an active highway of ministry: the Rev. Shirley Andrews of St. Johns had now planted the seed and the innate response of the St. John's community [as it is in so many communities of faith] was immediately forthcoming, i.e., "What can we do to help?" The forthcoming stories within this growing ministry bordered on the 'unbelievable' but, in truth, were also a reflection of America's naiveté about the extent, depth and deep-rooted conditions of the inner-cities of America. Somewhere between [1] the realities of inner-city living conditions and the imbedded despair and risk and [2] the lack of political will in the educational and political hierarchies 'to do something constructive, meaningful and enduring' persists as one of America's darkest secrets and it remains that way.

A 1996 telephone conversation between Shirley Andrews and Mother Martha became the next 'dot'. Shirley Andrews asked Mother Martha "What can we do to help?" Mother Martha inquired about the ministries that are active within the St. John's community. There was the usual spectrum of church ministries: altar guild, community service, pastoral care, food and clothing drives for the hungry and homeless,............. and a home repair ministry that was extremely active and expanding in 1995 and more so in 1996. This latter ministry apparently caught Mother Martha's interest and she asked about it. The Home Repair ministry was a weekend program that involved twenty to thirty parishioners, families and friends that would do a spectrum of home repairs for those unable to do or to finance those very badly needed repairs that accumulate when there is a long-standing lack of required maintenance. Basically, the Home Repair team functioned as a home repair contractor; the parish provided the financial resources for the needed materials, local businesses also donated some materials and the home repair team provided the tools, necessary skills and the willing 'hearts and hands'. Once the ministry was initiated the requests for home repair grew exponentially; requests came from social workers, visiting nurses, senior groups, case managers, relatives, friends and neighbors et al. The individuals requiring some sort of home repair were usually elderly, alone, often disabled and without the ability or funds to do the repair. It was a very successful ministry for all involved in it. There are many 'stories' that came about within this ministry; each reflect that quality of goodness mentioned earlier. These are two of those stories that reflect goodness, making a difference and an eye-opening experience which became a sort of 'baptism' for both participants and observers of the ministry efforts.

Home Repair Story #1

One of the earlier home repair efforts was the exterior painting of a modest ranch house for a 77-year old woman who had wanted it painted for several years but could only afford the paint but not the labor. The labor included significant 'prep', e.g., extensive scraping, sanding and the replacement of some exterior woodwork. As the work steadily progressed from one weekend to another, a need for an additional extension ladder developed and a neighbor of the woman was asked "Could we borrow one of the ladders in your yard for a few hours?" In a very neighborly manner, he agreed to that. When the ladder was returned, the neighbor inquired about the identity of the home repair team. A general description of the team's origins and activities was willingly provided including the fact that we were all volunteers doing this 'pro bono' work. The neighbor was somewhat surprised that the work was cost-free for the elderly woman and home owner. Interestingly enough, that same neighbor returned on the next weekend and asked "Are you guys really doing this for nothing?" It was an opportunity to talk about the reason and rationale for 'service to others'; it was, in fact, a baptismal moment for that neighbor! This type of opportunity presented itself quite frequently with many individuals: both observers and volunteers. It was a moment when 'giving', Mitzvah, 'service to others' et al became one and the same. One of the more eloquent and compassionate writings on **Giving** is found in **The Prophet** [Kahlil Gibran, 1984]; because of its powerful yet gentle message it is also provided in Appendix I. The process of giving albeit reluctantly is simply another name for 'baptism'. But this story doesn't end here; as the house painting effort was coming to an end, some members of the home repair team had found it necessary to do some of the 'finish work' around the windows from the interior of the house. It was discovered that there was a lot of darkness in the kitchen, bathroom and the bedrooms because, as the owner told us, the lights were not in working order. The team members inquired as to the length of time that the lights and outlets in those three rooms were not working. The elderly woman's response was "It has been at least three years or ever since an electrician had installed a ceiling fan." which, itself, was not working. At that time it seemed incredible that [1] this elderly woman had lived in darkness in the three major rooms of her modest house for three years and through three winters and [2] the 'electrician' who installed the fan and clearly left a trail of damage and inconvenience to this elderly woman represented a case of abuse to the elderly-another common occurrence in society. As was very common in this ministry, the home repair team responded immediately and looked into the problem; simply put, it took another weekend of effort to correct the problem. The woman's obvious joy and gratitude was simply 'amazing'; this story had been transformed from a heartbreaking one to a heartwarming one for the team members as well as for the woman; the outcome had given new meaning to "Let there be light!"

Home Repair Story #2

This story is about a couple with four young special-needs children who lived in a very modest house and who struggled daily with family and financial challenges. The first floor of their small house [really, their home] had a variety of small pieces of rugs of different sizes, shapes and colors as floor covering over an unfinished plywood floor. The family had always hoped to have a more reasonable floor covering but never had the needed dollars; there were a number of additional projects but the family deemed the floor as their top priority. The home repair team recommended that the entire first floor be done as soon as possible because the array of rugs was saturated with sand, dirt and other assorted substances that, collectively, represented a health menace to the entire family. In the removal process of these rugs, the team learned that [1] they were excessively heavy with accumulated sand and dirt and [2] the father had acquired them over a period of time from the trash cans of his neighborhood. Let the reader keep in mind that this is a family living in America! The rugs were removed, the plywood floor was cleaned and sanded and the floor was prepared for the installation of one foot square tiles chosen by the family from a local Home Depot. Since the house was somewhat dated and lacking in maintenance, it was important to draw some guidelines as a reference rather than the uneven walls. This took an entire afternoon but the team did have time to install six tiles that formed a 2' x 3' space in the middle of the kitchen. The team planned to return the next day to finish the job. That evening I received a telephone call from a sobbing mother; I immediately thought that something very wrong had befallen one of the four children. The tears in the mother's eyes [and mine] quickly became tears of gratitude because the children were so excited about the new floor that they had insisted on having their evening meal on that 2' x 3' space of new tiles. A special footnote of this story is that some members of the home repair team were 'youthful offenders' doing court-mandated community service for their youthful transgressions; these young adults were some of the more talented and committed members of this ministry. They, indeed, acquired a new perspective on life and responsibility and, to be sure, their own goodness and the inevitable 'joy of giving'. Some had then remained part of the home repair team even though their required hours of community service had been completed.

Mother Martha's interest in St. John's home repair ministry was a reflection of the enormous amount of repairs and maintenance required at St. Ann's in its historic structure, classrooms and grounds surrounding the church. Let the reader recall that St. Ann's is a safe place for the children in their after-school and summer hours of vulnerability on the streets of the South Bronx. One of the many continuing challenges confronting Mother Martha is the upkeep of the entire church property in order to provide the most functional and safe place for the children. It is not an exaggeration to say that this was and remains an almost insurmountable task. On a spring day in 1996, the Rev. Shirley Andrews, my wife, Marion, and I made our inaugural trip from St. John's to St. Ann's to meet with Mother Martha to plan some 'home repair' at St. Ann's. Despite its obvious need for repair and maintenance, St. Ann's presented itself as a beautiful, impressive and historic church and landmark that sits upon a rocky knoll amongst the many types of apartment buildings, varied store fronts and street activities and scenes.

We all agreed that something could and would be done by some members of St. John's home repair team; during a tour of St. Ann's a list of repair and maintenance tasks was compiled. This list was so long that it appeared 'endless'; more than two hundred individual tasks of varying complexities and challenges were identified. The interesting and compelling question was "Where would we begin?" Part of the answer to that question included some insight into those conditions that had led to the then current situation. Clearly, the historic path of St. Ann's had included some rather glowing and impressive growth during its earlier years but was eventually followed by years of increasing need for repair and even minimum maintenance as the entire South Bronx transitioned into 'third world equivalence'. St. Ann's Church celebrated its *170th anniversary* in July, 2011; Appendix J provides a historical summary of the rich and relevant history of St. Ann's Church. The totality of the ***minimum required repair and maintenance, i.e., those many high-priority tasks needed to sustain church use and functionality,*** was simply overwhelming and that's a very generous understatement. It was really beyond overwhelming! However, the commitment by the St. John's home repair team 'to do something' had been made and some activity did follow. As those repairs and maintenance were completed two realizations developed: [1] it was somewhat like 'shoveling against the tide' and [2] incredibly so, other more urgent requirements other than repairs and maintenance would present themselves daily. Of course, it was also a baptismal process for the members of the home repair team because we witnessed first-hand the enormous love, commitment and efforts of Mother Martha to daily-and often hourly-manage the innumerable tasks associated with the operation of the church proper, the advocacy and befriending so necessary to assist so many to simply survive each day and/or those so many personal, family or community issues and concerns that arise and/or develop within the St. Ann's community. *[Author's note: ....and this was the late 1990s; this book is being written in 2011 and 2012 and this observation remains just as valid fifteen years later if not more so!]*.

As indicated earlier, the ministry at St. Ann's enjoyed a steady growth during the mid-to-late 1990s via some 'home repair' efforts complemented by efforts at St. John's to provide some much needed items such as clothes, blankets, books, toys, etc. for the children and families at St. Ann's. The interest, compassion, commitment and, most importantly, the participation in this evolving ministry grew with each experience at and exposure to the St. Ann's community. There was certainly a 'buzz in the air' within both communities; a growing awareness that bordered on being charismatic or a feeling that 'this is what dreams are made of' because the dream of making a difference in our lives as well as the lives of others was achieving reality before our very eyes. The innate passion of doing something good because 'it is the right thing to do' is best described by Vice –President Joe Biden who said on March 24, 2010: *"History is made when passion is matched with spiritual principle."* He may have been referring to the passage of a national health care reform bill but it also has relevance to the developing ministry at St. Ann's. Some of the ministry events are described in another section that provides a litany of 'stories' that found their genesis and the needed fuel by combining 'passion' and 'principle' within this ministry

Another surge in this ministry came about in the spring of 2001: my wife, Marion, and I were driving home to Rhode Island via New York City when a series of violent storms prevented any further driving on Route 95. We remained in New York City for several days until these storms subsided to allow safe driving; however, while in New York City, I was really led to discover and acquire another book that provided some additional dramatic and moving insight into the plight of the children in the South Bronx; the reality was almost unbelievable so I called Mother Martha and asked her if the situations in this book were actually true. Her response was an astounding one to this author; she mentioned that the conditions were, indeed, true but probably worse than the written descriptions. These conditions were like an accelerant for the now innate response of the St. John's parishioners to the needs at St. Ann's. Again, it was so disappointing and even profoundly sad to learn about the huge spectrum of disadvantages of residency in the South Bronx [and, of course, many inner city environments across America] and the great need for so many items that are readily abundant elsewhere. One category of much needed items was 'school supplies'; we are not talking here about computers, smart boards, up-to-date textbooks et al but about pencils, erasers, notebooks, paper and all those very basic items needed by the children in their classrooms. The classrooms, per se, did not provide a healthy educational environment and left much to be desired; they were a sharp contrast to those classrooms found in most schools beyond the 'walls' of the inner-cities. One doesn't need a great imagination to visualize a teaching and learning environment without these basic items.

A drive for school supplies was initiated at St. John's and, on a hot day, August 9, 2001 [the temperature was 104 degrees F in the South Bronx], the first delivery of school supplies was made. This visit also gave the representatives of the St. John's Outreach Team and the Youth Group to see and 'experience' this moving ministry amidst the social and economic chaos of the South Bronx. Each of these representatives were touched/ moved in some way; as one of the younger representatives exclaimed: "This is quite different from Barrington!" During the years that followed, school supplies-especially, composition notebooks that are treasured items both in the after-school programs at St. Ann's and at its summer Freedom School. These school supply drives were complemented by efforts to enhance the library facilities at St. Ann's; the provision of 'books' became an annual staple for the ministry and continues to this day [July, 2012]. It is another of the wonderful 'stories' that are detailed in the coming pages. Another collateral story that followed that initial delivery is that of Allison Javery, first-grader and daughter of parishioners at St. John, who initiated a very special effort to gather additional school supplies; it is an effort that reflects the spirit of this ministry-a ministry in which many parishioners and friends of St. John's were becoming active participants. Allison requested that rather than give gifts to her on her 7ᵗʰ birthday, her family and friends could donate some much-needed school supplies for the children at St. Ann's.

This apparently coincidental experience during a totally unexpected delay in New York City had led to the outcome of creating a pipeline for school supplies during the summer of 2001 and one that continues today. "Hmmmm!", I said, "Is this really a coincidence?" or "Is it something more?" The answers to these types of questions will manifest themselves- abundantly and with clarity- in the forthcoming 'stories'. There are, of course, 'stories within stories'; each ministry story explicitly addresses an activity that is integral to this developing ministry. However, within each story there also exists a subtle and subliminal story about those individuals involved from both communities. The readers may recall the author's comments from **What Feeds My Soul?** and their linkage to this ministry. These comments certainly reflect my feelings and my spirit but it is the aggregation of the hearts, minds and spirits of so many individuals within the St. John's community that have provided the foundation and the continuity of this ministry. Three such stories of three very special individuals follow as an entree into those stories to come:

Ministry Story #1

"It is difficult to write about one's reasons for a passionate endeavor, as the reasons usually spring from a number of sources. One is prone to ramble. As a painter [artist[my creations are more about arranging elements, each having their own genesis; the composition being a balanced assembly of individual parts with serendipity being the glue. Such is my motivation for my work with St. Ann's.

A conversation I had with some of the young adults from St. Ann's in 2009 might explain my own relationship to New York City and the source of my motivation. I was discussing New York and how it has changed over my lifetime. I was a bit nostalgic; telling stories of going to Yankee games with my grandfather, what the City looked like then. I have memories and experiences reaching back to the1950s; they are peppered with stories from grandparents pushing my knowledge back much further. I was creating a tableau from my own experience, the West Village before the [Twin] Towers, to the city as it was before cars. I remember Joey picking up on my sadness over what was, mistaking my reverie to be about how much better it was then. It was not better then, I told him, it is not better now. My point was the city never changes, in it is always changing. New York is a fluid city. Like the river that defines it, it meets the sea and pushes back the tide; it then succumbs to the ocean's superior strength and is pushed back again. Cycles run their natural course. The City at its worse is the City at its best. When it is at its lowest point, people get creative,when economic collapses make the City uninhabitable, De Koonings, Warhols and Pollacks surface and the cycle begins anew. New ethnicities move in where previous ones have left to be assimilated into the greater America. It is the great melting pot. Falafel is sold where we always bought canoles or limpa bread or reubens.

I spoke of my roots there, but another element arises; my deep roots represent only half of my ancestry. My mother was of immigrant origins, the European immigrations of 1900 brought her family here. And their descendants are among those who left for distant cities.

I had the good fortune to visit the land of my mother's parents, meet my cousins, aunts and uncles there. One thing that strikes me is a number of my aunts and uncles were 're-pats', they came home. More to the point the 'old country' never ceased to be home. I had a similar experience moving to Washington State where my sister, my parents, and later my grandmother, had moved. My sister is totally assimilated in the West Coast, now with grandchildren; the Jersey girl she was is only known to me. My wife and I could not make the leap. We remained homesick and returned to Rhode Island after 10 years. For some reason, the East Coast never stopped being home. I have a feeling, had my wife, my son and myself stayed in Washington State, the events of [September 11] 2001 would have been unbearable and, surely, would have brought us back."

"The seed of meeting Mother Martha had germinated from our growing awareness of Mother Martha and her ministry at St. Ann's in the South Bronx. This awareness, while still on the West Coast, was enabled by some reading *recommendations of our Pastor in our parish [St. John's Olympia]. Perhaps the tipping point in our decision to move back were these readings. A reminder of the city of our origins, the minutia describing New York City was familiar with Liz and me as it would never be in Seattle. We longed to be in a place that we understood. Serendipity, however, is the unquantifiable element that brought our relationship to flower. We had barely been in Rhode Island a year, were still exploring how we want to live our lives, finding the right school for our son, a church, etc. St. John's Church in Barrington, a neighboring community,*

provided the lively environment we were seeking. The people at St. John's had also been on a parallel course of awareness about Mother Martha and her ministry at St. Ann's and had felt the pull to action. It was serendipitous and we felt a need to throw our efforts there. We found ourselves with like-minded people and an open door that pulled at our hearts. When the tragedy struck New York [and Washington, DC and in the skies over Pennsylvania], a chain of events formed.

Mother Martha readily offered her Church as a base camp for us as the daughter of St. John's Acting Rector connected our people with the organizers of the relief efforts at The World Trade Center in New York. The South Bronx was not the South Bronx I had always remembered from my childhood, I said.

*However, these young adults had no memory of that wonderful City. It was the City at its worse and **we had come home!**"*

[Steven Lippincott, October, 2010

Steve and his wife, Liz Hallenbeck, are quiet and unassuming in their way of life and living but are so representative of the character, commitment and spiritual courage that are the unspoken icon of those involved in this dual-church experience. Steve is a Viet Nam veteran, an artist, a man of faith, a man of action, a good person who [like so many others] breathes life into the ministry and provides a special enrichment to those who serve as well as those whom are being served. Liz is an effective complement to Steve and, together, they are an integral part of the commitment by the St. John's community to 'make a difference'. They have always stepped up-to-the-plate to do what must be done-to do 'the work that God has given us to do with gladness and singleness of heart'. And they do it so very quietly that relatively few within the St. John's community are aware of it but there are so many in the St. Ann's community that consider Steve and Liz as part of their families.

They have performed a wide variety of duties, tasks and labors of love during the many mission trips to St. Ann's, initiating and managing field trips for the children there [and some of the adults!] to various sites in New York City. Bear in mind that most of these children [and some of the adults] had never ventured beyond the walls of the South Bronx. Steve and Liz also were active in the many repair and maintenance projects; Steve was also an experienced wood craftsman; they also did some of the driving of the children to and from summer camperships in Rhode

41

Island. They opened the doors of their home to provide a safe place for the children to stay when necessary.........and so much more. Steve and Liz represent the epitome-a very quiet epitome-of 'faith in action' through their spiritual passion, commitment and 'doing the right thing' regardless of the hardship and/or inconvenience. I know that they would object to my use of the words 'unsung heroes' to describe them [and many others] but that description and their expected objection are also part of this story [and many others].

Ministry Story #2

Another 'dot' or, if the reader so wishes: another 'coincidence' is the story of **Curtis Barton** of Barrington, RI who entered the world on March 20, 1979 as the younger brother of Jed and Bradford Barton. I had initially become acquainted with Curtis during several of the multi-day mission trips to St. Ann's during the early 2000s. Curtis, perhaps, was somewhat reserved but always courteous, always smiling, helpful to the tasks at hand and possessed with an inner peace that he was doing what his heart, mind and soul was asking of him. He was a valued member of the St. John's Outreach ministry team at St. Ann's. However, amongst the usual busyness and tasks of the days at St. Ann's, I did have several opportunities to share our thoughts and feelings about community service and living the good life.....and each of us learned a lot. These are the times during which I developed a growing suspicion that there was more-much more-to Curtis than meets the eye. He would provide me with little subtle pieces of information about his life and activities that strongly inferred that he was an individual who chose to live life to its fullest! Just how much more wasn't fully realized until June, 2011 when I spoke with his Mom, Debbie Barton, because my sixth sense had been telling me that Curtis was a special individual for all the right reasons. The Barton family had already faced and coped with the parenting of a blind child, i.e., Jed starting with his 1974 birth. At that time, there really wasn't a lot of literature, references or medical expertise available or addressed to the raising of a blind child; this situation was made more challenging for all concerned because blindness is so frequently accompanied by collateral disabilities and challenges. There was a growing awareness that Curtis may have also possessed some learning disabilities with the typical derivatives of avoiding homework, academic focusing difficulties, areas of interest beyond the work of the classroom, etc. But there was more to Curtis than having a learning disability: he was well-behaved; he carried himself with assurance and self-confidence; he was courteous to all along his path of life and, in return, he was well-liked and respected as an individual. He was truly likable! He spent the 7th through some of the 10th grades St. Andrews School in Barrington and then transferred to Barrington High School to complete his secondary education. He loved 'hands on' projects rather than the traditional 'book' exercises. This ability became an asset to him as he successfully transitioned from a Life Scout to an Eagle Scout with the Boy Scouts of America. As the transition from one merit badge to another became more challenging, Curtis positioned himself to complete a 'service project' which would enable him, finally, to become an Eagle Scout.

The time allotted for the completion of the required 'service project' was rather limited so he had to find a project that was doable within that allotted time window. Now, are you, the readers, ready for another 'dot' or 'coincidence'? Curtis was a member of the St. John's congregation and sought out the advice of the assistant Rector there for some project advice and guidance. It was the very same time that the Assistant Rector, Shirley Andrews, had brought some readings to the attention of the parish and especially the book groups at St. John's. The inevitable discussions followed and, then, impact of these readings steadily lifted the awareness of inner city needs and the parish commitment to action. This was the very same time frame that Shirley Andrews and Mother Martha were talking with each other about the possible roles of St. John's ministry and outreach efforts within the mounting challenges at St. Ann's. It was within these discussions that the initial awareness that the St. Ann's community really 'needed everything' to cope with these daily-and sometimes hourly-challenges. A full realization would come to exist as the ministry continued to grow. This information was passed on to Curtis as a very promising area for his required 'service project'. Curtis' response was textbook goodness; he created his own network for the collection of a spectrum of items that could be used at St. Ann's. He was literally a 'one-man ministry' as 27 crates of items were collected from various sources including many solicitations within his immediate neighborhood. The task that now confronted Curtis was the transportation of these 27 crates to the South Bronx from Barrington, RI. Fortunately-maybe even coincidentally-the Barton family had this cabinetry business and made the family truck available for the needed transportation. It goes without saying that the 27 crates were received with much enthusiasm and gratitude at St. Ann's.

But the story doesn't end with that delivery of items to St. Ann's. Unknown to Curtis and to those who were involved in the previously described and growing ministry within the greater parish, there were two mutually exclusive efforts in progress that were mirror reflections of each other. The service project efforts and success of Curtis was, indeed, a parallel model for the collaborative ministry between St. Ann's and St. John's that has existed for more than 15 years. ***It is only fitting and quite appropriate to refer to Curtis as an 'outreach pioneer'.***

In his own very special and unassuming way, Curtis had single-handedly provided a special enrichment to the ongoing ministry work at St. Ann's. Curtis completed his earthly journey on August 21, 2005 due to a heart condition but he had accomplished more than most in his 26 years of 'living the good life' and 'making a difference as his heart, mind and soul had guided him to do so.' His outreach and ministry colleagues were always honored by his presence. I was also honored to be in attendance at a memorial service for Curtis at St. Ann's in the spring of 2006.

Ministry Story #3

Some background is helpful to place this story in a meaningful context for the readers. In the days immediately after the events of September 1, 2001, a number of St. John's parishioners [adults and members of the Church Youth Group were volunteers, periodically, at St. Paul's Chapel in Lower Manhattan immediately adjacent to Ground Zero. The Chapel, like the legendary St. Paul's Chapel of London, had survived the attacks from the air. St. Paul's had developed into a safe haven for the first-responders, the various police authorities, firemen, rescue personnel, medical personnel et al that were part of the extensive recovery efforts at Ground Zero. It is sufficient to say that the Chapel and Ground Zero settings provided their own litany of 'stories' that represented the very best that America had to offer. The proximity of St. Ann's ['across the East River'] to Ground Zero and the on-going ministry efforts there provided not only a place to sleep [albeit the gym and classroom floors] but, so much more importantly, the opportunity for these volunteers at Ground Zero to view first-hand, experience and understand the profound dynamics of the ministry efforts at St. Ann's and their positive impact upon that community-especially, the children! Upon the initial arrival of the St. John's volunteer contingent at St. Ann's on the evening immediately prior to their deployment the following morning at 6:00 AM at Ground Zero, we were met by a small energetic woman who was so openly gracious and welcoming that it was immediately obvious that this woman, indeed, was 'Mother Martha'. There are many individuals who have, persistently, raised questions about the children of the inner cities of America, in general; the South Bronx certainly qualified as a representative model. What is the most likely outcome for these young children who grow up in an environment of instability, poverty, educational deprivation, poor health, a lack of social and civil order, etc.? Simply put, the answer is that they are out 'on the streets' and struggling to survive. However, this is the question to which Mother Martha decided to provide an answer. She started a 'freedom school' which was modeled after those that were established and operated in some churches of the South; most recently, during the civil right days of the 1960s and 1970s. In addition to the summer 'freedom school', Mother Martha initiated an after-school program as an alternative to the streets of the South Bronx. This safe place not only provides the gathering of the children from the various public schools, an opportunity to enhance their education but also a meal prior to departure for their homes. For many, this is the only real meal that they will have for the entire day. Clearly, this was not the traditional setting found in middle-class America.

More than a few sources have identified the ministry of Mother Martha as the single, most positive influence upon the lives of the disadvantaged children of the community. This ministry has both motivated and even inspired a wide spectrum of volunteer efforts [and their wonderful gifts of *time, treasure and talent*] from the local neighborhood, from Manhattan, from some colleges and universities and, most certainly from the parishioners of St. John's Episcopal Church of Barrington, RI.

She works endless hours and her continuing efforts approach miracle status. Her devotion to these children and to this ministry comes right from Mother Martha's heart and spirituality. She is often referred to as the 'Mother Teresa of the South Bronx'. When watching the children around her and interacting with her, one can not only sense but experience the love that exists between Mother Martha and the children. She really makes a difference. She continues to be a source of inspiration and motivation for those whose paths take them to St. Ann's. She breathes life into these words: "Love your neighbor!" and "Whatever you do for the least of your brethren, you do for Me!"

Having said that, let us return to **Ministry Story #3**: after a long, challenging and heart-breaking and, at times, heart-warming and, yes, gut-wrenching day working at Ground Zero, the volunteers from St. John's prepared to return to St. Ann's via subway and then the drive back to Rhode Island:

"We worked until well past 8:00 PM that first day. We were tired beyond tired as we trooped out of St. Paul's Chapel to the subway station to headback to the South Bronx, St. Ann's Church and our long ride back to Rhode Island and home.

Our trusty guide once again, Al Colella, got us safely aboard our trains and helped keep the twenty of us together as we made our subway connections. As we neared our stop, it was evident that our twenty suburban, middle class, white faces were indeed the minority on that train. The train was stopped and we were anticipating getting off at the next stop-the stop at which we had boarded in the early morning hours. Suddenly, the conductor [via the intercom]and all the other passengers on board were frantically telling us to get off the train immediately! Believe me, we flew off that subway train. [Apparently, the station of our anticipated stop was closed during the late evening hours.] We found ourselves on some very unfamiliar streets of the South Bronx in the closing hours of a very busy and draining Saturday. Unfortunately, we hadn't a clue as to where we were or what to do next!

It is important to note that this was in those days prior to having a sharper awareness of the power of **Amazing Grace** *and its linkage to those perceived 'coincidences'. However, a kindly woman unexpectedly appeared and approached our exhausted and somewhat confused group and asked where we were headed. When we explained that we needed to find our way to St. Ann's Church, she laughed and said: "Oh! You are some of Mother Martha's people. I would be happy to lead you back to the church."*

As we trooped along 138th Street, approximately eight blocks, that night she explained that she had been on the train with us [another 'coincidence'?],watching us and wondering to herself: "Where in God's name do these pilgrims think that they are going?" She handed us over to Mother Martha with a "God Bless" and walked off into the night. It was evident to me then that God had sent us an angel to guide us safely back to our destination as these were truly the meanest streets of New York City. [Author's note: this woman, we later learned was Phyllis, one of a number of family members active at St. Ann's; one a manager of the after-school program there [and to whom I referred as the'Kommandant'] but also a true care-giver as well as a caretaker of the children of the after-school program at St. Ann's]. We quickly packed our things into the vans, hugged and kissed Mother Martha; we were on our way back home. Safe and sound again in my home, I realized that all of my clothing, my skin and my hair still smelled as though I were still standing there at Ground Zero. I might be able to wash the superficial smells away but I would always remember them…. and the experience will forever live with me."

Jan Malcolm, April, 2002

Chapter 7
Birth of the Summer Camperships

The genesis of the summer camperships in rural Rhode Island for the children of St. Ann's lies within the initial and very emotional trip to Ground Zero as relief volunteers. Understandably, the preparations [mental, emotional and logistical] for this trip were foremost in our minds and spirit. Plans called for the St. John's volunteer team to arrive at St. Ann's on a Friday evening, sleep there and then report to St. Paul's Chapel adjacent to Ground Zero for an early Saturday morning orientation followed by a surreal day of work-probably, the most unique work of our lives. It has been described elsewhere as one of those times that the very best in America 'stepped up to the plate' from every corner of the country and beyond.

The St. John's contingent arrived at St. Ann's in the South Bronx in the early evening and was met by Mother Martha. Some members of the St. John's volunteer team were involved veterans of the outreach efforts at St. Ann's and, then again, others found themselves at St. Ann's for the first time. The 'lodging arrangements' were settled and, then, all gathered for an evening meal in the basement 'cafeteria' of the church. There were only two points of interest upon which each and every person could focus: [1] the hopes, fears and expectations of the coming day at Ground Zero and, inevitably, [2] the 'So this is the St. Ann's environment?' Attention then focused upon the ministry at St. Ann's and the passion and love with which the 'veterans' told of their involvement and the many stories of the disadvantaged but beautiful children of the South Bronx. There was the inevitable explanation to the 'why' of their individual and collective involvement; surely the readers now have some understanding of the 'why'. As the details of this growing ministry for the children at St.

Ann's virtually came alive, there also developed this awareness about the many realities and disadvantages of life in the 'prison' called the South Bronx. This newly acquired awareness included so many 'things' [for the lack of a more descriptive and appropriate word] that were commonplace throughout America but totally absent in the environment at hand. This was so extraordinary when one considers that the South Bronx is 'just across the East River' from a thriving Manhattan. Questions were asked-and answered-about the availability of this program and that program; for example, are the St. Ann's kids able to travel beyond the South Bronx to that very different world beyond the South Bronx? My response to that particular question came from some conversations that I had with many of the children during our trips there; I would often ask "How many of you have traveled?" The typical response was that few, if any, really understood the realities of 'travel' and, therefore, not aware of life beyond the South Bronx but there was one hopeful response from an eight-year old: "I went to Brooklyn once!" Later in this book, there are 'reflections' from members of both the St. Ann's and St. John's communities; one of these 'reflections' is very relevant to this discussion; it was written on May 27, 2011 by a young lady [Alicia Brule] initially from the South Bronx but who moved to Providence, Rhode Island with her family that included two younger sisters and a considerably younger brother.

It is so relevant to note that Alicia is a 2009 graduate of Rhode Island College and is professionally employed in the area of early childhood development. Her complete story-indeed, the story of the four Brule youngsters will come later. Theirs is truly a success story that gave rise to the book title candidacy of *Let's Start With the Children* but her commentary on the recent 'Journey to St. Ann's' in 2011 follows: *"I'm so happy the children from St. Ann's are meeting the people of St. John's. That's how their horizons are broadened and they realize....like my sisters and I did that there's more to the world than our [South Bronx] community!"*

The conversation then gravitated to the feasibility of summer camps, e.g., the Fresh Air Program of New York City, for the children; there was one limited effort to take the children out of the South Bronx but only on an occasional basis. What was really needed was a summer camp program on a more sustained and comprehensive effort; an effort that would embrace a recognition of the humanity of these children and their need to be validated as 'important'. This principle would become the bedrock of the forthcoming camperships, i.e., that the children are important and, regardless of the specifics of any ministry activity, time, attention, and sincere, caring minds, hearts and ears that would listen to the children [and, inevitably, some adults] were the needed ingredients for an effective advocacy for the children ….and the adults. Of critical importance was the commitment to provide these ingredients on a sustained basis rather than a 'pit stop' basis. It was within this sustained environment that family-like relationships between the two communities would thrive. "Where could we take the kids?" bubbled up as the critical issue. Then one of the 'veterans' of the ministry, Liz Crawley [Parish Administrator at St. John's] said, "Wait a minute, now, we have a summer camp right in Rhode Island at the Episcopal Conference Center [aka ECC]; could that be a possibility?" It's important to remember that the Outreach Team had earned a reputation for just getting things done rather than explore the reasons why something couldn't be done and, at times, not seeking formal permission for what their hearts, minds and spirit were individually and collectively saying "This is the right thing to do!" With the perception and hope that such summer camperships at ECC were, indeed, feasible, all of those present-veterans and newcomers-responded enthusiastically with positive statements, e.g., "I'll send a kid to summer camp!" or "What can I do to help!" *The summer camperships at ECC in Rhode Island were born that evening in the basement cafeteria at St. Ann's.* Volunteering at Ground Zero and those evening activities in the basement of St. Ann's Church are also two additional 'dots' along the path of this developing ministry.

Upon our return to Rhode Island from our initial Ground Zero experience which yielded a second litany of 'stories' throughout the year of volunteer service there by many parishioners from the St. John's community, the task immediately at hand was to determine the realities of summer of ECC camperships. However, those 'stories' of service at Ground Zero are to be addressed at another time and, much like the stories of the ministry in the South Bronx, they are enriching, motivating and compelling stories that need to be documented for those who lost their lives there, those who served there, their families and for those who follow.

The next 'dot' along this ministry path manifested itself as Liz Crawley, Liz Hallenbeck, Steve Lippincott, my wife, Marion, and I met with Sue Henthorne, ECC Director, to explore the possibility of summer camperships. Sue listened intently and politely; we talked of the opportunities as well as the responsibilities involved inherent in such a venture with inner-city children. We were 'making our case' as best and persuasively as possible; our obvious passion and commitment were very much in evidence. However, our task was made much easier by Sue's forthcoming and enthusiastic response: "That's what the ECC summer camp program is all about; providing opportunities for children, especially, disadvantaged children. It's really the right thing to do! I agree with your ideas and let's move ahead with the program!"

All that was left to do was [1] rally the time, treasure and talent resources of the parish and [2] implement some summer camperships in the summer of 2002. The following was excerpted from the December, 2001 *TOWER*, the monthly publication at St. John's:

Let's Light Some More Candles

All of us are aware that St. Ann's Episcopal Church with the Rev. Martha Overall [aka Mother Martha by the children, parishioners and community] represents the only candle that sheds some light into the lives of many of the children of the South Bronx.

All of us equally aware that there is a proud history of St. John's support-generous support-for the wonderful and always challenging ministry of St. Ann's. On December 2, [2001] the Mission team will provide an informative presentation of its efforts, goals and plans for the coming year at the Adult Forum. One dimension of the presentation will be a plan to support some of the children of the South Bronx at the Episcopal Conference Center [ECC] during the summer of 2002. Such an opportunity for the children will inevitably be a strong complement to the existent efforts at St. Ann's throughout the year. Specifically, the goal is to raise the visions of life for these children and their own expectations for success. This effort will involve both adults and members of the Youth Group. Some parishioners have already 'stepped up to the plate' and have volunteered their time and/ or sponsorship for this effort. As one individual commented "I couldn't ask for a better investment with a greater return!"

As a result of the installation of a computer system [with the assistance of Johnson & Wales University] and the delivery in August, 2001 of a wide spectrum of educational goods donated by the St. John's community [as a direct result of conversations earlier in the year with other Martha about the spectrum of needs at St. Ann's] to support the 'keep the kids off the street' program, the candle burned a bit more brightly in the South Bronx.

Maybe-just maybe-we at St. John's could light a few more candles.
Come to the forum on 12/2.

Then, there was the following article also from the TOWER publication of January 18, 2002:

Send A Child To Camp

Our latest project is a dream that is slowly evolving into a reality. The Episcopal Conference Center [ECC], owned by the Episcopal Diocese of Rhode Island, and its Director, Susan Henthorne, have enthusiastically agreed to enroll some of the youth from St. Ann's in the summer camp program at ECC. They have allotted six spaces per session [about seven sessions] for these children. The camp holds sessions for grades 2 through high school, divided into segments by age and, when appropriate, gender groupings.

Why are we telling you about this? Because we need some help in various ways:

- Financial support to 'sponsor' a child-sponsorship can be met by individuals, by groups or by corporations. The cost per child is $200.00.
- We plan to provide the means of transportation to and from NYC-we need drivers, offers of donations of vans to use or donations to help support the cost of renting vans.
- In some instances some of the children might be our overnight guests for a night or two; they might spend the night at St. John's or at one of our homes.
- We could use some people to cook a few meals at St. John's or you could open your home to them for dinner.
- Donations of sleeping bags, blankets and other items they might need for a week at camp that they don't already have available.

To date we have six families from St. John's that have already come forward and sponsored a child and another six have pledged a full scholarship. Both full and partial scholarships are welcome. Almost all of these kids have a zero percent chance of graduation from a high a school and not much more of a chance of ever getting beyond the South Bronx.

We want to offer them a glimmer of hope, that they may have a week in the country; that they may have the chance to meet 'our kids' from St. John's and see that there is something beyond the walls of the South Bronx.

The Episcopal Camp and Conference [ECC] site is a center for Christian ministry on an old New England farm with 180 wooded acres and beach frontage on beautiful Echo Lake. It is located in the northwestern corner of Rhode Island. It offers eight week-long summer camping sessions for children and young people in grades two through twelve. Each camp session has a flavor all of its own. Work and worship, study and play are blended in a way where it is hard to tell where one ends and the other begins. The summer experience includes traditional outdoor camping, swimming, singing, cookouts and sleeping in cabins.

The 2011 summer sessions follow: *Young Adult Conference, Music & Creative arts, Teen Camp, Camp for Older Boys & Girls, Camper's Choice week, Younger Children's camp, Summer's End* and, finally, *Family Camp.*

Once again, the parishioners of St. John, as they would on occasion after occasion, 'stepped up to the plate' and put their faith into action in a direct response to the aforementioned 'help' that was required to make this particular dream a reality. Let there be no mistakes about it, this reality assumed dream dimensions from the kids' perspective; it certainly did so for those involved in this ministry. As time would pass during the coming decade, this dream-and others within the ministry-took on its true identity of ***Amazing Grace.*** This willing and loving donation of ***time, treasure and talents*** was also described in the following words of the June publication of the TOWER.

Thanks to the generous response of the parish, the ECC Summer Camp experience will become an opportunity and a unique reality for 36 children from the South Bronx. About 95% of the budget is in place; the logistics of transportation are being resolved; each of the children will receive a disposable camera with which to capture and memorialize this unique experience; 2 of the 6 camps end after dinner at ECC, so it will be too late for the return trip to the South Bronx. We've made plans for a sleep-over in Field Hall [St. John's] for 6 children on July 21 and 8 children on July 31 [2002]. All in all, this program is progressing well and even better than anticipated; this is a direct result of the generosity, availability, initiatives and work of the Outreach Commission, the Mission team, the Youth Group, Episcopal Church Women* [ECW], the administrative staff and, of course, the many parishioners of St. John's Church who answered the call of this amazing effort. But, of course, it all started with a spiritual awareness, faith and action and it moves along with such Amazing Grace!

These initial campership efforts in 2001 and 2002 resulted in 36 children from St. Ann's participating in the 2002 ECC summer camp experience. Within this experience and the years of campership to follow until the present time, there lies a wealth of 'stories' about the children and, more importantly, about the impact of their experiences upon their lives. Some of these 'stories'-each of them is a success story-are described in the next section of this book. However, there are two summary descriptions of this impact upon the life journeys of each of these children follow; the first offers the comments of Mother Martha on her trip to St. John's on September 27, 2002 following the first year of summer camperships. Bob Wexler, St. John's parishioner, former Chair, Outreach and active participant with his wife, Bobbi, their two sons, Greg and Kevin and daughter, Lisa, wrote this article in the TOWER [October 11, 2002]:

*More will be said later about the very generous and supportive role of the St. John's chapter of ECW not only in the ministry at St. Ann's but also in a very wide and impressive spectrum of Church, Outreach and local community service efforts.

ST. ANN'S + ST. JOHN'S = AMAZING GRACE

On Friday evening, September 27th, 60-70 members of St. John's came to hear the Rev. Martha Overall share her thoughts on how the 'ECC Camperships' program had affected the lives of the children of St. Ann's in the South Bronx. {I don't know that anyone actually counted but it was a tremendous turnout.} Her message was powerful.

For those not familiar with the Rev. Martha Overall [a.k.a. Mother Martha], she is the pastor of a small Episcopal Church in the heart of the South Bronx. The neighborhoods around St. Ann's are said to be the poorest in New York City and are some of the most dangerous. Mother Martha's ministry at St. Ann's includes after school programs where the children find a safe and welcoming environment, help with their homework, a nourishing meal and the love of a remarkable individual, Mother Martha. Our readings and research and, most importantly, our continuing experience and involvement at St. Ann's provided a continuum of insight into not only the difficult circumstances of many of the children but also the significance of Mother Martha's ministry.

The ECC Campership program, the dream of our own Al Colella, became a reality this past summer. [Author's note: I was simply the spokesperson for the entire team of parishioners who embraced, advocated for, supported, participated in and actively encouraged this summer camp program!]. Through the tremendous support of the people of St. John's and the Episcopal Conference Center [ECC], 36 boys and girls from the South Bronx were able to spend a week at ECC summer camp. Prior to hearing Mother Martha, there were probably others, like me, who wondered if it would really make a difference. This was great that the kids had a chance to get away for a week, but then what?

Listening to Mother Martha we heard answers to some of these questions. While, one minute, our hearts were saddened by stories of hardship, the next they were warmed with stories of courage and accomplishment.

"YOU MATTER! Even though we've never met, you still matter to us. You are important!"

According to Mother Martha, the people of St. John's communicated this very significant message, loud and clear, to the children of St. Ann's and their families!

The ways that many of the children [and parents] responded to this message were significant. Some children came away from the experience simply more confident and self-assured. Others came away with the sense that they did have some control over their futures. They didn't have to be a victim of their circumstances. One young man, who had missed over 40% of his classes last year, had yet to miss a day of school-he is now committed to taking control of his future. [Author's note: The common thread through the minds and hearts of all those children who have attended and will attend the summer camperships at ECC [or elsewhere] and experience life within a family setting is exactly and simply what Alicia Brule offered a few pages ago, i.e., *"......there is something beyond the walls of the South Bronx".* Yes, there is another life beyond the South Bronx environment! More importantly, there is 'hope'!

There were many other heartwarming stories-too many to discuss here [but will follow in the coming pages]. The message from Mother Martha to the people of St. John's and ECC was clear:

"THANK YOU! What you did made a difference!"
[Bob Wexler, Co-Chair, St. John's Mission Team]

Then there was this response to Bob Wexler's article from an independent observer; the Reverend John Hall wrote the following in another issue of the TOWER:

Letter to the Tower-Note from a one-time Curate

"In reading the October 11 issue of The Tower, I came across the article about the children from St. Ann's in the Bronx who, thanks to St. John's, came to ECC last summer. I happened to be at ECC one day during Music Camp and got to meet some of these kids. I remember especially one who came to the director saying, "I have got to come back here this summer!" As far as he was concerned, this was important and this was going to happen. Later in the summer, on the one other day I was at ECC, I found much to my delight, this same boy. He was back and he was having a blast. Who knows what this experience will mean to his whole life! If it turns out to be pivotal, this will not be the first time that an ECC camper has experienced a major life change there. What a blessing that St. John's sent those children to ECC!"

On August 22, 2002, Kristen Rasmusen, Providence journal Staff Writer, offered the following:

'It's a chance to expand the horizons for these kids'

About five or six years ago, several members of St. John's Episcopal Church read a book about Mother Martha's ministry. This summer, 36 students from the South Bronx reaped the benefits.

Several books had depicted the lives of children who grow up in the South Bronx, according to St. John's parishioner Albert M. Colella.

The portrayal is an ugly one, Colella said: in terms of health, life expectancy and poverty and education levels; the lives of these inner city children across America parallel with those of children in many Third World countries.

But bright spots, aka 'candles', do exist across America and, in the South Bronx, it is St. Ann's Episcopal Church and other so-called 'freedom schools' where children go after school to learn reading, writing and civics, receive a balanced meal and a ride home.

When St. John's parishioners read about St. Ann's, they wanted to help, Colella said: "We've always had a strong outreach. We've always reached a little bit farther than most. If there's a need, we go there." Colella said:

"And we saw this as the chance to raise the vision or expand the horizon for these kids."

And thus began the unique ongoing relationship between the two congregations.

Colella, in conjunction with Johnson & Wales University-where, at that time, was the Chairman of the School of Technology-set up a computer lab for the students at St. Ann's. One parishioner [Curtis Barton] had made St. Ann's his Eagle Scout project. St. John's contributed $5,000 toward a new floor at St. Ann's. Last year, the Barrington church donated 100 back packs [another remarkable and moving story!] and other school supplies for students.

But this summer, for the first time, parishioners from St. John's paid for all 36 St. Ann's freedom school students to attend camp at the Episcopal Conference Center in Chepachet. The 100 or so parishioners paid the $200-per-person camp costs, transported students to and from the Bronx and bought camping necessities, including bathing suits, flashlight and sleeping bags, for the students.

One family [Cheryl and Richard King] volunteered to purchase disposable cameras for the campers and pay to develop the film. St. John's parishioners even footed the bill for long-distance phone calls placed from homesick campers or a trip to the emergency room for one camper.

"St. John's just tells us to put everything on their bill." Said Susan Henthorne, Director of the camp. "They just say, 'Let's make it work.' "

Each summer, about 800 students, from grades through 11, from Rhode Island nearby states attend the camp during eight one-week sessions. Henthorne said. This year, six spaces per session were allotted for the freedom school students' one-week visit, she added.

It was a chance, these students said, to participate in several new activities, including improvisational comedy, swimming and anti-violence demonstrations.

"It's very calm and nice here and not so hectic." Said 16-year old Chuck Cooper, of the Bronx. "I definitely plan to come back next year."

But the St. Ann's students weren't the only ones to benefit from their time at camp in Rhode Island.

"It's been different because they come from a different place than we do, and they've experienced different things," said 14-year old Amanda Shurtleff, of Smithfield. "Plus, they bring that New York flavor. They're just really cool to hang out with."

There is one additional 'dot' that would completely define the path to St. Ann's by the parishioners of St. John's in Rhode Island. At this point, the readers have certainly become increasingly aware and the compelling stories of the plight of inner-city children especially with respect to those educational shortcomings for which they are not responsible but bear their burden……..*for life!* The reader has also read about the linkage of the inner-city environment for African-Americans to history. They have also read about 'voices' throughout the years included those who represented the non-existent 'voices' of those inner-city children and the efforts of St. John's parishioners [and others] who so willingly became the 'voice' of these children. On April 15, 2002, I was privileged to speak at an ECW [Episcopal Church Women] luncheon at St. John's. They also heard what you have been reading but I also added "Let's talk about the children and their environment-it is not a pretty story-indeed, it is a devastating one!" As it was difficult to relate to ECW a complete story in such a relatively short time-it is equally difficult to tell a complete story in a relatively few pages. However, at that time, I chose to share some thoughts, experiences and reflections with them-piece by piece, bit by bit-in order to bring some cohesiveness to all the pieces.

The steadily increasing awareness about the children of the South Bronx was the genesis, the wake-up call, the fuel, the launch pad, the motivation for this ministry. As we read, understood and experienced these 'pieces', the reason and rationale for this book of stories, slowly but steadily, were taking shape.

The children we meet through the deepening relationships that evolve between the children and their families certainly contradict the stereotypes of urban children, youth and families too frequently presented on TV and in newspapers.

More specifically, our experiences at St. Ann's, our discussions and sharing with the members of that community and our personal observations brought the honesty and defensive persona, the perseverance to survive, the courage to make the best of any situation and the cloud of anger and sadness as well as an innate joy that permeates this inner city environment. It is an environment of contradictions. It is, in the eyes of the author, a virtual prison with all of its impact upon humanity. It is an environment that is not necessary!

Imbedded within the conversations with both the children and adults are signs that they are aware that 'something is wrong here'. Perhaps, it is their individual and collective humanity speaking out!

The lack of reasonable health care shows its ugly head in a variety of ways, e.g., the level of AIDS upon adults, both men and women, and children, asthma and respiratory situations that are related to the environment. Personal experiences with those who exist amongst very substandard housing, a collateral lack of pest control, the ever-present threat of gang behavior and, in the experience-based opinion of the author, there exists a general *wherewithal* to address a wide spectrum of inner city issues that, for the most part, do not have a substantial existence beyond the walls of the inner city. Some of these issues are a lack of information and guidance about available resources, income tax conflicts, legal situations, an inability to interact with the various levels of government, crime et al. Then, of course, there are the usual predators of society that leverage these issues for their own benefit.

There is an uncanny ability, especially amongst the children, to create alternative games, activities and playgrounds from items that the rest of America simply throws away. There is a special level of creativity [perhaps, out of necessity] and an admirable resilience amongst the inner city residents in order to make 'survival' a 'successful process'.

I would be remiss in my responsibility if I do not mention the outward and obvious expressions and acts of faith so omnipresent in the inner city. There is a strong belief in a greater power, in God, that is such a huge contrast to the daily survival challenges of the inner city. Perhaps, they are related to each other! Of course, the ministry-as reflected in this book-provides an abundance and irrefutable evidence of **Amazing Grace**.

The continuing lack of an educational program that is parallel to those programs beyond the walls of the South Bronx is particularly discouraging. This is one of the driving forces for supportive efforts, e.g., the after-school and summer Freedom School programs at St. Ann's.

Hopefully, some sort of picture is forming in the minds of the readers that reflect the realities of life in the inner cities of America, e.g., the South Bronx. Allow the author to complement this picture with a simple question: *"How would you feel if these were your children?....and..... What would you do about it?"*

It becomes so appropriate at this point to interject two stories so relevant to this particular excerpt. [1] Following the ECW luncheon meeting, one of the very senior citizens at St. John's approached me very quietly and humbly and said in absolutely firm words "I want to send a Christmas card to a child in the South Bronx!" That following Christmas [2002], the families of St. John's sent more than 300 Christmas cards to the families at St. Ann's. Each card had a personal message enclosed. [2] During a home stay with Steve and Liz after a summer session at ECC, eight-year old Jamal Rodriquez exclaimed that "Today is my birthday!" Liz and Steve had a houseful this weekend as Jeffrey Goodwin and Edward White were also staying there. In a textbook response of St. John's Outreach team, and its reach beyond its borders, Dennis Demessianos and his wife, Lelani Kratowill were coming over from Middletown, RI; they have a longstanding relationship with Jeffrey and Edward and wanted to see them. A sheet cake suddenly appeared and the spontaneous birthday party was on. This was truly a memorable occasion for Jamal; upon his return to the South Bronx he commented to Steve and Liz: "You know, I never had a birthday party before."

These reflections and, indeed, the entirety of the stories within this book do represent an undeniable and compelling motivation for action by those who recognize and value their individual and collective social and humanitarian responsibilities. Imbedded in the St. John's Outreach Experiential Model [Appendix H] and in other similar functional models is the principle that outreach and community service are no longer optional activities of scheduling convenience but rather they are a social, ethical, moral and spiritual mandate.

Somewhere along that time line of education-based industrial, technological and social progress and development, continually improved living conditions and valued humanity for most Americans, the process of education for inner-city children became ***devalued*** for most inner-city children and, combined with other inner city factors, resulted in a sustained ***devaluation*** of the children. The resultant decline in priority, therefore, made a meaningful education increasingly unavailable-indeed, denied-to many, e.g., the inner-city populations. There is a 'twisted' and sad irony to this because Horace Mann, esteemed and enlightened educator, [1796-1859], also commented on this triad. He provided the following 'reminders':

"A human being is not attaining his full heights until he is educated."

"Education then, beyond all other devices of human origin, is the great equalizer of the conditions of men, the balance wheel of the social machinery."

"Be ashamed to die before you do something for humanity."

Clearly, Mother Martha, almost 200 years later, gave life and meaning to these paradigms via the after-school and summer programs at St. Ann's. At the risk of repetition, Patterson, in Appendix B, commended Daniel Patrick Moynihan not so much for saying "This is what we must do." but rather advocating that something must be done about those social conditions that suppressed those African-Americans trapped in the inner-cities of America. Certainly, Patterson et al have been and remain an iconic 'voice' for them. The Outreach Team at St. John's has responded to this consistent and compelling message and the many 'voices' throughout the years but the essence of Horace Mann's messages are emphatically imbedded in the outreach efforts at St. Ann's that embrace a recognition, a validation of the individual, an emphasis on the value of education and an alleviation of some horrific social and daily living conditions. Collectively, these provide a view of a better future and the priceless commodity of *hope*.

Chapter 8
Stories from the Summer Camperships

Spending a week or so at a rural summer camp in New England may sound like just another week of typical activity during those warm, lazy summers between school years for most American children. However, for inner-city children, summer camp is like life on another planet-a totally different world-a very different environment with very different societal 'rules' and protocols. Simply put, summer camp activities and especially the interactions with other similar-aged children were dramatic 'eye-openers' for the inner-city children *and* those children from middle-class America. As time moved on, the summer camp experience also became 'mind-opening' and, of course, 'heart-opening' for all concerned. In fact, it an upcoming section on 'reflections' there will be some very moving examples of this multilateral impact upon the lives of all involved: children, observers, adults, parents and staff personnel. Summer camp became a gateway to that awareness that there is another life beyond the walls of the South Bronx and, maybe, just maybe, that life may be achievable. The transformation from one world to another for these inner-city children now had its genesis! Momentum would soon follow!

The scenario for the summer camperships included [1] the 'earning' of a week of summer camp at ECC by the children at St. Ann's, [2] the transportation of the children from the South Bronx to the summer camp in rural Rhode Island, [3] the many logistics associated with the transportation to and from St. Ann's, ECC and Barrington, [4] the development of the expectations and mindsets of the children during these trips about the forthcoming camp experience and its inherent opportunities and responsibilities, [5] picking the children up at the weekly endings of the camp [usually a late Friday afternoon or early evening] and bringing them to Barrington since a Friday evening departure to the South Bronx would mean a 10:00 P.M. arrival there and that was practically unacceptable for many reasons, [6] overnight accommodations and activities with the younger set and their families and friends from the St. John's community and [7] the return trip to the South Bronx.

The transportation times were viewed as opportunities to interact with the children via listening, mentoring, answering a myriad questions, addressing fears and concerns and, in summary, further developing a sense of 'family' between the two very different communities but with the very common bonds called humanity and dignity. An undeniable and much-valued outcome of these summer campership 'scenarios' was the enhanced view of the world beyond the South Bronx within the minds, hearts and spirits of the children. This outcome would be translated into an increased hope and grounded reference for each of their lives. Individual stories to follow in the coming sections of this book are representative of the many that have and continue to provide a substantial confirmation and validation of their 'new' mindsets. Over the nine years of camperships from 2002-2010, the parishioners of St. John's have sponsored nearly 200 ECC camperships; some children attended the ECC summer camp more than once during the summer and some of those were due to the risk of spending their summer in the South Bronx. This scenario did achieve some level of 'smoothness' interspersed with those inevitable issues and concerns inherent in this segment of the ministry. However, these issues and concerns were 'golden opportunities' for discovery, mentoring, resolution of fears or differences and a bonding predicated upon the innate goodness and humanity of all the individuals involved in this ministry: those who choose to serve and for those we are honored to serve!

Although, the level of trust of the St. Ann's community and the credibility of 'those tourists from Rhode Island' had enjoyed steady and significant growth in a few short years with each outreach activity, the initial campership trips, understandably, were characterized by excitement and hype but also with a good dose of reluctance and even a fear of the forthcoming unknown. The dominant component of *all* the ministry activities was the care and concern for the children while the activities, per se, while important, were given a secondary priority. This priority for the children became an integral part of the informal orientation provided to the 'rookie' travelers from St. John's going to St. Ann's for the first time.

Regardless of the particular activity in progress, e.g., painting, cleaning, repairing, etc., whenever there was an opportunity to interact with the children, i.e., listening, answering their questions, asking questions about them, simply being with them, etc. that volunteer-child interaction assumed a top priority because the aggregate effect of these interactions were, in a sense, a process of validation for the importance [and the humanity] of each youngster [and more than a few adults]. We always wanted our actions and behavior to make the statement *"You are important!"* As the initial trips from the South Bronx got underway [there were seven such trips in 2002], the innate excitement of children going to their very first summer camp together with that inevitable 'bravado' of inner-city residents, steadily transcended into an uneasy quietness as the van came closer and closer to ECC. It was during these trips that the outreach adults [aka drivers] took the time and effort to enable the children to visualize their impending arrival as best as possible. The goal, simply put, was to minimize their fears and anxieties and to maximize the reality of their expectations. Of course, with the passage of a few years and the learned experience of the children attending camps in previous summers, this cacophony of sounds did not diminish but rather became constant. Additionally, the sound level increased in intensity and volume as the vans left the hardened environment of the South Bronx and the children showed their increasing delight with the transformation from the 'cement' of New York to the Connecticut countryside and then to the rural environment of Rhode Island and ECC. Exclamations of discovery became a staple of these trips, e.g., "Hey, I just saw a real cow!" or "Look at all the trees!" or "Wow, there's a real lake-with boats and all!" The unveiling of 'life beyond the walls of the South Bronx' had begun! To the ears and hearts of those outreach members making these trips, the 'cacophony' sounded like a beautiful symphony.

Laranda Jones

Laranda had come into our lives several years prior to the initiation of the summer camperships in 2002. Laranda was and remains a delightful young lady: enthusiastic, bright, interactive and full of energy and questions. There were times, though, that the trials, wounds and difficulties of residency in the South Bronx did surface but Laranda's unbridled spirit, enthusiasm and perseverance overcame these disadvantages; Laranda was, very much, a determined young lady [as the readers shall see!]. The outreach team members who frequently went to St. Ann's prior to 2002 had really bonded with Laranda [and others]. Whenever, it was time for the Outreach team members to board their vans after a day or several days at St. Ann's, they would always find Laranda-and other children-already sitting in the van. Laranda's request was always "I want to go back to Rhode Island with you guys!" Of course, the time for trips to Rhode Island had not yet arrived; but when the summer camperships were announced, Laranda really was excited-and that's a major understatement-about the possibility of staying in that van and going to Rhode Island. When Mother Martha selected her as one of the girls making the inaugural trip to the ECC summer camp, Laranda literally told the world of Mother Martha's 'wonderful selection.' In the days prior to this first trip, Laranda became the cheerleader for the rest of the children making that trip. She told them about the many wonderful activities that would happen at summer camp as well as the opportunities to share this summer experience with children from what was perceived as another planet called Rhode Island!

However, on her first trip from the South Bronx to ECC summer camp, the usual excitement and hype would inevitably diminish into this awkward quietness despite the efforts of the St. John's outreach ministry team accompanying the girls to alleviate the 'fear of the unknown'. Part of the trips to and from the South Bronx always included a stop at a McDonald's in Connecticut. When we stopped the first time on the first trip, all the children thought that it was simply great! Those stops at McDonald's became the highlight of the driving trips. However, I noticed that Laranda was unusually quiet-even subdued-with a few tears in her eye as she hesitated getting out of the van at McDonald's. I asked Laranda if there was something wrong and if there was something I could do to help. Clearly, the situation called for some one-on-one befriending. I asked the other St. John's adult to take the other girls into McDonald's. I suggested that Laranda and I just take some quiet time sitting under a tree as it was a very hot day; we didn't have to talk about anything but we could just sit together and, if she ever wanted to talk about anything, I would certainly listen. The eternity of 10 minutes went by and Laranda offered that she "wanted to go back to the South Bronx". I told her if that is what you really want, we'll make it happen but I would also be interested, without questioning the reasons why she wanted to go back home. Laranda's fear-based response was that "I may not like it at summer camp." I said that I certainly do understand that and that I would also be a little concerned and worried leaving my neighborhood to go to a strange place. "Let's see, Laranda, if we can come up with a solution." "Hmmmmm" I said "I'm sort of in the middle of a dilemma now because I've got to get the other five girls to camp this evening and I also have to get you back to the South Bronx!" "How would you feel if [1] we took the girls to summer camp and [2] I would then drive you back to the South Bronx this evening." She looked at me and said "Al, You would really drive me back to New York tonight?" My response was "Absolutely! But first let's get these kids to camp; the sooner we do that the sooner we can get you back home." Her concerns quickly faded as she said "I'm hungry."

As our van approached the entrance to ECC, it became apparent that Sue Henthorne and her staff at ECC had prepared well for our arrival; members of the staff and the counselors had prepared welcome signs for the children from St. Ann's and extended a sincere and warm welcome to all. The girls from the South Bronx became immediately enamored with this unexpected-in-their-minds reception. It also provided a firm validation of what we had told them to expect on the van ride from St. Ann's. There is a check-in process at summer camp that involved some paperwork, a health examination, an assignment to one of the camp cabins that housed about eight children and two experienced counselors; it is important for the reader to recognize that these activities were taking place in a green, rural environment with tons of fresh air. Following the check-in, the children, counselors and staff would gather for the evening meal. Seating would be at tables corresponding to their cabin assignments. Of course, Laranda went through the entire process and it appeared that she was becoming increasingly taken with and involved in the events of the arrival and the warm reception. Keeping in mind her request and our 'agreement' to return to the South Bronx that evening, I sought out Laranda during the evening meal. I found her with her cabin team; she had become the 'hit of the table' with her energy, joy and engaging smile. However, an agreement is an agreement and I had to remind Laranda about that and that we should be leaving for the South Bronx. Her response was immediate and clearly emphatic: "Al, I just love it here with all my new friends and I really would like to stay." I asked her if she was sure of this and her response to remain at camp was even more pronounced. As I departed ECC I was whispering words of gratitude and thinking "Wow, isn't that amazing?" Of course, this was but one of many 'amazing' events that would follow throughout the next decade. Laranda's innate enthusiasm and fueled by her experiences of this ministry has enabled her to dramatically improve her life and academic worlds and, according to the neighborhood network, she is currently living with her uncle in Queens and certainly seems to have lifted herself to a better place.

Mariah Lamont

Mariah [in 2002] was a 13-year-old young lady going to the summer camp at ECC for the first time and came to St. Ann's for her pick-up and transportation to ECC. Mariah is one of four siblings; she has three brothers: George, Chuck and Philly. The story of this family, the Morrisons, especially the journey of Chuck, comes later in this book. Again, one must remember that 'going to summer camp' was a new experience for the children who simply didn't have a reference point for a summer camp. It was perceived as an unknown world, very much like one's first day at school, going away to college or the military service, starting a new job, etc., with all the collateral fears and anxieties. I cannot imagine what thoughts, perceptions and expectations were going through their individual minds and their imaginations as well. Mariah came to St. Ann's with enough luggage and bags and 'stuff' for an entire summer-and even longer; she also came with what might have been perceived as a 'chip on her shoulder.' Time and Chuck would tell us differently, i.e., that this perceived 'chip' was really a defensive and self-protective practice for safety on the streets of the South Bronx. As with the initial trip with Laranda and her fellow passengers, the adult Outreach members made extended efforts to provide a visual picture of the camp, other campers of their age and camp activities so unknown in the South Bronx. They also made efforts to relate the 'success and satisfaction' experienced by those in Laranda's group who always and enthusiastically provided immediate emotional and exciting feedback to the St. Ann's community upon their return from ECC several days earlier. In spite of these efforts, Mariah continued to verbalize-in a variety of ways-her fears, doubts, suspicions et al about the upcoming summer campership experience. These verbalizations took on an added intensity as we drove from the South Bronx, through the rolling hills and woods of Connecticut and into rural and picturesque Rhode Island. When we arrived at ECC we followed the established protocol of parking the SUV in one of the available parking lots and prepared to go onto the registration area for cabin assignments and to meet the assigned counselors for their respective cabins. Once registered and having their cabin assignments, the procedure was to return to the van and drive each of the six youngsters to their cabins with their 'luggage'. However, as we started to walk to the registration area, this group of six young ladies and I moved very carefully and gingerly as a single body or a single cluster of people. As we moved in such a strange fashion, Mariah said: "Wow, look at all the white people!" Believe me; this observation was very understandable after living in the African-American and Hispanic colors of the South Bronx. My response to Mariah and the other five girls was: "That's OK because all those white people are probably saying "Wow, look at all the black people!" and they may be even more concerned than you. Don't judge people by their color-white or black-because, as you will soon see-they only see six very nice young ladies coming to summer camp." Of course, in a fashion so similar to that experienced by Laranda Jones and probably many others, the fears, doubts and suspicions faded away as that special magic of children getting along with other children came into play.

These and other similar experiences provided a dramatic introduction to those campership drivers and co-drivers from St. John's of the feelings and fears of so many children from St. Ann's. These feelings and fears are common derivatives of inner-city residence and environments. Presently, Mariah still resides in the South Bronx and is an unmarried mother. Her future, at best, is somewhat uncertain. However, experience over the past decade has made the point that the benefits of the summer campership experience are latent within the individual.

One of the more dramatic developments in the ministry at St. Ann's and back in Barrington was that the children from two very different communities bonded rather quickly and naturally; this dynamic was and continues to be a very moving experience for all concerned. The children provided an excellent model-for all to see- for the power and benefits of seeing through all the differences and just seeing each other's humanity.

As mentioned earlier in the historical perspective of this book, the failure to see the humanity in another person, another community, another ethnic group, etc. is a costly inhibitor to personal, group, national and social progress. This blindness to another's humanity inevitably leads to [1] a devaluation of life and [2] a wide spectrum of abuses. History and the world we live in today provide an abundance of horrific examples. Inner-city conditions in America are such an example; the absolute horror of ethnic cleansings throughout the ages certainly are mega-examples of a 'blindness to humanity'; domestic abuse is another; bullying is another; . . . . ; and let us not forget the inherent abuses of the 'slave trade', the resultant racism and the conditions of inner-city life in America.

Ryona

I met Ryona in 2004 during one of the mission trips to St. Ann's; as usual, each mission trip included a menu mix of planned and unintended activities. During this particular trip one of the planned activities was mentoring and tutoring for those who wished to participate. My tutoring session was in the basics of mathematics and Ryona was one of my 'students'; Ryona was 10 years old, attentive, willing to learn, courteous, articulate and quite capable in mathematics. Simply put, she was a delight to have in class and quietly served as a role model for other students.

I could not help but think about Ryona living in an environment other than the South Bronx, e.g., in Barrington or any other place in middle-class America. My expectations quickly gravitated to Ryona thriving and achieving a full, safe and meaningful life and having all of its many inherent 'gifts of life' as compared to the inherent disadvantages of birth and residency in the South Bronx. The lottery of one's birthplace creates both 'instant winners' to some and 'instant and life-long challenges', i.e., 'rocky roads,' to others. Ryona, like the other children at St. Ann's, was a constant reminder of the potential and promise of children and, of course, the motivation for this rich ministry.

During our trips to St. Ann's, Ryona had heard about the summer camp at ECC from previous attendees so she often expressed a growing wish to go to summer camp. We talked with Ryona's mother about the feasibility of sending Ryona to summer camp that forthcoming summer; her mother was adamant in her polite, soft refusal in choosing to withhold her approval. Ryona's mother and I talked about the demonstrated advantages of a summer campership for those children who had already attended. However, a major reason for not allowing Ryona to attend was that her family, like most, had endured a variety of losses and her fear for 'losing Ryona' was unbearable. Ryona-as I-was very disappointed. I talked with Ryona about the challenge and difficulties of 'change' experienced by every individual. Our talks also included that perseverance in pursuit of a worthwhile goal is another 'key of life' that eventually opens a door. However, one must keep trying! Ryona and I agreed that we would again pursue that summer campership in the following year

Prior to the summer of 2005, preparations for the upcoming ECC summer camperships were in evidence at St. John's and at St. Ann's. The opportunity for a continued perseverance was at hand. Again, we sat and talked with Ryona's mother who still remained somewhat reluctant but definitely not adamant. The advantages of a summer campership were put forth in a somewhat different context. First, we indicated that summer camp was truly a gift to Ryona-as it was with others who had attended in 2002, 2003 and 2004-but it was a gift that only she, her mother, could give to her. The mother's slight smile indicated that the reluctance was slowly diminishing. I pointed out to Ryona's mother that we understand and value the concerns of every caretaker [mothers, aunts, grandmothers, foster mothers et al] and we could make the claim that "You know, we haven't lost a child yet; we have returned every summer camper for three years now!". Again, her mom smiled a bit more and said that Ryona could go to summer camp in 2006 if she 'earned' it. Ryona, now very enthused by the progress, asked her mom just how she could earn it. Her mom said that "You will need 50 points to go to camp; I will give you a point for each good act that you perform during the coming year." Her mom then reviewed the candidate agenda of 'good acts' for Ryona to do. The deal had been struck with the power of Amazing Grace. As we shook hands and exchanged hugs, I could see Ryona literally dancing so very happily in the background.

It is important to note that Ryona earned those required 50 points in less than two months and did go to summer camp the following year.

However, there is more to Ryona's story than summer camp. During those early years, Ryona and I would share our respective thoughts and ideas about myriad topics. She would often test me by saying that she had something very important to share with me. My response, each time, was that "There is probably nothing that I haven't heard before but when you are ready, Ryona, I will listen because whatever you wish to share must be important to you and, therefore, it is equally important to me." Months later on a rainy afternoon, when the outreach team was at St. Ann's, Ryona asked me if we could take a walk around the church property because she 'wanted to tell me something'. We walked and we walked and had a lot of small talk about this and that and we walked in silence; she then shared with me in quiet terms that "She trusts me!" and told me that her Dad was in prison and she really did not want to go there to see him. I didn't want to ask any questions at that point but I did address the benefits of verbalizing your feelings; perhaps, you could share with whoever is asking you to go to prison to see your Dad your feelings. Perhaps this person assumes that you may want to go based on their view of the situation; you may be helping them by asking them to listen to your 'feelings' and concerns." "Whatever the outcome", I told Ryona, "You have been true to yourself, you have stood up for yourself and asserting oneself is good for you and helpful to the other person."

Another aspect of Ryona's story is that it highlights a very treasured commodity that simply cannot be purchased anywhere-not even at the most upscale malls. It is a commodity that is priceless and one that must be **earned** by an individual or a group of individuals; it is a human commodity that makes one's life journey a bit more smooth, enjoyable and meaningful. This commodity is either very rare or very common in the South Bronx; it is called **trust**. Ryona certainly discovered that members of the Outreach ministry could be trusted because of **what we did** and not by **what we said.** Indeed, the building of that trust with each member of the St. Ann's community took time, energy and even creativity. **Trust**, we learned was clearly rare amongst the chaos of disadvantages in the South Bronx and the other inner cities of America; probably, because so much was always promised but never really provided. Mother Martha, probably the most trusted individual in the South Bronx, is an iconic figure of trust in her community. Of course, there also exists in the South Bronx strong personal faiths and a **remarkable trust in Amazing Grace** despite this continuing chaos of disadvantages in the South Bronx.

Ryona's story is not an overwhelming one but it is a very important one because it –like the story of each and every child at St. Ann's-is an opportunity for mentoring and enhancing the hope, knowledge and expectations of each child. Admittedly, each story, realistically, cannot be a success story, but, more importantly, there are success stories albeit relatively few as compared to those myriad children who have little hope or opportunity for some path to success. It is appropriate at this point to shed some light on the enormity of the challenge, sustained effort and commitment that are, collectively, both necessary and sufficient to [1] provide guidance to and advocacy for the individual inner-city child to even visualize and believe that there is access to a pathway to success and [2] enable each child along that pathway **for as long as it takes!** That journey is not for the weak of heart, mind and spirit whether you be the child or the child's advocate. Like so many children with enormous potential, I can only wonder, hope and pray that Ryona is on a safe and meaningful path within her life.

Chapter 9

What Is 'Success'?

The definitions of 'success' are as varied as are their words alluring. It may be helpful to recall that foundational definition provided to us by Nelson Mandela in his 2011 book *Conversations with Myself* [Picador]. On page 211, he writes "In judging our progress as individuals we tend to concentrate on external factors such one's social position, influence and popularity, wealth and standard of education. These are, of course, important in measuring one's success in material matters and it is perfectly understandable if many people exert themselves mainly to achieve all of these. But internal factors may be even more crucial in assessing one's development as a human being. Honesty, sincerity, simplicity, humility, pure generosity, absence of vanity, readiness to serve others-qualities which are within easy reach of every soul-are the foundation of one's spiritual life."

It is quite remarkable that these same qualities also accurately characterize the residents of the St. Ann's community in the South Bronx!

I can recall a television commercial about the financial investment firm, Smith Barney. In it, an obviously older, experienced and knowledgeable gentleman and corporate officer is asked the question: 'Just how do *you* measure success?' His response was very brief but utterly profound "We measure success one client at a time!" In a nutshell, then, the title of this book, ***Let's Start With The Children***, takes on a more comprehensive and clear meaning. This incremental approach, i.e., one-client-at-a time, carries the message that [1] every 'client', every child, is important and time is required to transition to success [albeit in financial terms but, so much more importantly, in those intangible factors that give definition to one's humanity and character] and [2] success for a population of 'clients' will, indeed, take a much longer time. In very much the same manner, that same measure of success applied to disadvantaged inner-city children also means that every child is important. Specifically, when the impact upon the life of a single child in a very disadvantaged, devaluing and harmful environment is countered via a concentrated and comprehensive process of social and political effort, compassion, advocacy and commitment then-and only then-will a 'unit of success' be achieved. It is important to understand that the time that it takes to achieve 'success' for a single child is measured in years. The time to achieve 'success' for an entire inner-city family, community or neighborhood is then measured in decades or longer!

What is the message at this point? *It is precisely that it literally takes a huge, sustained effort to 'save one inner-city child'; there are no quick and convenient solutions.* This message will probably be foreign to those-whether they be aware or knowingly unaware of the immeasurable gravity of the human costs of residence in the inner-cities-who continue to sit on the sidelines and address other issues perceived as more important than the humanity of those children trapped in the inner-city. Let us recall what Daniel Patrick Moynihan offered in *The Negro Family: The Case for National Action* [1965], i.e., "that something must be done". And that was almost a half of a century ago! This message of the required long-term sustained effort surely seems to be enormously intimidating and even frightening to many and this situation will be addressed in more detail in the concluding pages of this book. Specifically, the ironic difference in the costs in terms of time, dollars and humanity of 'doing something' and 'doing business as usual' will be highlighted. Conversely, this message is thoroughly understood by those who choose to 'enter the arena' and persistently and faithfully serve, support and advocate for the inner-city populations-especially, the children.

A Note on the Educational Arena

One of the more interesting observations that permeate the last five or six decades is the persistent efforts of the 'educational engineers that modify the curricula of the primary, middle and secondary schools. It almost seems like there is a need for these modifications that are somewhat analogous to those marketing strategies and schemes to promote a 'new and improved' product. This search for an 'easier' path to academic skills seems, to this author, to have lost its way! With some modifications-especially in the area of mathematics and reading and writing-there is a movement away from those long standing principles of 'reading, writing and arithmetic' so prevalent prior to the 1970s. The successful path to these very necessary academic skills is found in the fields of effort, work ethic and perseverance.

This book-and others-have made references to the role of one's education to one's forward movement along the path of life. The educational statistical data base tells many stories of the status of education in America. The global ranking of America's math, science and reading scores have plummeted over the years. Stories about the rate of high school drop outs-especially in the inner cities-are disturbing. ***The challenges facing America's educational system are nothing less than significant; the challenges facing the schools of the inner city are well beyond significant!*** There is a tendency to immediately focus upon the performance of the teachers as the arena of interest; I would respectfully suggest that the school systems' administrators, the self-promotion of the unions and the politicians at local, state and national levels be added to the arena of interest. There is some movement in this direction but let us keep in mind that there are students still falling from the educational mainstream of America and the foregone opportunities that could have been available to them while the well-meaning educational engineers search for a 'solution'

Now, let's talk about the children of the inner cities, e.g. the South Bronx. Having been in the educational arena for five decades or so in a spectrum of capacities, I had myriad opportunities to recognize the many academic hopes, dreams and, yes, the inherent abilities of inner city children. One such position was as an adjunct professor at the University of Rhode Island; two young ladies in one of my math classes were from inner city Providence and were average students but each had the 'eye of the tiger' with respect to obtaining a college degree. At the conclusion of one academic year, it was their intent to enroll in the next level of math in the forthcoming fall semester. As their mentor and advocate, I suggested that doing some additional math work during the summer might be a worthwhile preparation for the math challenges of the forthcoming semester. Of course, these words about 'doing math in the summer' are not the words a student immediately embraces but these two students agreed. However, we established a schedule for meeting throughout the summer in the University's extension division in urban Providence.

Following our first meeting, one of the students asked if her brother could also attend the next meeting. I readily agreed to that. At our second meeting, there were five rather than the expected two students plus one brother. Prior to the third meeting, I was driving to our classroom and took notice of a rather large group of children of varying ages walking along the train tracks that separated the University complex from downtown Providence. I thought that they were putting themselves at risk but then realized that the initial two students were amongst this group. I arrived in the classroom before the students; what an unexpected surprise that there were fifteen tired, sweating and very eager students in class on that especially hot and humid summer day. Talk about eager and motivated students who truly embraced the opportunity to learn! *This was one of a litany of experiences that emphasized the opportunities to make a difference in the lives of inner city children.* Their abilities, motivation, dreams and hopes were no different from those children living in environments beyond the inner city. The literature is abundant with examples of African-Americans who have made contributions to society and, certainly, some of these individuals started their lives in an inner city of America. For the doubters, the author recommends *And Still We Rise, The Trials and Triumphs of Twelve Gifted Inner-City Students* by Miles Corwin [Harper Perennial, 2000].

Experiences, stories and even movies have addressed the challenges, risks and rewards of being a teacher in the inner city. Teaching *is* an honorable profession that history tells us-again and again and again-that so many success stories begin with a particular teacher. Teaching is challenging and rewarding in every classroom throughout America. However, in the inner cities, as great and formidable as the challenges may be, the opportunities and rewards are even greater or, more accurately, *could be greater, much greater.* Simply, have a conversation with a teacher who has served within the inner city. These teachers have answered the call to their educational duty while other candidate teachers lose their voices [Ah! that word again!] and sit on the more comfortable sidelines.

Perhaps, just perhaps, this story within the story will be heard not only by those in the teaching and educational arenas of America but also by those in the collateral areas of politics, school administrations and government.

More than a century ago on April 23, 1910, Theodore Roosevelt at the Sorbonne in Paris gave us an early warning of those who neglect their responsibilities:

"It's not the critic who counts; nor the man who points out how the strong man stumbles, or where the doer of deeds could have done better. The credit belongs to the man {woman} in the arena whose face is marred by dust and sweat and blood; who strives valiantly; who errs and comes short again and again because there is no effort without error and shortcoming; who does actually strive to do the deed; who knows the great enthusiasm, the great devotions, spends himself {herself} in a worthy cause; who at the best knows in the end the triumph of high achievement; and who at worst if he {she} fails at least he {she} fails while daring greatly, so that his place shall never be with those cold and timid souls who know neither victory nor defeat."

I shared Roosevelt's words-at different times and places- with various family members, students, professional colleagues et al who emulated the spirit and meaning of his quotation. Without question or exception, the credit and commendations really belong to that individual who is 'in the arena'. Make no mistake about it these are the individuals who strive daily to survive in the inner-city as well as those who choose to serve there and try to make a difference-and more often than not, do make a difference! I later added to the above quotation for my children and grandchildren, friends, students and colleagues my response to the inevitable naysayers and those who make acquiescence to futility a career:

"Always listen to your own heart, mind and soul rather than those individuals 'outside the arena' who have taken life memberships in the 'woulda, shoulda, coulda' clubs!"

Recall that the effort and time that is required to make a difference in the plight of a single inner-city child is huge, challenging and intimidating; let me add the following quotation:

"Nothing in the world can take the place of persistence. Talent will not; nothing is more common than unsuccessful men with talent........ genius will not; unrewarded genius is almost a proverb. Education will not; the world is full of uneducated derelicts. Persistence and determination alone are omnipotent. The slogan "press on" has solved, and always will solve, the problems of the human race."

Anonymous

This basic foundation provides some sort of a rational and realistic context for that challenge facing not only the inner-city child but also the American society in total in order to realize that there is another life beyond the virtual walls of the inner-cities of America, e.g., the South Bronx and, then, to find the 'road' out of this virtual disadvantaged imprisonment.

In order to provide just a 'hint' of the magnitude of the effort required to meet this challenge, let's look at the current efforts of Edward White, Jr. [16 years old], Jeffrey Goodwin [13 years old] and the Brule children [Alicia, Jennie, Liola and Frank]. It is probably safe to say with some confidence that the stories of the Brule children are now taking shape as remarkable 'success stories' whereas those journeys of Edward and Jeffrey are moving in a good direction but there exists risk and uncertainty with their respective journeys. Once someone said: *"It is not so important as to where you are but as to the direction in which you are moving!"* However, history is abundant with myriad similar personal and national journeys in which faith, self-confidence, principle and knowledge are the 'weapons of choice' that certainly diminish [1] risk and uncertainty with the passage of time and, also, [2] those long-standing disadvantages. Then-and only then-will personal and national hope, confidence and progress inevitably follow.

Edward White, Jr.

How does one begin Edward's 'story'? Let it be first said that he is truly symbolic of residence and upbringing in the South Bronx; it is equally symbolic of one person's ongoing journey and struggle and that moral and pragmatic guidance provided by both the St. Ann's community and the St. John's community as well as a concerned and loving dad, Edward White, Sr. The transformation of the persona of Edward, Jr.-when in the South Bronx- from a perceived hip-hop gang member with an 'in-your-face' attitude to a typical, family-oriented 'gentle giant'-when in the Rhode Island community almost defies description. Let the reader understand that the tough persona assumed by so many in the inner-city environment is really a defensive mechanism for self-protection; this 'lesson' was very articulately explained to me by Chuck Morrison whom we will meet in the next few pages.

In November of 2010, there was a flurry of emails within the St. John's community about Edward White, Jr. One parishioner, also an Outreach member, specifically, asked the question: "Who is Edward, Jr.?" In order to properly answer this question, it is necessary to look at that email that was the genesis for the flurry.

On Saturday, November 13, 2010, I sent the following email to Mother Martha:

Good morning Martha:

There were two events yesterday wrt Edward:

[1]   I stopped by to see Steve L. [he's a Viet Nam vet and I missed him on Thursday-wanted to chat and thank him for his service {in Viet Nam}] and Liz H. Steve was out but Liz and I talked about Edward. I briefed her on the activities and emails of the weekend of 10/30 and 10/31. My thoughts after that weekend were to advocate for Edward as a CIT [i.e. **C**ounselor-**I**n-**T**raining at ECC] but also to do some firm mentoring, guiding and reality testing for Edward. Bottom line [and I know that I'm probably preaching to the choir] is that Edward has 'potential' but also has been somewhat irresponsible in some of his actions in the past, e.g., not getting his application in to ECC as required for the [ECC CIT] orientation weekend of 10/30 and 10/31. My bottom line is that Edward should be informed of the 'rules of the engagement' should he get to ECC as a CIT. Specifically, this is an opportunity for him and, if he screws up, the impact would be that my credibility and that of others would suffer; other kids to follow could not have our advocacy and support because 'Edward screwed up' and, most importantly, he would have blown a wonderful opportunity to move forward in his life. My thought was to sit down with ECC, put everything on the table and determine the feasibility of Edward going with the condition that he is history should he cross that line that separates responsibility and irresponsibility, i.e., no second chances. Edward would be told of this condition prior to going to see if understands it, accepts it and is willing to accept the consequences of his actions.

[2]   The second event: Marion and I attended the induction of Robert Marshall as the new SJ Rector. Great and moving ceremony! However, the Rev. Susan Carpenter

was an invited guest having been the Associate Rector at SJ under the interim Rector for more than a year-Susan is now the ECC Director [author's note: Hmmmm! Another coincidence?]. We had a private conversation: I briefed her on the events and knowledge to date including what I have shared with you in this email. Her bottom line:

a.   His application must [I repeat 'must'] be in by 12/15/10.

b.   Edward would be favorably considered for a CIT position.

c.   She agrees with the no nonsense condition and, actually, it is applicable to all who attend-campers and CITs alike. Also, that Edward should be informed-clearly and concisely-that the ball is now in his court.

d.   I believe that there is a fee to attend camp as a CIT [but, personally, that would not be an issue]. [Author's note: the $500.00 CIT fee-simply unaffordable by an inner-city family-was quickly, quietly and anonymously forthcoming from two individuals who believed in the St. Ann's/St. John's ministry.]

e.   Another concern [of Susan's] is that the CITs are ECC camp residents during the week but must find accommodations elsewhere on weekends. Steve and Liz are the most likely and qualified candidates to do this. They are willing and most qualified because of their years of experience housing some kids during the summer campership programs for different durations of time. Susan-because of the safe-church policy which bans related adults from being the caretakers-would require that parental permission be given to Steve and Liz {perhaps similar to that given for Jeffrey {Goodwin}. I'm guessing that Edward Sr. has enough faith and foresight to provide this permission.

What are your thoughts? Of course, someone there {I wonder

Who?} would have to move his application along; also, there is time to share our thoughts, guidance et al wrt Edward Jr.!

As always, the best to all in the SA community.

Al :o)

Steve Lippincott's email response follows:

Thank you, Al

First, let me say the battle is not merely about an individual. It is about culture. The Bronx is, or at least in my childhood's eye, one of the great and beautiful cities of the world. It is a ruin now. It was a great city then because people like my Aunt Tekla and Aunt Ruth loved their city. There is little that we can do about things on a scale needed to restore the borough to its former glory. But that isn't our job [as I see it]. Culture begins with an individual. In the past decade we saw what Mother Martha's love for her city and its peoples has accomplished.

The old metaphor of the mustard seed comes to mind. Mother Martha has a bag of them. Here's our job: just as in our community garden, our job is **not** to make the plants grow. That is taken care of for us. Our job is to provide the healthy environment for the process to take place. Edward Junior lives in a culture that is about survival. How does one consider the possibilities of a long, rich and productive life when just getting through the week is an accomplishment?

So it is about an individual. Many individuals! I love my adopted city [the greater Providence area]. Nurturing that love is the children I have come to love in my city of origin; this is my weapon in the battle over the culture that ignores potential and defies love.

We've had setbacks and disappointments. I don't know how things will turn out concerning Edward Jr. and his cousin Jeffrey [Goodwin]. We are not given a master plan and we have to keep in mind that our expectations are just that: our expectations. But we can love these children. And guess what, folks? They love us!

Peace, Steven

My responsive email to Steve follows:

AMEN! Steve: and right now the individual of interest and care is Edward [Jr.]. I guess it's time for us to have faith [again] and let Amazing Grace push our fears and inabilities aside!

Thanks, Steve; your words and thoughts are always grounding for me and those beyond me.

Al :o)

A few days later, Steve wrote the following:

"Edward White Junior is one of our kids who have attended ECC for at least nine seasons. Junior is also at the heart of our St. Ann's ministry. The fact that one needs to ask suggests that this ministry has evolved to a point [where] the stated mission at St. Ann's and its applications have gone in different directions. To those of us in the center of all this, our ministry has become personal. We have watched these children grow. These are not just anonymous children whom we have made ours {ours, I hope, in the greater St. John's family}. Not only are these children known to us, their families know us and our relationships extend to them. As of now it breaks down to the Praza family [Daniel, Shadrack, Abdnego, and Meshak] who are the concern of the Judge family. The White family [Edward Jr. and Jeffrey] who are Liz's and my concern and the Brule family who are Jan Malcolm's [concern]. Then there is Gladys Mercado, mother of Ralph DeJesus and grandmother of Jamal Rodriquez [Liz and me again]. Gladys is the senior warden of her church, a grass roots activist on getting guns off the streets [see the YouTube] of her accepting the credos and well-deserved awards. Al coordinates this all.

Now the White story: Edward Sr.'s wife died some years ago. She was the sister of Jeffrey's mother, Shirlee. Edward Sr. lives in the [South Bronx] projects. Jeffrey used to live there as well. Shirlee now [or, at least, as of this 2011 summer] lives in a shelter with Jeffrey. The reason Jeffrey was returned to the South Bronx came of Shirlee's eligibility to get a better shelter for herself if she had a child living with her. [Author's note: several years ago, Steve and Liz-with advocacy and support from the Outreach membership at St. John's-arranged to have Jeffrey live with them in Riverside, RI and to attend St. Andrews school in Barrington, RI. After one successful year at St. Andrews, Shirlee used her motherly 'leverage' to have Jeffrey returned to the South Bronx.] Shirlee has issues. She's schizophrenic with substance abuse [crack, cocaine, etc.]. Jeffrey was an easy choice; he's brilliant, curious and quite malleable. Edward is a different story. We are worried for him because he has two sides. The side we see at my home, at ECC and at St. John's is a side he does not show in the South Bronx. Consequently, I feel he is at high risk. The side one sees when he is in the Bronx is a side that would cause one to dismiss him for more gregarious children. But the side we see is real. He is intelligent, sweet and caring. I feel he is of the highest risk. I support any effort to hold on to him as much as we can because I have known him since he was 5 or 6 years old. [Edward is now 16]. I know the risk involved and have a good understanding of his potential. I am also concerned I have gotten too close to all this and I worry that I risk doing more harm than good in this case so I am advocating for Junior through ECC. As you will see, there is no shortage of affection for Edward at ECC. Susan carpenter [ECC Director] and the counselors at camp know his good side well.

I will be glad to speak to you more on this. Impossible to cover all this in an email. This is a well thought out ministry [shooting from the hip is part of it] with transparency and ethical considerations a very high priority."

There is more-much more-to Edward Jr.'s journey and his growing awareness over the years of 'life beyond the walls of the South Bronx'. This awareness is most certainly an integral part of the St. Ann's and St. John's ministry and collaborative relationship but the dominant influence has been uniquely provided by Steve and Liz during Edward's residence at their home during the many years of ECC summer camperships. This influence-as we shall soon see-impacted Jeffrey Goodwin and others in a very similar manner. It was mentioned earlier that Sue Henthorne of ECC and the outreach team at St. John's had embraced, without hesitation but with faith, the opportunity to provide summer camperships for the children of St. Ann's and, as 'part of the package' the responsibilities of advocacy, mentoring and support that would inevitably be needed within the interaction with inner-city children in a completely different culture and environment in which the same rules and protocols simply did not apply as they may have in the inner-city. As it is for every individual, there is no journey without 'bumps in the road'! Edward was no exception. To be sure, there were some 'bumps' in the road for Edward and his journey. For example, Edward had to request a day's leave from his role as a Counselor-In-Training [CIT] at ECC to return to the Bronx for a court appearance for a previously issued citation for a 'trespassing' violation; citations for a variety of reasons are very commonplace in the inner-cities of America and the South Bronx is certainly not an exception. When a NYPD officer had asked Edward to 'move away' from school property, Edward had apparently failed to either move sufficiently fast and/or sufficiently far enough away from a school where he was 'waiting' for a friend. To Edward's credit and as an indication of his trust in Steve and Liz, he had shared that upcoming court appearance with them upon his arrival at ECC. Children from the South Bronx are more than likely quite hesitant to openly discuss personal issues, e.g., fears, concerns, needs, wants, hopes dreams et al. The inner-city environment of suppression, social and family trauma and simply 'crushed' dreams and expectations eventually takes its toll upon the residents of the South Bronx but especially and so unfortunately upon the children there

On the day of his court appearance, Steve, Edward and I left Steve's home in Riverside, RI at 5:00 AM to insure a timely arrival at The Bronx County Hall of Justice at 265 East 161st Street. We were joined there by Mother Martha, Edward White, Sr. and, quite unexpectedly, by Jeffrey's mother, Shirlee. The experience of that court appearance and seeing the hundreds of individuals being there for any number of reasons was absolutely sobering for me! Although we had to wait more than several hours for Edward's appearance before a judge of the court, it was also an opportunity for Edward to experience the support, presence and love of those who were there for him; I suspect that it was a new experience for Edward. The judge ordered Edward to just stay out of trouble for a specific time and the citation would be automatically expunged.

Prior to this court appearance, there was some misinformation and, therefore confusion, about a second citation and court appearance. Apparently, Edward had been involved in some sort of an altercation with some other teen-agers but there was talk of a felony offense. There was also talk of the reduction of that felony to a misdemeanor. Edward, Sr. had also told Edward, Jr. to 'pack all his things when leaving ECC for his return to the South Bronx for his second court appearance'. Clearly, the message was that he would probably not be returning to ECC; this fear was absolutely devastating-even traumatic-for Edward, Jr. It is fair to say that his entire being was shaken at the expectation of not returning to ECC and the opportunity there which he had embraced. From one person's perspective, the steady and obvious improvement in Edward's confidence as reflected within his interactive skills seemed to take a major step backward to that cautious, withdrawn, quiet and suspicious persona acquired in the South Bronx. Simply put, Edward was one very fearful individual!

This time Steve [Lippincott] and Liz [Hallenbeck] accompanied Edward on his second return to The Bronx Hall of Justice; they were joined there by Mother Martha, Edward, Sr. and Edward Jr.'s court-appointed lawyer. After some confusion brought to the situation by this court-appointed lawyer who actually had two clients with the same name. This was the source of the inconsistency between the felony and misdemeanor charges. Upon hearing of Edward's participation and progress at ECC's summer camp, he continued the case until September, 2011. It is the hope of all concerned that the misdemeanor charges will be dismissed or made eligible for eventual expunging. It is also expected that Edward will return to school to complete some 9th grade requirements and then move on in his high school and then return to ECC as a Counselor in the summer of 2012. His journey continues!

On Monday, August 1, 2011, Sandy Connor, long-time participant and facilitator of the ECC summer campership program, had just driven two boys, Ricky and Carlos, from the South Bronx to ECC. Here's an excerpt from her email: "Had a great trip bringing the boys to camp today [I have to admit, I'm exhausted-but, it's a good tired]. Pat Judge and Eli Seltzer [students at Barrington High School and young veterans of the ministry at St. Ann's] were a big help and made the trip fun for the 2 young boys and they were great co-pilots for me, too. *It was really wonderful to see Edward 'on-duty' as a CIT when we arrived at ECC....he was introducing Ricky and Carlos to everyone as 'these boys are from my church in NY.'* "

It has been mentioned earlier that there are two major critical phases for an individual to 'escape' the disadvantages of residency in the South Bronx or any other inner-city environment for that matter. First, there is that process that enables the individual to visualize and, hopefully, experience life beyond the inner-city and, secondly, the transition to a life devoid of so many undeserved and unfair disadvantages. The reader is asked to remember that this transition is virtually impossible without a supportive team that is committed to *a sustained advocacy* [aka 'for as long as it takes'] for the individual. It is now August, 2011 and Edward is in his closing days as a CIT at ECC and his weekends with Steve and Liz. Not so surprisingly, Edward has 'seen and experienced' another way of life and is now self-advocating for himself to remain in Rhode Island rather than return to the vulnerability of the South Bronx streets. His Dad, Edward, Sr., is well aware of the enormous risk of Edward's return to the South Bronx and is certainly supportive of this option but, understandably, doesn't have a plan to make it happen. The St. John's Outreach perspective is to consider this situation as an opportunity!

Integral to our ministry at St. Ann's, the Outreach membership of St. John's has also experienced many 'teaching moments'; one of these is a quite profound statement by the father of four children who came to ECC from the South Bronx. His response to a question asked by a parishioner during a visit to St. John's, i.e., "What is life like in the South Bronx?" was that "It's like being in a dark room, you want to get out, you don't know how to get out and there's no one to show you the way." This response accurately captures the essence of the challenge of the journey of an inner-city child, an inner-city individual and even an inner-city family to literally break free of the imposing disadvantages of the inner-city. It is also the essence of the collaborative St. Ann's/St. John's ministry! It is important to note that the St. John's effort is simply one of many that directly support the continuing courageous leadership efforts of Mother Martha and her team at St. Ann's.

Edward's wish [based on an innate feeling for both self-advocacy and self-survival] is to remain in Rhode Island or, somewhat more relevant, to *not* to return to the South Bronx; it is a major choice in his journey. As we all know, it would be great if one could just wave a magic wand to make his wish come true; it is also a choice that requires some careful thought and a plan that must be shaped by a long-term goal of successfully impacting Edward's journey, his life's journey! This is the current state of Edward's journey: the teams at St. Ann's and at St. John's need to develop a long-term plan that will essentially make Edward's wish come true but make it come true within a realistic timeline. Our next step is to, again, have faith in the magic of Amazing Grace and share our thoughts with Edward and move forward together. This plan is currently taking shape; it has three major components: [1] an advocacy and mentoring by the St. Ann's community while he necessarily completes his upcoming 9th and 10th grades in the South Bronx, [2] an advocacy and mentoring by the St. John's community in determining feasible academic and resident options in Rhode Island for his 11th grade in 2012 and [3] Edward, himself, and his willingness to embrace those self-responsibilities so inherent in this plan. Edward does have a growing awareness of these responsibilities, e.g., he has already suggested that he transfer to a different school where there would be a reduced risk to his success. He has also mentioned the possibility of volunteer work within St. Ann's after-school program to further reduce the risk to himself during those after-school hours during which the children are most vulnerable. Of course, a collateral benefit is that there are individuals within the St. Ann's community who, then, could provide a supportive umbrella for Edward. On October 26, 2011, Edward returned to ECC for that forthcoming weekend to participate in a training program that would enable him to be a candidate for ***Junior Counselor*** at ECC during the summer of 2012. Several months later, Edward received his confirmation that he had successfully passed the training program. This is a significant step forward in Edward's journey; one is tempted to look beyond 2012 to the summer of 2013 when Harold will become a Counselor in good standing at ECC. Yes, indeed, Edward's journey continues!

We are talking about a single individual, Edward, Jr.; one can only imagine the enormity of the effort required to turn the tide against the disadvantages of inner-city life across a neighborhood, a community ......across America! Hmmmm!

Jeffrey Goodwin

Jeffrey, like his cousin, Edward White, Jr., and so many other inner-city children, seem to present to the world a surprising and growing chain of previously hidden [or, perhaps, long unrecognized] 'positive' characteristics, skills, interests and dreams. One could even say just like those children from middle-class America and those above this middle-class population. From the Outreach perspective, it has become increasingly evident that the ECC camperships-indeed, all facets of this collaborative ministry-have provided that additional catalytic environment for personal awakenings and growth. It is important to note that this ministry is ***inspired by,*** ***collateral to*** and ***supportive of*** Mother Martha's ministry of more than 16 years at St. Ann's. As Steve [Lippincott] had stated earlier in one of his always very relevant and incisive emails: "Here's our job. Just as in our community garden our job is ***not*** to make the plants grow. That is taken care of for us. Our job is to provide the healthy environment for the process to take place." That's exactly what Mother Martha and her staff are doing at St. Ann's and it is exactly what St. John's outreach members do within this ministry.

Jeffrey has become a member of the Riverside, RI community via his many 'home stays' with Steve and Liz during his summer camperships at ECC. I do remember that Steve, Jeffrey and I were members of a team at St. John's unloading over 2000 pumpkins for the annual fall pumpkin festival. Jeffrey was a very willing worker but did display some of that South Bronx persona when he and another boy [from Barrington] of similar age had a difference of opinion about the best way in which to do a particular task on that Saturday morning. It was a physical confrontation in the making. I was able to take Jeffrey aside and, quietly and confidentially-as we have done numerous times throughout the years with numerous children- said that the 'rules' that may be necessary, practiced and accepted in the South Bronx are really not necessary nor appropriate in the St. John's and Rhode Island community. This practice of pointing out alternative solutions and pathways to conflict resolution is just another integral part of the required mentoring process. Most importantly, Jeffrey listened, understood and embraced this new way of living. Even at that early date, Jeffrey was considered to be a 'diamond in the rough'.

The polishing of that 'diamond in the rough' would be provided by Steve and Liz and their very nurturing stable and loving environment. Jeffrey was able to spend a year at St. Andrews School in Barrington, RI while living with Steve and Liz. This year was a special one for Jeffrey because it gave him a continuing view of life beyond the South Bronx. Unfortunately, his mother decided to have Jeffrey return to the South Bronx rather than allow him to continue for another year [or more] at St. Andrews. He had experienced a growth in maturity, behavior and compassion during that year with Steve and Liz and the St. Andrews environment. For example, while at St. Andrews, Jeffrey was as would be expected and quite appropriate for the situation was romping on the soccer field before a game. While rough housing with other students,

Jeffrey tackled a much smaller student. Actually, that smaller student was Frank Brule, a friend from the South Bronx. Frank went down hard. In what was not nearly enough time for Steve to react, Jeffrey was there with his hand under Frank's head, preventing injury. Jeffrey's compassionate side was coming to the surface. It was also noticed by neighbors of Steve and Liz at their neighborhood pool party that Jeffrey assumed the role of monitor, watching over and caring for the younger children. That year in Rhode Island also enabled Jeffrey to enhance and understand life beyond the South Bronx environment.

Jeffrey has become an avid reader over the years and one suspects that he has discovered that reading skills are one of the 'keys of life', i.e., reading competency, translates directly to classroom improvement across a wide spectrum of courses. One of the enabling factors in addition to Jeffrey's innate interest and appetite for reading is that Steve would read 'Harry Potter' books to Jeffrey practically every evening over the years.

Much like Edward White, Jr., Jeffrey's journey continues and with each passing day, week and year, the risk to each boy slowly diminishes and their confidence and hope increases. So does ours.

In the early days of the summer of 2011, Mother Martha asked about the feasibility of having both Edward White, Jr. and Jeffrey Goodwin remain in Rhode Island for the entire summer. The Outreach team at St. John's has always relied upon the advice and guidance of Mother Martha in order to effectively and properly shape the efforts of this ministry. She, in effect, is the 'on the ground' in the South Bronx and, therefore, was the most reliable and knowledgeable source of information. The Outreach team responded immediately. Edward would already be in Rhode Island for the entire summer either as a CIT [Counselor-In-Training] at ECC or in residence with Liz and Steve. Arrangements were also made to have Jeffrey attend as many of the weekly camp sessions as possible that were appropriate for him; when not at ECC, Jeffrey would also be in residence with Liz and Steve. Edward and Jeffrey were in a safe place during the summer of 2011.

Although there was a firm recognition that the streets of the South Bronx poise a risk to all-especially, to the children- it wasn't until September 16, 2011 [just 5 days ago!] that the enormity of this risk was brought so very close to members of the St. Ann's and St. John's communities. I received a telephone call from Steve Lippincott and an email from the Senior Warden at St. Ann's that a boy from St. Ann's who had celebrated his 16th birthday in early September died of multiple gunshot wounds on the evening of September 15, 2011 as he was walking his girl friend back home. The news was unexpected, tragic, sad, heart-breaking and so unnecessary because this boy was one of the four children of another mother from St. Ann's who was active in the school programs at St. Ann's and was successful in raising her four children despite the inner-city environment and all its overt and subtle threats to life. Eduardo had attended the ECC summer camps for several summers and certainly seemed to be headed in the right direction. However, the streets of the South Bronx were not safe for Eduardo during the summer of 2011; the environment-and its sad and continuing tragic legacy- had cast a dark shadow over the courageous efforts of family, church and community.

This tragic event emphatically underscored the strategy employed at St. Ann's to gather the children at the various public schools to escort them to the after-school safe haven provided at St. Ann's. Similarly, it also speaks volumes for the Freedom School provided each summer at St. Ann's. The after-school hours and summer break are the times during which the children are most vulnerable. Within the collaborative ministry context, providing maintenance and school supply logistics were deemed critical to ensure to the maximum extent possible that this safe haven would remain functional and available to the children.

Gladys Mercado was initially mentioned in one of Steve Lippincott's letters to me; more will be provided about Gladys in the coming pages in *Reflections from the South Bronx.*

Brules [Alicia, Jennie, Liola, Frank]

The members of the St. John's Outreach team that were involved within the St. Ann's/St. John's collaborative ministry initially came to know the Brule 'girls', Alicia, Jennie and Liola, within the context of the ECC summer camperships. Following Jennie's initial summer camp experience at ECC in rural Rhode Island, the parishioners of St. John came to better know each of the three Brule girls via a variety of events: additional summer experiences, van drives between the two communities, home stays with families in Barrington, St. John's parish events and mission trips at St. Ann's. As the years went by, their mother, Beatrice, and father, Greg, and their 'little brother', Frank came into our field of view. This extension of a relationship with an individual child from St. Ann's via interaction, tutoring, mentoring, sharing et al to the child's family was becoming a natural dynamic within the ministry.

During these early years, Alicia attended the Legacy School of Integrated Studies in New York; in 2006, she relocated to Providence, Rhode Island with plans to pursue a college degree. She had been accepted at Johnson & Wales University in Providence but opted for Rhode Island College because of its history of education majors and programs. At that time, Alicia had expressed her interest in 'giving back' [aka 'paying it forward'] via teaching-perhaps teaching in the South Bronx. She received her baccalaureate degree in 2010 and is currently employed as a pre-school professional. Jennie was attending St. Hilda's and St. Hughes School for grades 5-8 and, then, at the Mother Cabrini School for the 9th grade in Manhattan. Jennie, in 2005, then attended St. Andrews School in Barrington, RI for grades 10-12; she graduated from St. Andrews in 2008 and is currently a student at Rhode Island College where she is majoring in [Elementary] Special Education. Liola completed her primary and middle school grades of education in New York City's public school system in the South Bronx. She then attended St. Andrews School in Barrington, Rhode Island and graduated in 2010. In the fall of 2010, she entered Mitchell College in New London, Connecticut and is doing very well academically. In the summer of 2011, Liola was busy working several jobs two of which were in her professional areas of interest, i.e., law-enforcement. She served a summer internship with the Barrington Police Department and was also a 'shadow' to one of the officers at a Connecticut correctional facility. At first glance, one would perceive that their respective academic journeys reflected the traditional middle-class and beyond transitions from secondary schools to the university/college arena and then into their respectively chosen professional ranks. However, there is more-so much more-to their story! It is a story of hardships and struggles, an unwavering commitment to their visions and goals and an outstanding level of perseverance and determination to break the bondage of the South Bronx environment. It is a story that others have experienced and that more children, e.g., Edward, Jeffrey et al, will, hopefully, also experience. It is a very sad realization that myriad children have not had such an experience and many, e.g., Eduardo, who had been denied their right to a safe passage to safety and a meaningful life.

All three Brule girls were involved in the after-school program at St. Ann's as well as its Freedom School during the summer months. In retrospect, it becomes readily obvious that the St. Ann's environment was a 'foundational' experience of life for some of the Brule children; one could even say that the St. Ann's experience was a launching pad for some of the children and, then, with the passage of time, more children. Given that St. Ann's was a foundational experience for many children including the Brule girls then the ECC summer camp experience could surely be called a 'turning point' for the children. The factors included [1] the drive from the South Bronx through suburban and rural Connecticut and Rhode Island, [2] the ECC summer camperships and [3] the collateral association, interaction and bonding with children and adults other than South Bronx residents, collectively, shaped a very new view for the children from St. Ann's.

Although this book has provided some description of 'life in the South Bronx', there may be some useful insight into that environment which is really the starting point for the Brule children and so many other children. Another excerpt from *St. Ann's Covenant* [Volume 6, Number 1, December 2010] provides another layer of relevant insight in the form of an update:

Updates

The neighborhood of Motthaven, which St. Ann's serves, is the area which was referred to originally by the label "South Bronx". Over the past 10-15 years, people have come to use "South Bronx" to describe areas as far as three miles north. These other areas have improved some, but, especially with the drastic cuts in city, state and federal programs, conditions in Mott Haven have gotten worse.

The 38 apartment buildings known as the Diego Beckmans had an especially difficult year. Federal rent subsidies expired and were to be taken over by the city, but the unprecedented massive conversion was not smooth. The Chief Executive Officer was removed and several cronies went with him. Fortunately, new officers have the situation well in hand. Tenants are working with the new board to lower electrical usage for both the budget and the environment. The local police department and the district attorney are protecting law abiding citizens from the tyranny of gangs and drug dealers. Sadly, Shirley Flowers, a long time leader of the Diego-Beckmans died from complications of diabetes.

Jennie used to live in the Diego Beckmans. Her family lived next to an apartment where drugs were being sold, and they were miserable. Jennie's mother, Beatrice, agreed to stay in the United States only until her daughters got their education. Now, her eldest, Alicia, who wants to be a teacher, has finished college and is taking a short break from graduate school to support her family. Jennie, who wants to be a math teacher or a social worker, is in college. The youngest daughter, Liola, just started college with a large scholarship. With a great deal of help, Jennie and her family moved out of the South Bronx; her mother has now moved back to Guatemala. Carlitos, one of Jennie's cousins, was sent back to Guatemala, where his education ceased, although his father lives and works in the United States.

Cliffie has been graduated from college. His devoted mother took an overnight bus to his graduation and watched him receive his diploma and awards. Cliffie worked at St. Ann's Freedom School for the summer, and is currently planning to work as a security guard at night in hopes of getting an acting job from daytime auditions.

Ariel and her brother both have babies. Ariel works as a corrections officer, which gives her good health and education benefits.

Chuck Morrison, who used to be in what was sometimes called "Mother Martha's gang" is married and has a baby boy, Kyle. He and his wife aspire to careers in health care. Meantime, Chuck is working hard as a caretaker at St. Ann's. Having grown up in the church, he understands well the importance of all the programs.

Author's note: the reader may have gained some sense of the family dynamics in the South Bronx but the following additional two excerpts may add to that picture:

[1]   **Out of Broken Dreams**-PATH, the clearinghouse for all the homeless families is just three blocks from St. Ann's; many tragic families come through our doors. Recently, a pregnant woman with her five year old daughter, three year old son and the father of her unborn child came seeking food. The family had travelled by bus from the Midwest looking for work; the person who was supposed to meet them never showed up.

They weren't allowed to stay together because they weren't married, and she didn't want to be separated from him. We persuaded her to go to the family shelter for the sake of her children, and we got him a bed in a nearby shelter run by

Mother Theresa's order. We managed to get them bus tickets back home, abandoning their dream for now. Anthony, Mother Martha's assistant reported that, "Before they left, they said that when the baby is born in December, if it's a boy we're going to name him after you [Anthony], and if it's a girl, we're going to name her for Mother Martha."

[2] **Males in Trouble** -"All my life I've been advocating for the rights of women and girls, but now Black and Latino boys really need help," said Mother Martha, "and our programs address the needs of such children in a high poverty neighborhood through small classes [usually no more than 10], after-school and summer programs in a safe, enriching environment." Mothers recognize the benefits of starting their children early; we have more applications for first grade than any other. This year, 60 per cent of our children are boys and 40 per cent are girls.

So these two stories are symbolic of the 'starting point' for so many inner-city children. If nothing else, they do serve to emphasize the spectrum of cruel and disabling disadvantages of inner-city birth, living and their life-long impact. Many voices, e.g., Abraham Lincoln, John F. Kennedy, Daniel Patrick Moynihan, James Patterson et al have brought light to this dark side of America. However, the reality is that despite this light, despite those individuals, organizations and efforts who have mentored, advocated for and enabled some children to life beyond that of an inner-city environment, *there are hundreds of thousands-perhaps, millions-of children who-over the years-have remained literally condemned to inner-city life. Let us not forget those many more young adults, adults and seniors who have also never had the opportunity or political support for life other then the inner-city environment. This continuing situation has not only carried an enormous and continuous human and social cost beyond one's understanding and imagination but it also represents a mountain of foregone opportunities for the individuals and for America. The inner-city virtual prisons have long denied to America the talents, gifts, creativity and even the excellence and genius of so many inner-city individuals.*

There is a significant distinction between that understanding that is derived from conversations, reading stories, analyses and the never-ending litany of social and educational program descriptions and recommendations for this very, very long-standing inner-city situation and that understanding that is derived directly from first-hand experience when spending time [as opposed to a political or curiosity based visit] within the inner-city. In particular, listening to the voices of the inner-city population: their concerns, their issues, their fears........and, yes, their dreams!

Earlier in this book, the concept of 'dots' was introduced and that a sequence of 'dots' eventually forms a scenario, an experience, an awakening, a journey and, essentially, a shaping and definition of one's individual journey. Each 'dot' represents both a decision point and a milestone along one's life journey; an individual moves from 'dot' to 'dot' as a direct outcome/consequence of his/her choices and decisions. These choices/decisions, then, determine the meaningfulness-or lack of meaningfulness-of each associated milestone. To a very significant extent, one's station in life can be positive and meaningful or 'nothing to write home about' or negative and even destructive-it all depends upon the choices that an individual makes as he/she moves from 'dot' to 'dot'! It is an American legacy that both adults and children have the opportunity to make those decisions which directly shape their life's journey. Is it not now appropriate to say that most inner-city residents have been denied their opportunity to make their life-shaping decisions rather than having their lives shaped by a disabling environment?

For the Brule children dot #1, so to speak, was their involvement in the Freedom School at St. Ann's; dot #2 was probably their participation at the ECC summer camperships; dot #3 certainly could have been their growing relationships with the Outreach members of St. John's and, then, with practically the entire parish community. As Alicia has so profoundly stated-and I am sure that it is equally true for each of the Brule children-that the summer camperships and these relationships did provide a view of 'life beyond the South Bronx environment.' The choices, collectively to date, made by the Brules have been outstanding ones and have created a meaningful journey-albeit difficult and challenging- for each of them. Alicia, Jennie and Liola, individually and collectively, embraced this view of life beyond the South Bronx and chose education as their next 'dot' as described on the preceding page. This general description of their educational journeys doesn't really do justice to the realities of their difficult path for Alicia being a college graduate and professionally employed, Jennie soon-to-become a college graduate and Liola entering her second year at Mitchell College and preparing herself well for a career in law enforcement.

As offered earlier, it's important to realize that there are two very necessary steps in escaping the trauma of residence in the South Bronx: [1] having the *experience* of the view/vision of life beyond the walls of the South Bronx and [2] transitioning and actually achieving that better life. It is important to note that this 'better life' can take place both within and beyond the South Bronx. Please understand that there are more than a few individuals who have successfully experienced this very challenging two-phase process. ***It is the commitment to, the advocacy of and support of these two steps that is the mindset, heart and soul of the ministry at St. Ann's and, without question, it is also at the mindset, heart and spirit of those many supporting ministries, e.g., St. John's Outreach.*** The Brules had come to experience, accept, embrace and achieve that first phase of their journey, i.e., to have a view-however provided-that could be theirs! The second phase, i.e., actually making the transition to a better life, is really a challenge that is even intimidating beyond description-as it has been for those who came before the Brules and, most certainly, for those who will inevitably follow the Brules. It is probably no less challenging or intimidating-but probably more so due to the historical context of the inner-city - than it was for those legions of immigrants who came to America in the 19th and 20th centuries and for those who continue that same journey in the 21st century. To those immigrants the lady of Liberty in New York harbor silently said "Give me your tired, your poor, your huddled masses yearning to breathe free, the wretched refuse of your teeming shore. Send these, the homeless, tempest-tossed to me, I lift my lamp beside the golden door." Making the transition from the inner-city to middle-class and beyond America is not unlike those journeys of the immigrants who really, literally and figuratively, built America. The journey of these young Brule women is so similar to a journey from one country to another totally different country. The physical environment, the educational system, the culture, the societal rules, practices and protocols, even the languages are vastly different. What works and is acceptable and appropriate in one country [or community] is more than likely quite different from what works and is acceptable and appropriate in another country [or community]!

In 2006, Jennie was a student in residence at St. Andrews School in

Barrington, RI and Alicia was in her final year of high school at the Legacy School of Integrated Studies in New York. At this point in time, Jennie was the prime recipient of advocacy and support from the Outreach team at St. John's but that emphasis would change dramatically. As mentioned earlier Jennie was innately a special young lady with outstanding interactive skills, an endless reservoir of smiles, care and courtesy; she was very popular with the faculty, staff and other students at St. Andrews School-as much as she was popular with all who came to know her especially so many members of the Outreach team at St. John's and the faculty, staff and other summer campers at ECC.

The move from the inner city South Bronx to suburban Barrington is so much more than a geographical and physical move; it is very much a move from one country to another, from one culture to another, from one environment to a radically different one, from. . . . . ! An interesting exercise for the reader is to imagine being relocated to a completely unfamiliar foreign country where resources, local guidance and protocols, advocacy and mentoring are simply not available and you are not at all prepared for nor knowledgeable of life in this somewhat strange environment. It is not unlike being in that room of darkness to which one father of children in the South Bronx had referred.

Jennie had completed her first year at St. Andrews School and was preparing to return for the 11th grade there in the summer of 2006. Alicia had just finished high school in New York and was looking into colleges; as a former faculty member at Johnson & Wales University, I was able to advocate for her there. She was accepted there on her own merits and academic performance and was the recipient of an outstanding financial aid package. However, Alicia's professional and personal interests oriented her to the educational arena; such a program was not then available at Johnson & Wales University. As her mentor and advocate, I recommended that consideration be given to Rhode Island College, an institution with a solid history of preparing its graduates for the arenas of education and social work. She was readily admitted for the forthcoming semester.

For reasons, e.g., an understanding of the timeline-based requirements of the admission and matriculation processes, Alicia did not qualify for on-campus availability for dormitory residence. However, she was able to locate a third-floor apartment reasonably close to Rhode Island College. With support from the Outreach community at St. John's, the apartment was outfitted with gifts of used furniture and household items. It was a very humbling and lonely beginning in her first 'home' away from the South Bronx.

During the year that followed, the Brules – mother [Beatrice], father [Greg] and younger son [Frank] were able to reunite as a family in this very limited 3rd floor apartment. Additionally, Frank and Liola were coming to St. Andrews School as Jennie was moving on to Rhode Island College following her graduation from St. Andrews School. The entire Brule family then moved to suburban Barrington in order to be in that neighborhood that also included St. Andrews School and St. John's Church. The move was facilitated by members of the Outreach team, their family and friends.

The following years were financially very stressful-to say the least-but, in addition to the demands of the academic arena and the marginalized budget, there were struggles concerning the 'culture' of suburban Barrington and it's important to note that the Outreach members also struggled with the 'culture' embraced by the Brules for so many years. Simply put, there was a lack of understanding within both communities about a culture that was different. However, this lack of understanding also transcended into wonderful learning opportunities for all those involved. For example, during these years, Greg Brule would often leave Barrington unexpectedly to return to Guatemala for undetermined lengths of time. This travel activity seemed to put those very necessary employment responsibilities and opportunities at risk as well as the support of those individuals who advocated for employment for Greg and also for those who chose to offer employment to Greg. Ironically, one of these positions seemed to leverage both Greg's skills as a chef's assistant and the financial needs of his family; this particular position [with health benefits] was at St. Andrews School. For a family with financial difficulties, this position was a major step in the direction of much-needed financial stability.

However, this coming and going and the obvious expense of air travel to and from the Caribbean area raised some eyebrows-including mine. What was not known by the Barrington community-at-large were the father's requirements and responsibilities that necessitated frequent travel out of America and back. I asked Alicia about this situation and it is my understanding that Greg was a *Buyei*. Spiritually speaking, the Brules were firm and faithful in their belief in God but their spirituality included a belief in a connection to their ancestors. The link or communication medium is realized through a *Buyei*. It is a form of reincarnation through the *Buyei*. Greg's ministry embraced not only the Caribbean area but other Central and South American areas. It is in some of these areas that medical/health resources are not really available and that the ***Buyei***, for the lack of a more accurate term, is somewhat of a healer using medicine from herbs. The latter practice of herbal medicine has a long history of success in other geographical areas, e.g., Southeast Asia and the Asia continent itself. Greg's ministry included being responsive to a cadre of clients who requested his assistance and who would offer to finance his travel.

The Brule's financial struggle was a daily one despite the variety of jobs held by Greg and Beatrice and those part-time jobs held by his daughters while attending their respective schools. The parishioners of St. John's truly understood the need-the moral imperative, if you will-to advocate for and provide support to this family who were on a most challenging journey of its own. The parishioners 'stepped up to the plate' without hesitation but with enthusiasm and commitment; e.g., text book funds were provided, a [used] laptop was also provided, gifts were provided from St. John's 'Giving Tree' at Christmas. The Giving Tree project at St. John's is a beautiful tradition and provides gifts to children and families in great need especially during this holiday season. Much needed income tax advice and administration were also made directly available to the Brule family on a *pro bono* basis. However, the more meaningful advocacy and support came not from the material items made available but from the intangibles of advocacy, confidence, faith, love and emphasis upon a 'keep on moving forward' attitude.

When the Brule family had first gathered in that 3rd floor apartment in Providence, they did have a car that was in its final days of life; a family of one of the parishioners sold a very functional van to the Brules for the astronomical but very affordable price of $1.00. Indeed, several days before Jennie's graduation from St. Andrews School in 2008, this same van developed a water pump problem followed by motor overheating and a gentle demise. Let us remember that Jennie's graduation was a very proud milestone affair for the entire Brule family and their friends who would come from New York City to the graduation en masse. Again, the community would 'step up to the plate' and provide a properly registered and financed van in less than 24 hours. It was a time in which the soft and gentle strains of ***Amazing Grace***, once again, became louder and clearer.

The spring of 2010 was a special time for the Brule family: Liola would graduate from St. Andrews School and be heading to Mitchell College in Connecticut; Alicia would graduate from Rhode Island College and enter the professional work force. Again, the entire Brule family and friends would gather in Barrington for that wonderful cross-cultural cookout so reminiscent of the cookout at Jennie's graduation in 2008.

Beneath this surface of success were the daily struggles that were matched in intensity by the individual and collective determination and efforts of the Brule family. The family had accrued some significant debt over the past few years out of the sheer necessity to continue their educational journeys and to sustain themselves. Each member of the Brule family had survived-and that's an appropriate term-the financial struggle, the cultural differences, the societal challenges and the academic demands. One reflection of their tenuous journey is an incident that occurred in Alicia's undergraduate years. She had received a college bill that was light years beyond her capacity to resolve; she was, in her sadness and disappointment, planning to leave college. Another opportunity for mentoring and advocacy had presented itself; again, it was also one of many 'teaching and learning' moments. This situation came to the attention of the Outreach membership; their perspective-based on experiences within their own families-was that Rhode Island College or any other university or college just didn't accept 'leaving college or university'. Rather, once an individual is admitted to college/university, there is an imbedded responsibility to enable and facilitate that individual's college years to commencement. There are procedures and practices in place as well as supportive financial counselors to assist that student in financial difficulty.

I met with Alicia and Greg Brule after Sunday services at St. John's Church to review the Rhode Island College correspondence relevant to her outstanding college bill; I suggested that we meet with her college financial advisor and simply put everything 'on the table'-a strategy quite common in the American culture but, perhaps, not as common in theirs. It was just another 'teaching and learning' moment. The outcome of that meeting with the RIC [Rhode Island College] financial advisor was a solution that included some additional substantial financial aid that was readily affordable and that allowed Alicia to continue her journey toward her baccalaureate degree.

There were the inevitable additional 'teaching' opportunities [for the Outreach membership] and the 'learning' opportunities [for the Brules] about the realities of financial management, the risks of an entitlement mindset rather than an ownership mindset for financial responsibility,......... and the necessity to rise about the nuances and inconveniences of the real world and *'doing the right thing!'* The benefit of the latter is that *'doing the right thing'* will always and inevitably have positive dividends; in fact, the prime benefit is that a more sound and secure foundation for one's future is in the making. Mentoring and guidance are important pieces of Outreach's responsibility as well as the Brule's journey. Collectively, all concerned parties readily acknowledged the 'risk' in moving to Rhode Island but an equal amount of attention and emphasis was addressed to the imbedded opportunity of such a move. In the forthcoming section on *Reflections*, the Brules bring their personal views into the arena and they are, without question, relevant and meaningful.

As mentioned earlier, the spring of 2010 was a special time for the Brules: Liola was on a path to Mitchell College, Alicia was to graduate from Rhode Island College and Jennie was to return to her undergraduate program at Rhode Island College. However, the family had been considered for a legal eviction from their Barrington apartment due to a significant amount of unpaid rent over the last few years. The Brules had always paid the monthly rent but were often unable to provide a full payment. Again, the Outreach team and its friends in the community stepped forward to 'do what must be done'; Kim Anderson, CEO of a local company, **Ava-Anderson Non-Toxic**, stepped forward-as she and her family have always done for social and humanitarian causes. Their collective efforts are done, so to speak, 'under the radar' in a quiet, committed, generous and efficient fashion. Kim, again, quietly and quickly rallied her network community to alleviate the not-so-small amount of unpaid rent. This enabled a willingness of the apartment landlord to forego the intent of eviction and to enter into a pact that was socially and financially responsible for both the landlord and the Brules. Kim Anderson in her own special way located an appropriate apartment in Providence for Alicia as she was returning to Rhode Island College for her senior year. Kim then organized a huge yard-sale to further alleviate some outstanding expenses and provided some financial management and a sound financial strategy for the funds from the yard sale in order to further reduce the unpaid rent as well as putting into escrow enough funds to effectively reduce the rent in Alicia's upcoming 3rd floor apartment for a full year. Integral to this process was a negotiated 'handshake' agreement with the Brules' landlord that would allow the Brules to pay the remaining rent due whenever that would be possible. He, the landlord, understood the overall situation and continued to put any thoughts of eviction permanently aside in favor of this more humanity-oriented agreement. This was also another 'teaching and learning' moment for Outreach and Alicia, Jennie and Liola. Specifically, Greg, Beatrice and Frank would be returning to the Caribbean in the near future and the debt due to the landlord would be the responsibility of Alicia, Jennie and Liola; as mentioned earlier, it was referred to as a 'debt of honor'; more specifically, it was a matter of their honor and our joint credibility!. There were previous occasions in which a payment due for one reason or another simply could not be made because of the unavailability of dollars. It was during these occasions, we offered, that it's acceptable to be unable to pay [a universal trait] but it just isn't acceptable to ignore the payment due; such a strategy would only serve to diminish the credibility of the individual.

Additionally, it would most certainly raise the level of suspicion and distrust on the part of the creditor. An acceptable strategy would be to keep the individual or company due the payment informed. It's usually quite acceptable for all they want to really know is that you *will honor the debt* and not walk away from it.

Kim Anderson's commitment to community service and, especially, to the journey of the Brule children has continued well beyond the events of relocation within Rhode Island. She has been a consistent and active player for the advocacy, support and mentoring of the Brule younger set throughout the years and remains committed to the principle that 'all children are important'. She facilitated Frank's entry into the San Miguel School; the impact of her role can best be exemplified by Frank's love and commitment for the academic world and his mirroring the efforts of Alicia, Jennie and Liola. Alicia, speaking for the all the Brule children, offered the perspective in late 2012 as the Brules were preparing-via Kim's efforts-to move into a 'home of their own' that their life was 'like living in the middle of a dream'. Kim's husband has also embraced the mentoring role of another student at San Miguel. These unfolding events-and so many others-demonstrate that 'one ministry begets another'.

As the Brule girls continued to move forward on their respective journeys, there was often mention of giving back to their community of choice. This mindset was both encouraging and refreshing; it appears that *paying it forward* is on their agenda. The Outreach membership's signature response to "What can we do?" as always been "Your time and opportunity will come.....frequently!" All you have to do is *step up to the plate*. An example of this is Alicia's choice to gain custody of

Frank who was living with his parents on a Caribbean island but not really participating in the educational arena there. Frank returned to Alicia's household recently, entered the public school system but, with the assistance and advocacy of Kim Anderson, was admitted to the **San Miguel School**. Frank was positioned to start his meaningful educational journey, aka his first 'dot', at this outstanding school. The school's website provides the following descriptive information: **The San Miguel School of Providence** is an independent Lasallian middle school for urban boys from the Greater Providence area. The school is dedicated to the belief that education is the key to breaking the cycle of poverty.

Students experience a school culture that emphasizes citizenship, service and personal responsibility in a caring learning environment where academics are rigorous, expectations are high, and individual talents are nurtured. Students grow into young men with a positive vision for the future that leads them to effect positive change in their lives and their communities.

The motto/mission of the San Miguel School is *'We transform urban kids at risk into gentlemen who are proud of their school and who want to be successful and productive members of society'*. This school is really the antithesis of that disabling environment of the inner-city, e.g., the South Bronx or even Providence. More importantly, it is a school that enjoys a resounding resonance with the philosophy, principles and practices of the after-school and Freedom School programs at St. Ann's as well as the supportive and committed ministries.

Chuck Morrison

Chuck is a young man with whom we became acquainted during the early years of the ECC camperships. He attended this summer camp for several years and was usually present during the various mission trips to St. Ann's. Chuck stood out with his engaging smile, personality and conversation. The synergism of his exuberance accented by his articulation seemed to radiate confidence, commitment and, as we later learned, a strong measure of bravado.

Chuck's life was so similar to other teens and young adults of the South Bronx whose lives were inevitably shaped by their environment; however, Chuck seemed to have that intangible 'extra something'. He always had his mind and his conversations on his future-one could easily say that he was searching for something beyond that which was offered by the South

Bronx. Simply put, Chuck certainly possessed an unknown, undeniable and strong potential; simply put, if you close your eyes while sharing a conversation with Chuck, you would think that you were in the company of a young man in some outstanding private school in upper middle-class America. I have always described Chuck as an individual who, if he were born in a place other than the inner-city, would have been a natural candidate for Wall Street or corporate America.

However, Chuck is also somewhat of a self-admitted procrastinator. At first glance, one would think this characteristic a negative one until you take a longer look at Chuck and made efforts to understand and enable *his* journey and search; there was always a litany of reasons-explained with great articulation-for his lack of forward mobility. I asked Chuck about this with the condition that his wonderful and glib articulations [aka b_ _ _ s_ _ _] were no longer acceptable. What followed was a 'learning' moment for me and other Outreach members. His comments were very reminiscent of those experiences with Edward White, Jr. and Jeffrey Goodwin, i.e., the environment of the South Bronx necessitates the development of personae for the purposes of coping, defense and even survival. One must appear to know all, to be able to take care of oneself and to project a tough and capable image.

Chuck represents the often dismissed personal promise and potential of inner-city residents and their unrealized contribution to society; this dismissal, this denial is a contributing factor to the racism of poverty and neglect and, most importantly, the blindness to humanity. Chuck's moving thoughts and feelings are provided in the coming section on *Reflections*.

One additional note about Chuck: the many hardships of the inner-city have been previously mentioned; one hardship-then and now-has been the challenge of the cold months of winter in an apartment without heat. Chuck's solution in his unheated apartment was to take a donated hair-dryer to bed with him for some much-needed heat.

There Are Success Stories

I would be remiss in my responsibilities as an author if I did not bring center stage the fact that *there are success stories* amongst the chaos, danger, life risks and disadvantages imbedded in a South Bronx residency. The metrics for success in the South Bronx are quite different than those that are prevalent throughout middle-class and above in America. It was pointed out earlier that sheer survival from day-to-day is a very realistic measure of success in the South Bronx.

The question 'Just how do you measure success?' in the financial arena had the response 'We measure success one client at a time!' The latter response strongly infers that 'every client is important'. Moving from the financial arena to the inner-city arena, can we not then say that 'every child is important'? Having said that then encourages us to believe that success can also be measured one child at a time. Success is a hierarchy and most non-inner-city residents have a jump-start within that hierarchy because, for them, they do not have to climb the many inner-city rungs of survival. Conversely, most inner-city children-through no fault of their own-are faced with a far greater challenge to overcome the handicap of survival. They are, by necessity, dealing with the many faces of survival: survival of poverty, survival of unhealthy environments, survival of drugs, survival of street violence, survival of broken families and households, survival of forced shelter residency, survival of a faulty educational system, survival of malnutrition and more. It is safe to say that each and every inner-city resident has some 'mix' of these faces of survival.

The transition from *survival* to *success* requires a path unique only to the children of the inner-city; this difficult path often comes as a traumatic discovery for those from Rhode Island [and elsewhere] who have chosen to serve in the ministry at St. Ann's. Despite this challenging situation it is no less than remarkable that there are a variety of true success stories amongst the children, teens and adults of the South Bronx. Indeed, it is absolutely amazing! These success stories match up quite well with those achievements of children from middle-class America. *There are just not enough of them!* However, those who do make it through the survival maze make a strong statement that success comparable to others in non-inner-city communities is achievable. Imbedded within these achievements there is hope for others. Certainly the stories about the Brules, Chuck Morrison, Laranda Jones, Anthony Bonilla et al provide a strong confirmation that the children of the South Bronx are as capable as anyone. Even the stories of Edward White, Jr. and Jeffrey Goodwin reflect significant success in their setting of their life compasses to a direction leading to further success. The reader will also soon learn about Gladys Mercado who epitomizes success within the South Bronx.

There are a myriad success stories that have emanated from this disadvantaged environment; however, other than an occasional moment or two in the national spotlight, there is insufficient trumpeting of these successes. This insufficiency is also a real disservice to those who struggle daily throughout their lives within the maze of survival and disadvantages.

An Update on 'What is success?'

One very symbolic success story is that of Liola Brule. Her story provides an answer to that always interesting question: 'Can anything good come out of the South Bronx?' Here's one answer that arises from the iconic and always inspiring ministry of St. Ann's in the South Bronx. The context of this answer was set forth by the Reverend Martha Overall on the second Sunday after the Epiphany on January 15, 2012 when some parishioners made yet another journey to St. Ann's on this MLK weekend.

Mother Martha made reference to the Gospel passage "Can anything good come out of Nazareth?" but she also added "Can anything good come out of the South Bronx?" She made some comparative statements about the similarities between Nazareth and the South Bronx. We all know well about the 'good' that came out of Nazareth; Mother mother's response to "Can anything good come out of the South Bronx?" was "You bet it can!"

Liola Brule-as are Alicia, Jennie and Frank Brule- is well known to most parishioners from her several summers at ECC, her undergraduate years at St. Andrew's School, her matriculation to Mitchell College in New London, CT where she has just completed her second year as a major in law enforcement. Liola is a young woman of strong character and perseverance, she has an outstanding work ethic and, simply said, she is really symbolic of the 'good' that can come out of the South Bronx.

On Aril 25, 2012, my wife, Marion, and I were honored to attend the annual awards ceremony at Mitchell College for both students and faculty. It was, indeed, wonderful to share the following with her: she received three awards-an honor reserved for only a few students She received [1] the Darlene A. Mattis Shah '81 Memorial Scholarship for a student 'who has confronted personal crisis or adverse circumstances with bravery, dignity and optimism while working toward her educational goals; [2] The Law Society Association award for demonstrating a degree of participation above and beyond that anticipated by peers and mentors; and [3] the Outstanding Resident Assistant Award for the demonstration of a degree of participation above and beyond the job requirements to foster a positive community within the residence halls and throughout campus.

The members of both the St. Ann's and St. John's communities can take some well-deserved and quiet pride and satisfaction for their roles in the ministry at st. Ann's and their contribution to the growing litany of 'success' stories that found life and meaning within this special ministry.

"Can anything good come out of the South Bronx?" As Mother Martha said in her sermon [which can be found in its complete form in the *Reflections from St. Ann's*]: "You bet it can!"

Chapter 10
The Role of St. Andrew's School

This particular reflection is provided by Head Master John Martin:

"Missions work is often defined as 'going to' rather than 'coming to' because such work is easier to understand, is punctuated by time specific time periods and underlined by projects. But the best missions work occurs when the 'going to' is combined with the 'coming to' and, then, lives are changed. It is in that framework that St. John's Episcopal Church and St. Andrew's School, along with St. Ann's Episcopal Church in the South Bronx worked together-as a team-to change the lives of one family.

In the summer of 2002 representatives from St. John's came to St. Andrew's to talk with me about the feasibility but, more importantly, the opportunity to have a young lady from the South Bronx attend our boarding program. We at St. Andrew's have many requests for students who would like to leave the inner-city and attend our school; however, this request was quite different. First, there was a connection-historical and emotional-between St. John's and St. Andrew's in that our founder had been the rector at St. John's in 1893. Secondly, several of the individuals connected to St. John's Outreach ministry at St. Ann's were also connected to St. Andrew's either as Trustees, Donors and long-time friends. Thirdly, individual experiences wth inner-city education had influenced me for years; this really enabled me to have an informed perspective of the opportunity before us. All these combined with our own historic mission to help students who need assistance and advocacy in their search for 'success'. The synergism of these factors worked to create a special moment in time that subsequently changed a family's life.

The young lady who applied for admission, Jennie Brule, had some serious deficits in her education despite all the attempts by others to help her. We worried a great deal about [1] whether or not she could handle the academics at St. Andrew's and [2] if these deficits could be addressed soon enough to properly prepare Jennie for college. As with every opportunity, there is a measure of risk but St. Andrew's decided to accept her and provide significant funding along with some help from the St. John's community and other donors. After a somewhat difficult beginning, Jennie caught on and, with her positive personality and hard work, successfully graduated with a joyous smile that made everyone very proud. She went on to Rhode Island College where she is pursuing her dream of a college education. Soon thereafter, her sister Liola, followed her path to St. Andrew's and, despite some obstacles in the life including inadequate preparations, had a successful experience living at the school. This outcome certainly underlines the importance of just how the environment and hard work can alter a students's life direction and goals. A good student at St. Andrew's, Liola went on to Mitchell College where she, too, is pursuing her dream of a college education-a life-changing experience that she could only dream of a few years ago. It is important to note that their older sister, Alicia, has already graduated from Rhode Island College. This achievement of three sisters raised in the South Bronx but whose life directions took each of them through a supportive educational and community environment is nothing less than outstanding.

They also had a younger brother, Frank, who was in St. Andrew's Lower School for several years before he moved back with his parents to Central America. Frank found himself within an educational system that left much to be desired. However, his experience at St. Andrew's was so powerful that he has returned to the United States and is at the San Miguel School in Providence, RI: a school that offers the support and educational direction he will need for success.

Graduation Day is always an important day at St. Andrew's more so than many other schools. This is because every student has a 'story'-indeed, a very special story-and we at St. Andrew's, along with the families and friends of students, celebrate their abilities to overcome obstacles and succeed. With both Jennie and Liola Brule, we celebrated their success with tears and joy because, without the support of so many, graduation from St. Andrew's would not have been possible. In this sense, missions is a team effort and event and the 'coming to' of the missions experience changed not just the lives of two young ladies but a school, a church, a community!

Jesus has told us that we "should love God with all our heart, mind and strength and our neighbors as ourselves" and that, this, was in effect the whole law. By loving this family we learned what that law truly means and it opened our hearts and minds to just who are 'our neighbors' and what we can do to change their lives here, where we live as well as countless places of need around the world.

Missions came home to St. Andrew's through the Brule family!"

This special reflection breathes life, value and meaning into the *Mission* and *Vision* life-preparation arena of St. Andrew's School. The *Mission* and *Vision,* in turn, resonate with the spirit and essence of this book; from its website:

St. Andrew's recognizes the importance of preparing students to meet the challenging demands of our ever-changing world. As a community of learners, we strive to unlock the full potential of each individual, developing confident and independent lifelong learners. In doing so, St. Andrew's is completely invested in creating an atmosphere that gives students the tools to learn and focuses upon each student's learning style.

The **Mission** of St. Andrew's School is to reach out to those students with learning differences whose needs have not been met in public or private schools. Our student-oriented teachers are committed to identifying individual learning strengths and teaching to them. Since 1893, St. Andrew's has embraced social and economic diversity, offering a generous, need-based financial aid program. In a nurturing community, we emphasize moral and ethical values guided by our Episcopal heritage in preparation for each student's purposeful engagement in the world.

Guiding Principles

After many discussions and careful consideration, St. Andrew's adopted guiding principles as a way of pinpointing the overall *vision* of the School. Listed below are key points that reflect the core values of our community, and major components in fulfilling A St. Andrew's Education.

- We believe in and practice the concept of "students first" and strive to insure that all our decisions-academic, fiscal and philosophical-emanate from this conviction.
- We are committed to a curriculum that prepares young men and women for life and ensures that all who seek access to higher education will be sufficiently prepared.

- We value a community as diverse as the world in which we live and therefore accept students based solely on their capacity to learn, grow, and flourish because of our approach to education.
- We pledge to offer sufficient financial aid to fulfill our mission.
- We uphold the conviction that our students learn best in a small, intimate environment that allows for personal attention and ongoing interaction with faculty.
- We seek to create a campus-wide environment that fosters growth in all its dimensions-intellectual, emotional, physical and spiritual-and promotes learning in the classroom and beyond.
- We embrace the arts, athletics, and community service as essential elements of A St. Andrew's Education.
- We strive to enhance the spiritual, moral, and ethical development of our students by offering courses, programs, and activities that nourish just not the head, but the heart and soul.
- We recognize the importance of recruiting and retaining the very best faculty, staff, and we work diligently toward that end.

Chapter 11
Mission Trips

The goals of the St. John's Outreach efforts in support of Mother Martha's efforts at St. Ann's are to [1] provide an overall blanket of validation for the humanity, value and self-esteem of the children there, [2] enhance their view and self-expectations of what 'life could be' and [3] assist in the maintenance of the physical plant at St. Ann's and its crucial role as a safe haven for the children, their education and their spiritual growth. These goals would be largely addressed via the innate interaction and collaboration of the St. Ann's and St. John's communities via the summer campership experiences, the concept of consistency by always 'showing up' for *mission trips* and the imbedded support and advocacy for the educational process. Summer camperships have already been addressed; a variety of *mission trips* provided the foundation for this concept of consistency and their opportunity for additional bonding with, support of and advocacy for the children. One of the relevant *reflections* provided by a St. John's parishioner following the Spring of 2011 mission trip was *"....you simply need to show up and let God's work be done."* Supportive educational efforts and activities will be addressed following *mission trips*.

Mission trips could last for a day, several days or a full week; the initial step in each mission trip was to ask Mother Martha "What can we do to help?" There was always and there remains an outstanding menu of needs at St. Ann's; the Outreach membership would always defer to Mother Martha's insightful guidance and recommendation at any particular time. She was our most reliable resource for the identification of prioritized needs at St. Ann's; she would always be consulted to determine the relevance of a resource donation *as perceived within the St. John's community.* As the commitment and passion for the ministry efforts at St. Ann's grew, various parishioners would step forward and ask "Can St. Ann's use this or that?" Our response, of course, would be "More than likely but let's ask Mother Martha about that just to be sure!" One of the efforts that were initiated *without* asking Mother Martha was acquiring a number of used and new bikes for the children at St. Ann's. However, the realities of this effort were then brought to our attention by Mother Martha. Simply put, bikes on the streets and sidewalks of the South Bronx are risky, dangerous and a huge liability. *'Ask Mother Martha!'* became a crucial step in mission trip planning. The mission trip logistics would then be shaped around her recommendation. Part of the planning process included a general schedule of tasks and events for the mission trip. Of course, time and experience also shaped our efforts at St. Ann's. Despite the rigor and efforts of planning, the actual tasks and efforts inevitably included a menu of unexpected items; efforts there, by necessity, assumed a significant 'adaptive' characteristic. However, the bonding and interaction with the children [and adults] of St. Ann's remained the dominant constant throughout the varying dynamics of each mission trip. A corollary outcome of these mission trips would be the growing awareness on the part of the St. John's parishioners of the extraordinary level of need at St. Ann's; many would simply ask "Can St. Ann's use **this** or **that**? Our response was always "It may sound strange but St. Ann's always needs anything and everything [but not bikes]!" The following mission tasks are representative of the wide spectrum of those done and to be done but, in total, certainly reflect St. John's Outreach commitment and response.

Repair & Maintenance

The early mission trips addressed the basic maintenance needs, e.g., painting, an ambitious cleaning program for the grounds at St. Ann's, weeding, landscaping and an equally ambitious program for cleaning the much-used kitchen. Looking back at the latter effort, I can recall that a team of eight took the time [an entire day], effort and perseverance to clean that kitchen like it's never been cleaned before. Additional tasks included interior painting, refinishing some of the beautiful church doors, cleaning out a grass alleyway between St. Ann's and an adjacent apartment building. Apparently, the residents there used the alleyway as a convenient 'dump' for anything and everything, e.g., used diapers and a large number of needles used for drug injection. The variety of items would challenge one's imagination.

In those early mission trips of clean-up and maintenance, the amount of debris and refuse literally filled hundreds of large plastic bags; in addition, there was a potpourri of larger items, e.g., doors, furniture, plastic junk, old toys, well-rusted items some of which were unidentifiable. Trucks were required to remove these items that had accumulated for nearly a decade; however, trucks were not an item included in our logistical planning. But this is New York where much is accomplished via unofficial negotiation between unofficial individuals. All that I can remember is that Michael, the sexton at St. Ann's, said that he would 'arrange' to have all the debris, junk and rubbish removed if it could be stockpiled on the sidewalks of St. Ann's Avenue. I also remember that on the next day that curbside mountain of 'stuff' was, indeed, removed. Since those early days, a more concentrated effort by Michael and volunteers has maintained a very acceptable level of order and cleanliness throughout the grounds at St. Ann's.

Another major effort was a collaborative one between members of both the St. Ann's and St. John's communities to refinish the hardwood floor in the church itself; the floor had simply accumulated grime and grease for God-only-knows-for-how-many-years and had given the floor a very discouraging and very dark finish. The floor was completely scraped, sanded and refinished. It remains today as beautiful a hardwood floor as it had been decades earlier. These mission trips were/are a collateral effort of those programs and projects for church and grounds maintenance initiated and managed via the leadership of Mother Martha and the St. Ann's community. Some of the mission efforts follow:

Gardens, Grounds and Flowers

Once the ground cleaning efforts were completed, attention was focused on bringing a new life to a garden planned in previous years and was directly in view from the front doors of the church. A new and durable fence was erected around the garden; the garden, per se, was prepared to become both a flowers and vegetable garden. Four large planting pots were purchased at a local Home Depot and placed on each side of the three front doors of the church. Flowers appropriate for altar and church placement were then planted. A number of the St. John's parishioners were very skilled in garden arrangement, development and maintenance; flowers, shrubs and plants were transported from Barrington, Rhode Island and placed in garden areas throughout the grounds at St. Ann's. The efforts of Janet Scott from Manhattan deserve particular acknowledgement as the planner and overseer of all gardening projects.

As mentioned earlier, the mission trips to St. Ann's were always preceded by logistical, schedule and task planning and preparation. However, the modus operandi for these trips inevitably took on the flavor of 'The best laid plans of mice and men......'. These unexpected changes served to develop a very special adaptive capability for all concerned; 'We did what we must!" and what was ever accomplished bordered on the 'amazing'. This entire process also led directly to a greater personal and mission faith-as opposed to wasteful fear, concern and worry. One can call the mission team members naïve but, darn it! It was working and working well beyond our-and anyone's- fondest expectations.

The Story of the *'Human Rototiller'*

Mother Martha had amongst her menu of tasks, projects and plans for the St. Ann's community a plan for a community garden on the church property. The site chosen was adjacent to a well worn but always used basketball court on a grassy knoll behind the church itself. On a Spring Saturday morning, that community garden was one of the tasks on our usual 'things to do' list. Upon our arrival, the community garden team that was made up of members from both the St. Ann's and St. John's congregations gathered to visit the proposed site in order to 'do what we must'. There was shrubbery, tall grass and miscellaneous litter to be cut, bundled and removed; the garden site, per se, however, consisted of a hardened, rocky soil that would probably require some type of industrial-grade tilling machine. Mother Martha asked the garden ministry team "Where's the [tilling] machine?" Of course, transporting the tilling machine from Rhode Island to the South Bronx had been considered and then rejected as not being very feasible. Amongst the garden ministry team, there was a parishioner who had made the journey to St. Ann's as had numerous other parishioners; Lou Massa [and his wife, Anne, and children Stephen, Elizabeth and Emily] had also served at St. Ann's. Lou immediately took note of the look of disappointment on Mother Martha's face as well as my own because this particular site could only be tilled with the proper machinery. Lou stepped forward and, in a commanding voice, stated that "We will do it!" The effort put forth by Lou [now known as the 'human rototiller'] was, indeed, a super human one as he turned over the hardened rocky soil inch-by-inch with a series of hoes, shovels and other assorted tools most of which had become casualties by the end of the day-a very long, long and hard day. This 'victory' of one man's human effort, strength and determination carried the day as that hardened garden site was now free of rocks and debris and ready for planting. Indeed, a very unlikely community vegetable garden was born at St. Ann's. However, there's more to the story! In the days to follow, Lou had shared with me some of his thoughts and feelings about that difficult day at St. Ann's. During the rototilling effort, Lou had absorbed some of that noisy, chaotic activity that surrounds St. Ann's. That environment had even included an ongoing 5th floor fire in one of the abutting apartment buildings; it occurred to Lou that survival was the task of the day for many of the South Bronx residents. This awareness of the hardness of life within the St. Ann's community had really fueled his efforts and his determination to bring a reality to his earlier promise that "We will do it!" He also shared that the experience had transitioned his entire being to a very special 'place' of peace, satisfaction and gratitude for having had the opportunity to serve at St. Ann's. As time went by and the many mission trips throughout the years continued, it became apparent to many-as it had to Lou Massa-that the ministry between St. Ann's and St. John's lifts each of these communities to a better place for a variety of reasons. I kid you not, Lou's most descriptive adjective [as is so common amongst those who serve and those who observe] was that the entire experience was nothing less than amazing.

Another maintenance project was the painting of a beautiful [but clearly not maintained over the years but only by necessity fueled by the lack of funds] wrought iron fence enclosing the church property abutting St. Ann's Avenue. This fence really reflected the early beauty of the church property. A team consisting of the teen-agers from St. Ann's and St. John's, armed with their many hands and small paint brushes, 'attacked' the fence one Saturday morning; the task was meticulous and slow-moving. As was often the case, members of the local community would gather, observe and engage in a wide range of topics with the painting team. It is important to note that the consistency of 'showing up' and working at St. Ann's was acknowledged more and more by the local community. Simply put, the Outreach team [aka the 'white pilgrims from the North'] had gained wide acceptance; some members of the local community would even participate in the various ministry efforts. The fence-painting project moved ahead much faster when one of the local residents suggested wearing disposable gloves to dip into the cans of paint and simply running their hands over the fence bars rather than use brushes.

Kitchen Renovation

The kitchen [and the adjoining cafeteria style dining hall] located in the basement was utilized for a much-needed community meal-site and food-pantry, an evening meal for the children of the after-school program prior to going home, lunches for the children of the Freedom School during the summer, clothes collection and distribution for the community and a meeting and eating area for those groups visiting St. Ann's. This area was an extremely busy one operated by an efficient church team led by 'Ms., Daisy' [who is xx years of age.] This team literally performed miracles with that kitchen and dining area. It also served as an early-morning breakfast area for the Outreach membership and a gathering area for tutoring sessions with the children. The kitchen area had always remained functional despite the accumulated need for maintenance and repair very much like the other church grounds and properties.

One of the initial tasks was to simply apply some 'spring-cleaning-expertise' to the overall kitchen area. Other tasks involved the building of shelves for the storage of pots and pans, the installation of a ceiling fan to alleviate the overbearing heat and humidity of the kitchen both during winters but especially during the summers there, the installation of a wall air-conditioning unit to further provide some relief from this heat and humidity, the re-tiling of the entire kitchen floor with commercial tiles, etc. However, the 'miracle of the freezer and refrigerator' demands special attention. This busy kitchen included several large stand-up freezers and refrigerators that just lacked the capacity required for the demands of this kitchen. In fact, one of the freezers didn't really have a freezing capacity but, out of necessity, was still used as a freezer. The units certainly needed replacement with commercial equipment but the cost would be prohibitive for either St. Ann's and/or the St. John's Outreach budget at that time. I have mentioned that 'coincidences stop happening when people stop praying'. More than 400 miles to the Northeast in Providence, Rhode Island, there was the nationally acclaimed College of Culinary Arts within the Johnson & Wales University umbrella. Within this College, there was a Vice-President with a previous professional affiliation with the Paramount Restaurant Supply Company which now shared a professional relationship with the University. Once again, trusting in ***Amazing Grace***, I met with the Vice-President to explain the freezer and refrigerator needs of St. Ann's. I must confess that my expectations were very modest ones at best. The Vice-president listed with courtesy and contemplation. The meeting ended with a brief private telephone call by the Vice-President and a reference to a particular individual at a Paramount warehouse in Warren, Rhode Island. Jan Malcolm and I met with that individual and received a tour of the equipment there-some used but practically new but also very expensive. We expressed our budget limitations to our 'tour guide' and she suggested that we select what was needed rather than look at the prices; she then asked about our available budget and then firmly suggested that we select the equipment needed and we'll talk about the budget later. Well, Jan and I finally selected a commercial freezer and huge stainless-steel refrigerator that would meet the storage requirements in the St. Ann's kitchen. The combined cost was a multiple of our available budget! Our Paramount guide indicated that the available budget would suffice and the selected equipment was purchased. The next issue was the transportation of the equipment from this warehouse in Warren, Rhode Island to the kitchen at St. Ann's. Again, our Paramount guide added that 'her instructions' included transportation and delivery to St. Ann's. Jan and I expressed our enormous thanks, walked out into the bright sun of the day and simply said "Thank you!" I will leave the discussion about coincidences, prayers and ***Amazing Grace*** to the readers.

The Window That Was

Another project of maintenance and repair involved the outcome of a major fire some years ago that destroyed what had been a beautiful stained glass window on one of the larger walls of the church. This was referred to as *'the window that was'*. The window-again, by necessity-had been replaced by a wooden one that had deteriorated into a fire hazard. A hazard that was noticed by the church's insurance carrier and, in its present condition, posed a risk to further insurance coverage. After some inspection and planning, an Outreach team of six led by Steve Lippincott and Bob Tavares, team members with outstanding carpentry and construction skills, [1] cleared away the growth of brush, trees, bushes and the accumulated litter and trash which led to the discovery of a long-forgotten garden [2] removed the fire hazard of wood and [3] replaced it with exterior plywood and framing and a fresh coat of gray paint that matched the stone wall exterior of the church.

The above paragraph doesn't really capture the spirit of this project; Steve [Lippincott], who must now have some name-recognition amongst the readers, has provided a much more living and spiritual description. It follows:

It started out innocently enough. We got a call from Mother Martha asking our help. The insurance company wanted her to address some problems with, for one, the weeds growing in back of the church. Secondly, the plywood that covered the window openings where once hung stained glass windows destroyed by a fire long ago were de-laminating and constituted a fire hazard. Being a carpenter, it fell upon me and another similarly skilled friend, Bob [Tavares] to tackle the plywood problem. We removed the deteriorated plywood, packed insulation in the framing, applied primer to the new plywood and installed flashing where necessary. Overall, it was a neat professional job. One issue, however, arose for me. Besides being a carpenter, I am also an artist and a painter. And like nature's attitude towards vacuums, blank flat surfaces cry out to me. Especially considering what was there before the fire. An idea took root and when I came home I began the design of a new window.

St. Ann's, in a word, is about grandmothers. My relationship with the South Bronx began as a child with going with my grandmother to visit her aunt. The grandmothers of St. Ann's are today the very fabric that blankets the children in safety, love and nourishment in a world sadly lacking all these vital elements. So it was my inspiration to write an icon depicting St. Ann as grandmother of Jesus, and as the saint of literacy. I had her carrying the child and Mary holding a book. As I am not a glass artist, making a window to look like glass, is the best I could do. So with the help of the St. John's Youth group I made stencils and bought spray paint, and, yes, drop cloths and masking tape.

The Window That Might Have Been

A parallel story was taking place, however, as one could imagine, the church was in a terrible state of deterioration, deferred maintenance and a lack of money over decades had taken their toll. Fortunately, St. Ann's church is the parish and resting place of Governor Morris, the author of the preamble to the United States Constitution and also the final resting place of other patriots of the Revolution and Civil War. Consequently, The City of New York saw the place as a national shrine and came up with the funds to replace the steeple and *its iconic [as least for us] leaning cross, reroofing and re-pointing the stonework, painting the woodwork, hang new front doors and replace the [building] gutters. Unfortunately for us now, **our** project had to have the approval of the City. Somehow, the idea of teenagers from out of town with spray paint decorating the building [albeit with window-lookalikes] did not meet with the City's approval and we were prevented from going any further.*

The mockup-a scale version of the project remains at St. Ann's-and I still work on a final version. Icon making is writing, in a visual milieu but writing none the less. It keeps evolving, however. Like me.

This follow-on project created by Steve Lippincott, Outreach enthusiast, skilled carpenter but also an artist, also noticed that some other [boarded up] church windows could have been replaced by stained-glass-like windows of exterior wood. His idea was to merge his artistic and carpentry skills into a joint project for the youngsters of St. Ann's and St. John's. Steve took careful dimensional and shape measurements of the existing 'wooden' windows. His plan was to have the children at St John's create templates for these windows and, then, have the children at St. Ann's paint them. It was a project that had 'goodness' written on it. The outcome would be replicas of the original stained-glass windows. The project was progressing along and then necessarily terminated in part due to the code requirements for the church which had a 'historic' designation. We referred to this project as 'the window that might have been'. Although the project was never completed, like so many other projects at St. Ann's, the expected outcomes were always welcome, this project also had an imbedded intangible characteristic: the collaboration, the interaction, the team-building and 'togetherness' were priceless commodities for the members of both communities. If 'humanity' were to be included on the market indices of Wall Street, it would have experienced another significant surge! It became a common practice for every event or gathering-whatever the purpose may have been-to become a bonding and growth experience for all concerned. Each person-without exception-eventually came to see, understand and embrace the humanity of others as well as their own. Someone once stated that Jesus Christ would be proud of each of us, all of us!" Someone responded "I believe that He is!"

Pizza Ministry

Having some pizza may not seem like a ministry event in most places but, at St. Ann's, it became symbolic of the sharing and bonding between two very different communities each with individuals who are very much the same in human spirit and feelings. It was during one of the early mission trips during which members of each community were collaborating on some of the ground cleaning and maintenance efforts. The outreach team had ordered a number of pizzas from Raymond's [our off-site conference room at the corner of St. Ann's Avenue and E. 138th Street] to be delivered for the lunch break. When the pizzas arrived, most of the members of the St. Ann's community slowly and politely faded into the background not realizing that the pizza was for all-no exceptions. Of course, the process of growing friendships and bonding was well underway; members of the St. John's contingent sought out their St. Ann's counterparts to personally issue invitations to 'come to the table' together albeit a pizza table. It was one of the early iconic events of what turned out to be a continuing sequence that served as that bonding 'glue' solidifying the togetherness of the two communities.

We have heard of the song and movie 'Singing in the Rain' with Gene Kelly; the ministry at St. Ann's was the birthplace of 'Showering in the Rain'. Following a very busy, hot and humid Saturday at St. Ann's, most members of the St. John's Outreach team really wanted-in fact, very much needed-a shower of some sort. St. Ann's did have a single functional shower that provided one part of the solution for some. Some of us were invited into the residences of members of the South Bronx community to take a shower-that was the second part of the solution. The third part of the solution was provided by the teens from St. John's who took advantage of a thunderstorm/shower to simply 'shower in the rain'. Following all this shower activity, members of both communities gathered in the basement dining area at St. Ann's and enjoyed their evening meal together while recalling the events of the day. Again, it is important and relevant to mention that the invitations into the homes of some of the St. Ann's families were so reflective of trust, respect and togetherness enjoying a continuing development within this ministry.

Community Cookouts

Another special event that is becoming a tradition during these mission trips is the community cookout. During the first and following years of ministry at St. Ann's, it had become a welcome practice to 'break bread together' as a single, unified community. During these mission trips there was always an exploratory and discovery process with respect to the many rooms and areas of the church. One summer afternoon there some of the volunteers had planned to clean out the accumulated odds-and-ends in one of the underground passageways beneath the church. Actually, it was a sort of mini-catacomb which certainly hinted at the history of St. Ann's but it also added to the mystery, anxieties and excitement of the volunteers. One of the items found in the passageway was an old, rusted charcoal broiler that had enjoyed much better days. The volunteers agreed that this charcoal broiler could be repaired and cleaned and used for the then unplanned and now upcoming inaugural community cookout at St. Ann's. Last-minute logistics were never an issue or much of a challenge to the Outreach membership; some brought the charcoal-broiler to life, others did the food shopping and, still others from both communities that now acted as 'one' prepared the cookout site with tables and all those items needed for a successful cookout. There was really an 'excitement in the air' for this upcoming event. Also, the heady aroma of hamburgers and hot dogs being grilled soon filled the air. The cookout was underway and the grilling process had shifted into high gear as the waiting/serving line grew in length. However, after about an hour of grilling and serving the members of both communities, I took notice that the waiting line was just getting longer and longer rather than shorter; I remember asking my co-cooks, Richard Silva and Cindy Lomas, "Is it my imagination or is the line always getting longer?" Well, it was getting longer as the attractive aroma of grilling hamburgers and hot dogs had filled the surrounding neighborhood and members of the community had simply joined the line and others had asked if it was 'OK' to join the line. One of the well established practices and protocols of the Outreach ministry is that 'Everyone is welcome anytime, anywhere!'.............so more hamburgers, hot dogs, buns, chips and cold drinks were quickly procured at some of the local delis and grocery stores. What had been a cookout gathering of the St. Ann's and St. John's communities quickly-and very joyfully-became a neighborhood affair. Simply put, a great time was had by all. Other cookouts at St. Ann's followed with equally wonderful results as the two communities and the neighborhood merged into a larger 'one'; the 2010 cookout took on a special flair with the inclusion of a mini-American Idol contest. Interestingly enough, two of the better renditions included ***Amazing Grace*** and ***Let the Light Shine In***.

Sleeping at St. Ann's is always a special experience for members of the Outreach team for a variety of reasons; one of those reasons is those 'noises in the night' so common in the inner-city environment: fire and police sirens, traffic, boisterous individual and crowds, barking dogs, some strange noises and, in the wee hours of the morning, the crowing of roosters. Then, on the other hand, those individuals from St. Ann's sleeping in Barrington had to adjust to the unexpected 'quietness' of this suburban community; in fact, some of the St. Ann's children had an especially noted fear or reluctance about walking about the relatively quiet and dark streets and lanes of Barrington. For all sleeping either at St. Ann's or in Barrington, there was a marked difference in their respective sleeping environments. Mother Martha and other visitors from St. Ann's, on an occasion of sleeping at my home took special note of the difficulty in sleeping because "It was so darned quiet!"

Another very special celebratory event was the Sunday Eucharist at St. Ann's at the conclusion of each and every mission trip. Just being present at the Eucharist shared by these two communities: one from the inner-city of New York City and the other from suburban New England, was a unique experience. You would just 'feel' the excitement of this Eucharistic gathering. Mother Martha's sermons were always very relevant, on-point and meaningful to all. During the traditional offering of 'Peace' to one another, it seemed that each person would seek out every other person in attendance for this 'Peace' offering. The time for this particular segment of the Eucharist lasted several minutes at St. John's whereas it would last fifteen or twenty minutes at St. Ann's. Talk about bonding and togetherness: "Wow!"

The return trip from St. Ann's included two more special events that continued to add substance and meaning to these mission trips. The first event was the loading of the vans; however, it was typically the children of St. Ann's who would quickly converge upon the vans and load themselves into the vans once the word was out that our departure was minutes away. This was immediately followed by promises, pleading and negotiations with these 'would-be stowaways'. They would claim that they also wanted to make the trip back to Rhode Island but, in reality, we surmised that they just wanted the day to never end. We usually invoked that childish logic that we couldn't come back unless we left; that logic was acceptable for only a few departures though but they knew that we would always return. One of the staples of the ministry at St. Ann's was the fact that we *always* came back............. and we still do!

The departure process always included a note of sadness as well as a note of accomplishment for what was done and a note of gratitude for having had the opportunity to do it. As the return trip unfolded these feelings were replaced by a feeling of excitement as the events of the mission trip were recalled again and again in much the same manner of those 'return trips' of the children returning to the South Bronx following their ECC summer campership. Some of these feelings-and more-are detailed in the forthcoming section on **Reflections**.

Again, there are so many beautiful and very moving 'stories' innate to this ministry and time and space become necessary limitations; however, each story is truly symbolic of the meaningful substance of the ministry.

Photos

Group 1

Miracle of the Backpacks

Another special story includes elements of coincidence, goodness and the inevitable spirit of *Amazing Grace* and is entitled '**The Miracle of the Backpacks**'. In 2003, Mother Martha was asked "What do the children really need?" as part of the effort to gather and deliver a spectrum of school supplies to St. Ann's. Her response was another 'eye-opener' for the parishioners of St. John's Church. She told us that many of the children are not really settled into a single place that they can call 'home' but rather are frequently moving from here to there. What the children need are really 'backpacks' in which there important 'stuff' could be with them at all times.

That following Sunday another ministry announcement was made during the Eucharistic service about this need for backpacks. Typically, there are always follow-on questions generated by these ministry announcements- especially those pertaining to St. Ann's-at the fellowship gathering after the service. A number of parishioners indicated that they would readily provide either usable or even new backpacks for the children at St. Ann's. However, a visitor on that Sunday had come to Barrington that weekend to visit with some friends and had decided at the last minute to come to the Sunday service at St. John's. It turned out that she was the President of the Retired Telephone Operators [of America] and had been moved by the ministry efforts at St. Ann's. She asked me "How many backpacks do you need?" My typical response to that question was "St. Ann's can use whatever can be provided because theirs is a continuing need in the light of the continuing challenges." "Well!" she said "Our organization will provide some new backpacks and I'll purchase them tomorrow and bring them to St. John's!" On the following day [Monday], she arrived at St. John's with fifty new backpacks. It was a very generous donation and, when added to those donated by the parishioners, made it possible for a delivery to St. Ann's of more than one hundred backpacks. Mother Martha later told us that the arrival of those backpacks was truly an 'event' there and the children were simply ecstatic about them. Subsequent trips included additional backpacks each filled with school supplies.

Library Upgrades

Generosity to the needs of the children at St. Ann's never ceased to be anything less than amazing. During the Spring of 2011 *Journey to St. Ann's*, a delivery of more than 2500 books in the area of literacy improvement, e.g., reading and English comprehension with instructional 'flip-charts' took place. These items were made available and seemed like they were made for the academic needs of the after-school and summer programs there. This gift was made possible through the efforts, advocacy and facilitation of Bryan W. Cooper, St. John's parishioner. One of the tasks during this mission trip was to convert an available room into a library for the children and staff at St. Ann's. The logistics involved included a design of the library shelves and configuration by Steve Lippincott, the purchase of materials from a Home Depot in the Bronx, delivery coordination with the dates of the mission trip and, of course, the availability of a construction team of six led by Steve. Final result: the library was 90% completed during that mission trip and the experience brought tears to more than a few of the St. John's volunteers who were on their inaugural mission trip. Recollections and reflections for this particular trip follow in *Reflections from St. John's*. In a follow-on 2012 effort a number of high-school and college level textbooks were donated to this 'new' library; these books provided both references for high school students as well as another view of their future academic journeys. Apparently, Bryan wasn't finished with his supportive efforts either: during the summer of 2011, he had also acquired a huge number of pieces of fall and winter clothing, including shoes, for delivery to St. Ann's. Bryan had always heard about the collection of clothes for St. Ann's where clothing needs were never ending and he personally took responsibility for the collection of clothes that required three deliveries to St. Ann's by an SUV van. It is important to take note that the word 'trips,' has been used quite frequently. Whether the trips were for the children attending the ECC summer camperships, mission trips, delivery of school supplies, planning meetings with Mother Martha, etc., there was a cadre of drivers that always 'stepped up to the plate' to make these trips possible.

Christmas Cards

One more story of many: the Outreach Team is vary familiar with the soup kitchen at St. Ann's where there were usually twice as many children as adults in the several people there. A priest there shares his thoughts about these children: most of these children receive very little and certainly less on their special days. There are children here who don't get receive birthday presents, well-deserved acknowledgements and who rarely had a gift at Christmas time and or even had a Christmas tree within their home.

Recall that on April 15, 2002, I had provided a luncheon talk about the ministry at St. Ann's to the ECW [Episcopal Church Women] membership at St. John's and had talked about this sad situation and others. Following the many questions that followed, one quite elderly member made her way to the rostrum and very quietly-but very firmly-that "I want to send a Christmas card to one of the children." That woman had 'stepped up to the plate" and had put her faith into action. More than that *she had provided the 'seed' of an effort that culminated in more than 300* personally written Christmas cards from the children and adults at St. John's being delivered that Christmas to the children at St. Ann's.

Chapter 12
Educational Advocacy & Support

Countering the inherent disadvantages of inner-city life was the synergistic effect of education, self-esteem and self-value and self-responsibility, a view of a world beyond that of the inner-city and a faith in a greater power. In the proverbial 'nutshell', these factors were really/exactly what the collective efforts at St. Ann's were all about during the years of Mother Martha's leadership. These factors were also the necessary ingredients of the ministry efforts of those who came to St. Ann's to do whatever they could to complement the programs there. **Quality education**, however, is especially a critical factor for a reasonable, hopeful and meaningful life for inner-city children as it has been for individuals throughout history. The Outreach activities of the St. John's community at St. Ann's fully embraced this milieu. Each and every activity-without exception-fully integrated a sound and meaningful educational component, an extraordinary awareness of the humanity of the children, a very sensitive view and compass for their individual and collective life journeys and that 'glue' that just seemed to bind everything together. This binding force was/is **Amazing Grace**; there simply isn't any other way to explain the continuing success of the ministry at St. Ann's and the litany of pilgrimages of individuals, families and groups to St. Ann's from a spectrum of sources.

It is true that St. John's efforts have paid rigorous attention to those traditional needs for any school program, e.g., school supplies, books, writing instruments, notebooks , pads.........ad infinitum. As mundane and commonplace as these items seem to be for most schools, they were not so commonplace in some of the inner-city schools. In fact, they were rare and sometimes non-existent for a number of reasons that simply should not be. Although St. John's continues to respond to these school needs, the Outreach membership-indeed, the entire St. John's parish-also continues to respond quickly and generously to a particular need that may arise. Some representative efforts/activities that emphasize the importance of 'education' for the children follow:

I remember the response of Mother Martha to my then naïve question in the summer of 2001 about school supplies: "Mother Martha, what do you really need?" She, very politely, responded with a list of items that, at that time, brought a new light to the paucity of school supplies at St. Ann's [and in some of the public schools in the South Bronx]. She was referring to those 'rare' items, e.g., paper [even scrap paper to use for writing, drawing, etc.], paper clips, erasers, pencils, pens, pads, etc. Simply put, there was an outstanding need for 'almost everything' but especially for these very basic items; one can only imagine what the learning environment was without these basic items. It was certainly a learning moment for the Outreach membership; one of so many to come. I have already cited the 'school supply drive of 2001' and another initiated by Allison Javery who requested school supplies for St. Ann's rather than birthday gifts for herself. One never is not surprised that a standard composition notebook with an estimated cost of $1.00 [or less] continues to be a much-needed and appreciated item at St. Ann's. St. John's has consistently provided these composition notebooks for the after-school and summer programs at St. Ann's. The significant difference in the perceived value of a composition notebook in the St. Ann's and St. John's communities is so symbolic of the difference in their hierarchy of values.

During a 2002 mission trip in the early years of this joint ministry, an entire weekend was needed to sort out those books scattered about in the various classrooms located in each nook and cranny of this historic church structure. In addition to this potpourri of books, a collection of books previously gathered in the St. John's community [including many from two public libraries in Warren and Bristol both neighboring communities to Barrington in Rhode Island] mandated some semblance of order. It was during the sorting of books by topic and age groups that a litany if conversations were simultaneously taking place between the embers of the St. John's Outreach team and the children of St. Ann's. In accordance with our well-established protocol, the sorting of the books became less in priority and the opportunity to share, interact and listen to the children became our top priority. It was-as we learned in time-that these interactions and sharing became wonderful learning moments for all. For example, myriad questions were asked by the inquisitive children about life in Barrington and about the volunteers themselves. One of the St. Ann's younger set helping in the sorting and labeling process wanted to talk about her school; I asked her "What grade are you in?" She responded "I'm in the 5th grade" I asked her "What grade will you be in next year?" She thought for a very l-o-n-g moment and responded "I think that I'll be in the 6th grade!" "Wonderful!" I exclaimed and then asked "….and what grade will you be in after the 6th grade?" She paused for several minutes and with a somewhat perplexed look on her face, she said "I don't know." I sensed another very important learning moment in my very near future. I asked a number of the children similar questions and discovered that many of the children lacked a vision of school life beyond the 6th or 7th grades. Topics such as middle school/junior high school and high school and beyond were very much unchartered territory in their beautiful minds. This experience translated into our subsequent emphasis upon the value of reading skills not only in school but throughout life. National statistics reveal that [about] 25% of the country's population is illiterate; I can only imagine what it could be in the inner-cities of America and, more importantly and so tragically, the human cost of illiteracy. This two-way educational dynamic for the children and the volunteers became a trademark of the overall ministry; it remains so today!

During these verbal exchanges another general question asked of the children was "What do you want to be when you grow up?" A very typical question for most children but for the children at St. Ann's it provided an immediate gateway into their hopes, their dreams and their limited view of the realities of the present as well as the potential for their future. It provided a natural stepping stone into discussions and explorations of outcomes far beyond their limited view and, yes, the role of education as the road to a more promising future. The Outreach team provided them with a mental visual of 'what could be' which would soon be followed by an experientially based future via the summer campership program and time spent in the Barrington community. Simply put, part of the ministry was to enable them to actually taste vanilla ice cream rather than just hearing of it.

St. Ann's was very fortunate to have the services, commitment and expertise of Don Jenner, a computer professional. Don developed a 'master plan' for the recently acquired computers for a lab at St. Ann's. The lab consisted of [about] 15 work stations with desk-top computer systems including monitors, mice, keyboards and speakers; the lab also included a systems management and administration station as well as a ceiling mounted projection monitor. Clearly, this computer lab and the availability of Don Jenner and, later, Ms. Chen Lin were a giant step forward for all concerned. The Outreach team with a huge assist from some of the School of Technology students at Providence's Johnson & Wales University developed a second local network computer lab for St. Ann's. The students at this University needed to complete a degree-required community service component. It also turned out at that time that there was a significant computer turn-over for most faculty members; the 'old' computers, for the most part, were still very functional and in reasonable shape. It did not take rocket science to see that [1] there are available computers, [2] there is a need for a second computer lab at St. Ann's and [3] there was a team of highly technically capable University students who would welcome this type of community service. The project consisted of obtaining the University approval for the donation of these computers to St. Ann's, a thorough check of each individual computer system and the design, development and testing of this local area network system. This effort included the replacement of hard drives, power supplies, etc. as well as the installation of software for local area network [LAN] and internet capability. Of course, there were a couple of minor details: transporting the complete computer system to St. Ann's and acquiring the needed tables and chairs that were computer-lab appropriate. The School of Technology made several large vans available to the student team; the computer lab furniture was provided by the manager of the University warehouse and storage facility. He asked what we needed and simply said "Let's go take a walk and pick out some chairs and tables!" The rest is history but a very wonderful and *amazing* history!

Another component of the 'computer' story is the brokering of a similar agreement with Information Science students from Columbia University. The goal of this effort was to provide the tutoring, guidance and instruction for the use of the PCs as an effective educational tool [as opposed to their use as a 'game machine']. Topics included the spectrum of Microsoft Word skills in direct support of their academic classes in English, geography, history et al.

Within the St. John's community, the stories of the ministry at St. Ann's became a topic of conversation and pride and satisfaction that

Outreach was, in fact, making a difference. Time, opportunity and our experiences continually reinforce the fact that St. Ann's is a shining light in the South Bronx. Following the computer projects, someone later added "That light is shining a little brighter!"

As computers were becoming available from the School of Technology, they were also becoming available from the parishioners at St. John's. More than a few times, an individual or family would donate their 'old' computer [still very functional] to the continuing efforts at St. Ann's. The procedure for these computers was to ask Mother Martha to identify a family that could make use of a computer system in their apartment. Again, more than several were delivered but there is one delivery that became somewhat special, perhaps bizarre, but also another learning moment.

We had arrived rather late on one Friday evening for a weekend stay at St. Ann's and we had a single computer system to deliver and set up at the apartment of one of the St. Ann's families whom we had known for several years. Rather than wait until Saturday we contacted the mother of this family of four boys and one girl-some of whom had experienced a summer campership [s] at ECC in Rhode Island and asked if this part of the mission trip could be done that Friday evening. It would make the Saturday schedule less demanding. However, we needed directions to their apartment building; the mother said that she would walk over to St. Ann's and drive back with us. At the risk of repetition but still with a measure of reality and relevance it must be noted that the ministry was actually evolving into a real-world classroom and learning experience for *all* concerned. We-the Outreach team-had read and heard about some of the living conditions in the South Bronx but each experience within the South Bronx community provided the volunteers with visuals that went far beyond the spoken and written words. The family's apartment-a fourth floor 'walk-up'-was very basic and barren: devoid of furniture, small for a family of this size, beds were mattresses strewn about the apartment and there was a very small table that was to become the platform for the computer system installation. Bear in mind that laptop computers were not very common at that time; the computer system that we carried up to the fourth floor was a desktop model with a printer, a monitor, a keyboard, a mouse and a single speaker. Not exactly a functional work station. Adding to this challenge, the room had only a single electrical outlet which seemed to be already overloaded with several extensions each with multiple connections to other devices. The team proceeded with the installation/

connection/testing of the computer system. During this activity, one of the boys-let's call him Arnaldo-asked if the team would like to see *his* snake. Hmmmmm! "Where is this snake, Arnaldo?" I asked. We were told that it *was* in a nearby glass container; Arnaldo lifted the 12 inch or so very colorful snake from the container for us to see and admire. "That's great, Arnaldo!" we said but "It's getting late and we still have some work to do here." As we continued with the computer testing, another brother came forth from his bedroom and engaged us in some conversation and asked "Al, do you want to see *my* snake?" I asked if it were in the same glass container in which Arnaldo kept his snake. The brother's response was "Oh no! It would never fit in there; it's too big so I just keep it in my bedroom." Neither our experience nor the computer installation manual had prepared us for this moment. We employed the well known 'yadda, yadda, yadda' routine and suggested that we do that second snake viewing at another more convenient time. We finished the installation and testing in a hurried fashion and then made a strategic withdrawal back to St. Ann's.

Our learning experience eventually enabled the volunteers to place the snake incident in a more meaningful context. Prior to Arnaldo's initial trip to the ECC summer camp, he had inquired about the existence of snakes and insects at the summer camp. Our much uninformed reaction assumed [and we all know what that really means, right?] that the question was based on fear rather than a healthy interest. We learned that one of Arnaldo's early interests was entomology! Arnaldo has not been described earlier in this book but he is certainly a great example of the unrecognized potential of an inner-city resident that simply doesn't have the same opportunities so readily available beyond the inner-city walls.

This ministry was growing in ideas, enthusiasm and a renewed commitment to do whatever needed to be done at St. Ann's. Parishioner after parishioner would 'step up to the late' and ask questions about their possible involvement, e.g., "Can St. Ann's use 'this' or 'that'?", "When is the next mission trip?", "What can I do to help the children at St. Ann's"..........One of the St. John's parishioners, Matt Collins, wrote to me in April of 2008 about a donation for which there is no collection box. Matt had been a co-driver with Liz Crawley driving some kids back to St. Ann's from summer camp. He had started a website as a fun way to encourage his three school-age daughters to do their best in math. He also wrote a math primer that is website available but thought that many kids, e.g., St. Ann's, may not have internet access or skills. He made the primer directly available to the Outreach team. Copies are provided to St. Ann's as required. The title of the primer is ***Get Really Good at Arithmetic***. On the MLK weekend in January, 2012, 200 additional copies were printed and delivered to St. Ann's by Sandy Connor, an Outreach veteran and prime mover for that particular mission trip.

During several mission trips, it was noticed that the chalk 'blackboards' and 'green boards' in the classrooms at St. Ann's were well-used, covered with chalk dust and literally wearing thin. Recall the concept of 'connecting dots' as Matt Collins and so many others did; if one takes a closer look at the Outreach efforts at St. John's and elsewhere, one realizes that the 'dots of interest' are ***needs*** and a means of ***fulfilling those needs***. In this particular case, there was an outstanding need-from an educational perspective-to have usable writing surfaces within the classrooms at St. Ann's. More than 400 miles away at Johnson & Wales University, there existed a second 'dot', i.e., nearly new dustless 'white boards' were frequently replaced with newer models and put into storage for a future use. That use had arrived! ***Outreach, in basic terms, is about connecting dots.*** After the administrative details for the acquisition of these 'white boards' were satisfied, the Outreach team, led by Rik Deering and, once again, Steve Lippincott transported a van full of 'white boards' to St. Ann's and installed them.

There is a formal component to education, i.e., attendance in the classrooms at all levels of education, and there is an informal component about education beyond the classroom, i.e., skills that are needed for a meaningful life. These latter skills are traditionally acquired within family, faith and friendship environments. An integral part of this informal education is a reasonable measure of 'what to do' and 'what not to do'; simply put, 'what is appropriate and constructive' and 'what is not appropriate and inevitably destructive to the individual'. Simply put, the paradigm linkage of choices, actions and consequences was emphasized. In this context, then, the Outreach team has provided interactive informational sessions both on those one-to-one-basis opportunities provided throughout the many ministry activities and then to a larger audience made up of young teens, older teens and young adults. The former were usually focused on a very specific issue whereas the latter were, by necessity, more comprehensive and inclusive. Two of the latter were entitled ***Choices*** and ***Rules of Life [aka 'Keys of Life']***. The structures for each of these discussions are provided in Appendices F and G, respectively.

Although these activities are representative of the many educational opportunities that have been imbedded within every aspect of this collaborative ministry, there is one final example that deserves mention. One of the educational efforts at St. Ann's is to provide 'field trips' [aka mobile classrooms] to the children so that their perception of life is greatly enhanced. Mother Martha has been the guiding light for some of those field trips jointly experienced by members of the St. Ann's and St. John's communities. Field trips could simply include a subway ride and a walk around one of the boroughs of New York City or the more extended and separated summer camperships at ECC. During the various mission trips, joint field trips from St. Ann's were made to movies in Manhattan, Battery Park, boat trips to and around the Statue of Liberty, the Rose Planetarium, the Empire State Building and others. These field trips have become a very special part of the mission trips. Going to Barrington was considered by the children as a field trip in of itself. While spending time at homes of Outreach members either before or following their campership times, there were joint field trips around Barrington, per se and the waters of Narragansett Bay. *Again, these formal and informal forms of education affected the children of St. Ann's, the children of St. John's and all those who participated in the ministry activities!*

Chapter 13

"Givers Become Receivers And Receivers Become Givers"

A very special and even *amazing*, still continuing and quite unexpected outcome component of the educational advocacy and support process is embedded in the phrase *'Givers become receivers and the receivers become givers'*. This phrase isn't just a verbal cheer that was created in a minute of excitement, it is an observation and, indeed, a creed developed over a period of several years as a direct result of the presence at St. Ann's by the St. John's Outreach team. Without question there was an initial high expectation that this ministry would provide some added impetus and support to the on-going education of the children of St. Ann's-in fact, it was and remains one of the prime goals of the ministry. This educational component not only emphasized the life-importance of the academic world, i.e., reading, reading comprehension, math and writing [These should be very familiar to people of all ages] it also included an education about the intangibles of life which are scarce items within most school-oriented academic programs. This latter 'education' was/is especially important in the inner-city because that environment possesses an innate capability of 'teaching' those things that take away from the individual rather than enhance their individuality and humanity. The spectrum of collaborative activities amongst the St. Ann's/St. John's 'team'- 'family' is probably more appropriate – whether it be working together, playing together, studying together, discussing a myriad topics, etc. but always together. This 'togetherness' created a sort of mobile classroom without walls that was absolutely independent of time, season and location. As the ministry progressed through the years, the stream of questions from the children of St. Ann's seemed to be a catalytic agent for the St. John's volunteers to start asking their own questions; it was obvious that the communities really had no 'walls' between them but rather a very special respect and, so very much more importantly, **trust**. It is within this 'family bond' that 'education' took on a greater dimension and meaning for the individuals from both communities.

It is quite true that these 'visitors from Rhode Island'-both teens and adults-were able to see the vast differences in their living environment and that of those residents of the South Bronx. During the mission trips there was always a walking tour conducted by Mother Martha, Steve Lippincott and/or myself around the St. Ann's neighborhood for these visitors-especially the younger set; words and verbal descriptions were kept to a minimum. Simply 'seeing' and experiencing this neighborhood, its spectrum of residents, its many sidewalk activities and, unexpectedly for most of these obvious 'tourists', spontaneous conversations with the residents there. It was these tours, the litany of interactions with the residents and shop owners during the visits and mission trips, as well as the Rhode Island experiences of the children and adults of the St. Ann's community that provided the opportunity to look beyond the visual and gain a special perspective of and insight into the striking similarities between the two very different living environments: the view beyond the visual was that each individual shared the same *humanity*, i.e., the same feelings, pride, hopes and dreams, creativities, skills, innate intelligence but also the same fears, personal, family and financial challenges et al. The differences are really ones one of scale and opportunity! I cannot remember the source of the following prayer but it is so relevant: *"O Lord! Lord of my life and of everything in the universe! I affirm that all human beings are brothers and [sisters] unto one another."*

This chorus of activities provided lessons in history – past and present - that simply cannot be found in textbooks or classrooms. Whether it was an increased awareness on the part of the Outreach team members about the evolution of the inner-city to its present state or an equivalent awareness of the children from St. Ann's about the status of life in suburban Barrington, RI and their potential to achieve some measure of that status, it was history being discovered, learned and even made. These lessons were equally applicable to members of both the St. John's and St. Ann's communities; one of the more common *reflections* of those who made the journey to St. Ann's from the St. John's community was that they had been living in a bubble, a very comfortable bubble; their St. Ann's experience had forever altered their lens of life!

This chorus of activities also had a rippling effect into and throughout both communities; some of these rippling effects are imbedded in the forthcoming **Reflections** from both communities. The Outreach team from St. John's has a standard practice of not only advocating for the children at St. Ann's via what has become an endless list of requests to their parishioners for support, needed school supplies, clothing, funding , drivers and home accommodations for the summer campership program, the inevitable unexpected needs, e.g., a vacuum cleaner, books, etc. but, of equal importance, of 'reporting back to the parishioners' the impact of their individual and collective advocacy and generosity. For example, In the Spring of 2004, the following invitation was provided to the parishioners of St. John:

SOME SPECIAL VISITORS TODAY

This morning Laranda [Jones], Jennie [Brule] and Chuck [Morrison] from St. Ann's Church of the South Bronx will join us for the forums at 8:15 and 10:00 AM as well as the 9:00 service. These young people have attended the Summer Camp at ECC both in 2002 and 2003. With the advent of the warm weather of Spring! the minds and eyes of the Mission & Outreach team are looking forward toward the ECC Summer Camp for this forthcoming summer. The parishioners of St. John's have read about and heard about this wonderful experience for the children of St. Ann's and some have participated in the equally wonderful ministry. This morning we have the opportunity to share some time with Laranda, Jennie and Chuck to hear them talk of their experiences at ECC Summer Camp and, more importantly, what impact it has had on their lives.

These forums - and others to follow – provided a unique interaction between the children of St. Ann's – so well represented by Laranda, Jennie and Chuck – and those St. John's parishioners who couldn't make the trek to the South Bronx. Simply put, these forums were an integral part of the overall educational aspect of this ministry. It was commonplace for a very senior parishioner – or a very young one – to verbalize their desire to 'go to St. Ann's' and personally rather than remotely share this ministry experience. I do remember one particular parishioner, a woman in her late eighties, who always wanted to go but the rigors of travel by van or bus and the activities at St. Ann's including sleeping on a floor somewhere made such a trip unfeasible. However, as time went by, arrangements were carefully made to make this trip by auto and a single driver and all those factors that made it a comfortable trip. It became a virtual one person pilgrimage.

Chapter 14
Reflections

Probably some of the more relevant and poignant *reflections* that best capture the spirit of the collaborative ministry between St. Ann's and St. John's are those commentaries and insights provided by members of each community. However, before offering these reflections, there is an article, **50 Years Later, A Soul Struggles**, by Leonard Pitts that appeared in the Miami Herald in May of 2011, that serves an appropriate preamble for those reflections to follow.

50 Years Later, A Soul Struggles

John Seigenthaler should write a book.

Actually, Seigenthaler, former aide to Attorney General Robert F. Kennedy, has authored several books, including one on Watergate. But as near as can be gleaned, from a search of Amazon.com, he has yet to write the book he ought to write. Meaning, a book that struggles with the question that seems, in some ways, to have haunted him most of his life.

What does it mean to be a white person of conscience in a racist nation?

It is a question that is applicable to millions, of course, yet one that has seldom even been posed, much less grappled with in any meaningful way. Seigenthaler is uniquely qualified to do both.

This becomes clear in a poignant meeting with the 2011 student Freedom Riders at the First Amendment Center that bears his name. He is a decent man. You get that sense. He's the one the attorney general dispatched to the South to rescue the Freedom Riders after a bus was burned and a mob set loose on the defenseless college students who committed the "crime" of riding interracially on interstate buses.

He is the one who took a pipe blow to the back of his head while trying to rescue two black women from that self same mob.

So a decent man, yes. But he is a decent man who, not unreasonably, still wonders 50 years later, at 83 years of age, how the tragedy of American racism could have been so invisible to him and his contemporaries until movements like the Freedom Riders forced them to see. How could something so obvious now have been imperceptible then?

"I think back to my childhood," he tells the students. "Those two [African American] women, Lela Gray and Birdie Mai Liddle, at times were surrogate mothers to my siblings and me. And they were treated with great respect in my home. Once they were on the street and in a crowd...I don't mean I wouldn't have recognized them if I had seen them or been courteous to them or caring for them.

'Invisible'

"But I will tell you, like Ellison said, they were invisible. I don't know how many times I was on a bus or trolley car when I was a child or a young adult, not paying any attention to the signs. Lela Gray or Birdie Mai Liddle, Rosa Park's counterparts here, paid their fare and went where the signs told them. Some were carrying [burdens] maybe taking laundry home from some white woman's kitchen to press it during the night and getting it back in the morning. They struggled to the back, where they had to go. My parents had told me, if a lady needs a seat, stand up and give her your seat. It never occurred to me they meant a black lady. And indeed, my parents never meant a black lady." *[Author's comment: in the early days of the ministry at St. Ann's, I had on more than one occasion offered my subway seat to a lady or elderly person of color; I was initially surprised that the obvious facial reaction from the other passengers seemed to say 'My God, what are you doing?' Another learning experience for this author.]*

He is perched on a stool in front of the small room, arms folded inward, reflecting, "Until you read Ralph Ellison*," he says, "you don't understand what the invisible man or the invisible woman really were. We who are white, maybe went out of our way not to see them. That's not entitled to absolution. It's a condemnation of our ignorance."

*Ralph Ellison Wikipedia, November, 2011]: Ralph Waldo Ellison [March 1, 1914 – April 16, 1994] was an American novelist, literary critic, scholar and writer. He was born in Oklahoma City, Oklahoma. Ellison is best known for his novel *Invisible Man,* which won the National Book Award in 1953. He also wrote *Shadow and Act* [1964], a collection of political, social and critical essays, and *Going to the Territory* [1986].

Published in 1952, *Invisible Man* explores the theme of man's search for his identity and place in society, as seen from the perspective of an unnamed black man in New York City of the 1930s. In contrast to his contemporaries such as Richard Wright and James Baldwin, Ellison created characters that are dispassionate, educated, articulate and self-aware. Through the protagonist Ellison explores the contrasts between the Northern and Southern varieties of racism and their alienating effect. The narrator is "invisible" in a figurative sense, in that "people refuse to see" him, and also experiences a kind of dissociation. The novel, with its treatment of taboo issues such as incest, won the National book award in 1953.

There is wonder in his voice. "I look back at that time," he says, "and that's when I say, where was my head, where was my heart, where was my parents' heads and hearts? Never heard from my teachers about the indignity, the indecency. Not one time did I ever hear a sermon in my childhood or young adulthood, directed in any way at the injustice of a society that separated people by race. It was part blind ignorance and part blatant arrogance. And I confess that with great and deep regret and if I could change, I would. But you know, I'm 50 years too late from the time I first really started intensely thinking about it."

You sense the soul struggles of a good man who will probably go to his grave wondering how the society, the very soil from which we spring, could have gotten so much so tragically wrong.

In 1899, Rudyard Kipling wrote a poem *The White Man's Burden,* in which was described as a colonizer's obligation to the welfare of the colonized nation, "your new caught, sullen peoples." If Seigenthaler is any example, though, it might be argued that the white man's burden – at least the burden of the white man who regards himself as decent, enlightened, moral, good – is to figure out what to do with the legacy of injustice that attaches like glue to the very concept of whiteness in America.

Another Reflection

Many years ago, the late Michael Browning, a white Miami Herald reporter, wrote of his encounter with Rev. C. T. Vivian, an aide to Martin

Luther king Jr., who spoke of his white seminary students if they had ever prayed for forgiveness for the sin of racism. Browning felt indicted by the question.

"Southern irresolution," he wrote, "How, if I am as benevolent as I think I am, can black people see me as such a monster? Am I an inert part of some vast oppression? Do I injure blacks by breathing and just being white?"

And the answer is probably less important than the asking.

"You know," says Siegenthaler, "it was a cliché, maybe, when Jack Kennedy said each of us can make a difference. But it's no cliché to say each of us should try."

He grieves of things that were invisible to him a lifetime ago.

Perhaps the only sensible and moral response, then, is to wonder: What things are invisible to us now.

I could add another cliché to that one offered by John Siegenthaler; it was provided by the Irish philosopher, Edmund Burke who said "All that is necessary for evil to triumph is for good men to do nothing."

Chapter 15
Reflections From St. Ann's

The reflections from the St. Ann's community include a litany of observations, comments and written commentary of its reaction, impact and response to this continuing joint ministry between two very different communities that shared a common bond and belief. It just isn't feasible to provide the totality of these reflections –and it is equally so for the St. John's community-however, the reflections from both communities to follow do capture the spirit, mind and soul of those who serve and, more importantly, of those who are served. The stage is set with the reflections of Gladys Mercado.

Gladys Mercado

The inherent disadvantages of inner-city life have been addressed earlier in this book and elsewhere and are widely and readily acknowledged in the world of reality. There the efforts of individuals struggle to move forward and beyond these disadvantages [aka the maze of survival] have also been addressed; one's struggle can entail education and a residency beyond the South Bronx or it can mean an education and a return to and residency in the South Bronx. Both paths are difficult and very challenging but the latter deserves some added recognition because life in the South Bronx also carries some additional unique challenges that simply don't exist in life beyond the South Bronx. They return to/remain in the South Bronx to do what they can, what they must and, in keeping with those words found in the Episcopal Church's Book of Common Prayer: ......"And now, Father, send us out to do the work you have given us to do".......

or......."Send us now into the world in peace, and grant us strength and courage to love you and serve you with gladness and singleness of heart" There are so many individuals - some recognized but most are not – who continue to 'make a difference' on a daily basis to their community and its people. Certainly, Mother Martha is an iconic figure in that respect but there are also others. Gladys Mercado is such an individual; she was born in Harlem and relocated to the South Bronx in 1986. She has been an active parishioner at her church since 1993 and senior Warden there for ten years. She is also the mother of four children, three of whom have survived in the South Bronx. In 1986, her 14 year old son suffered an accidental death while *train-surfing, i.e., riding illegally on the exterior of a moving train, e.g., a subway train. In 2005, Gladys's ten-year old niece, Natasha Addison, was inadvertently shot and killed in a drive-by shooting.* The intended victim was shot five times while repairing a bicycle. Some relevant excerpts from Darrin Burgess's article in the Bronx Beat [*the bronxbeat.org*] entitled *Bronx Woman Persists Against Gun Violence* on March 7, 2009 follow:

It has been seven years since her ten-year old niece was killed by a bullet meant for another child, when New York media pounced on the tragedy and left quickly for another story. Gladys decided cases like these needed more attention. "I was infuriated with the fact that after she died, she was just a media event."

Gun violence is killing Bronx teens, and residents whose families have been affected complain that only fleeting exposure is given to the issue.

City records and census figures do show that the overall rate of murders in the Bronx was 52.4 percent higher than the city average.

Another disappointment for community organizers has been the failure of City officials to set up a successful gun buyback program in the Bronx, in which churches cooperate with the New York Police department to exchange guns for $200 debit cards. Mayor Michael R. Bloomberg announced last week that six Queens churches involved in the program acquired 910 guns over a single Saturday event. The program has been similarly successful in Brooklyn, Manhattan and Staten Island.

Bernard Smith, 58, whose 19-year-old son was shot and killed in 2001 following an argument among friends, has hosted a neighborhood gathering each year on the anniversary of his son's death. He closes off the streets surrounding his block in Morrisania [St. Ann's neighborhood], serves food, plays music, and hands out T-shirts and pamphlets about gun violence. "I don't have no funds, nothing. I don't care if I have to bring out my own grill." He said.

Each gathering ends with a candlelight vigil in front of a photo-collage of Bronx residents whom guns have killed since his son's death. There were 45 last year, he said.

Since these events, Gladys Mercado has emerged as an effective and proactive leader for the voice of the tragedy of gun violence. She raised the awareness of the tragic, unexpected and very personal outcomes of gun violence. She became the leader of the Bronx chapter of *New Yorkers Against Gun Violence;* this chapter has more than 60 members comprised of supporters, families including families of victims. She was the recipient of a three year grant from the Trinity Church at Wall Street and worked out of a small office at her church; her days have been filled with telephone calls to media outlets, reaching out to parents and arranging volunteers for rallies at City Hall as well as various speaking engagements about the harsh realities of gun violence. Once the grant funds were expended, Gladys continued her campaign as best as possible through donations. ***Through her efforts to date [2012] more than 1200 guns have been removed from the streets of the South Bronx.***

The Brady Center to Prevent Gun Violence [Washington, DC] and its sister organization the Brady Campaign to Prevent Gun Violence are dedicated to reducing gun deaths and injuries through education, legislative reform and litigation. The word 'Brady' is a result of the current chairperson, Sarah Brady, joining the group after her husband, Jim Brady, was shot and seriously wounded during the 1981 assassination attempt on President Ronald Reagan. While the commendable efforts of the Brady Center continue, the scarcity of funds for the efforts of the Bronx Chapter of *New Yorkers Against Gun Violence* have severely curtailed the continuity of this much-needed campaign.

Recently, Gladys Mercado became the recipient of the cherished ***Brady Award*** from the Brady Center. Her special ministry in the South Bronx continues to this day. During St. John's ***Journey to St. Ann's*** in the spring of 2011, Gladys made a presentation to members-most the younger set-of the combined St. Ann's and St. John's communities. [Several photos of her talk are soon forthcoming] Gladys's very effective and moving presentation involving the commentary and photos of some of the more recent victims of gun violence – from ages two to ninety-two - made a dramatic and lasting impression on this younger set. Sadly, though, the realities of gun violence are almost accepted by those from the South Bronx and somewhat eye-opening to those who are not. The experience of viewing a photo-collage is a dramatic experience whether provided by Gladys Mercado or Bernard Smith; it is a reminder of the horrors of street warfare.

In a recent discussion with Gladys, I asked about her view of the on-going collaborative ministry efforts of St. Ann's and St. John's. Her reply follows:

"Well, Al, I am a single parent living in a poor community; life is difficult and I haven't had any sort of vacation since 2000 but I am determined to have one more vacation before I die!' About what the people of St. John's do here at St. Ann's: the summer camperships have given our children a life-changing experience beyond the South Bronx; they have seen and experienced 'another world', a very different world. The children, teens and adults from St. John's have generously shared their gifts of *listening, caring and nurturing.* The children, teens and adults from St. Ann's consider that this sharing, their visits to Rhode Island as a safe place and the visits of the St. John's community here at St. Ann's are the *very best of times.*"

The Brules

Some very special reflective insight is provided by Alicia, Jennie and Liola Brule: they were residents of the South Bronx, started their educational life there, participated in the summer camperships at ECC in Rhode Island and, in 2006, initiated their transition to residency in Rhode Island. Having the experience of both communities makes their reflections very relevant.

Alicia Brule: "I feel blessed to be part of St. John's and St. Ann's. It has been life-changing for my family and me. My sisters [Jennie and Liola] went to a private school there [St. Andrews School]. Frank also attended that school for a year and is currently a student at The San Miguel School in Providence. People there [in Rhode Island] helped us in our times of financial need. They served as my family support."

"I was privileged to meet amazing and God-believing people who also believed in the gift of giving and helping those in need."

"Our relationship with St. Ann's began when Jennie was attending school at Public School 65. My sisters, Alicia and Liola and I participated in the after-school and Freedom School programs at St. Ann's; also, the summer camp opportunities."

"My family and I faced many financial challenges after we moved to Rhode Island in 2006 where we began our new life. My father again returned to help my Mom support our family. I attended my first year at Rhode Island College as Jennie continued her education at St. Andrews School. Liola attended St. Andrews School the following year and Frank followed."

"Prior to moving to Rhode Island, my family was comfortable. We had everything we needed. When we came to Rhode Island, this situation changed dramatically. With my mom working part-time and my Dad traveling frequently for cultural and religious reasons, it was hard 'making ends meet'; buying food and home necessities became difficult as well."

"God was always good to my family despite all our financial struggles; St. John's often helped us with gift cards to Shaw's [Supermarket] or my father's family would help us if they could."

"After I graduated from Rhode Island College, I became independent and got my first apartment with the help of the St. John's and Barrington communities. Shortly thereafter, I received custody of my brother, Frank, and I continue to support my family in any way that I can. I am very thankful for everything and all the blessings of my life-especially the people!"

On May 27, 2011, Alicia commented on those reflections made by the St. John's parishioners during their return bus ride from St. Ann's following the ***Journey to St. Ann's*** on April 30 and May1, 2011. She said "The reflections were great. Everyone gained something from their trip there. I would love to be a part of this next time.......I'm sooo happy the children are meeting the people of St. John's. *That's how their horizons are broadened and they realize....like my sisters and I that there's more to the world than our [South Bronx] community. Thanks for continuing these amazing trips.*"

Jennie Brule: "I feel very blessed because my family and I were given a once-in-a-lifetime opportunity. My siblings and I were able to go to a very good private school [St. Andrews School]; my older sister, Alicia, was able to attend and graduate from Rhode Island College."

"St. Ann's helped my journey get started by introducing me to people from St. John's."

"St. John's helped my siblings and I through school as well as financial help and when other things were needed."

"I feel like moving to Rhode Island is one of the best things that has happened to my family and me. My sister finished college. My younger sister improved in school. I also improved in school and learned to believe more in myself. The downside of moving is that I miss my friends and family."

"My motivation for wanting to become Frank's custodian and bring him back is so that he could have the same education we had. We want him to follow his dreams. He has a higher chance in making it here than in elsewhere."

Liola Brule: "The best thing that happened to me was moving to Rhode Island. If my parents didn't move to Rhode Island, I would be a high school dropout. I never thought about college but moving out of the South Bronx opened my eyes to a lot more things."

"I wouldn't say that there is a bad thing that happened to me in my journey because you learn and grow from whatever happens to you in life."

"The reason why this journey/experience has become such a success for my family and me is that we all have determination in our hearts."

In an email dated December 21, 2011, Liola [after completing the first semester of her second year at Mitchell College where she is preparing for a career in the law enforcement arena] provides a message that really 'says it all'; 'Happy Holidays! I hope that you enjoy your holidays; I just wanted to keep you updated on what's going on. I finished my semester and my GPA is a 3.66. Juvenile: A; Criminal law: B+; Logic: A; Human Services: B+; Social issues: A. *The hard work is paying off!*'"

From the Children [about time spent in Rhode Island]

"It's good to get away from the madness, the killing and the guns....I love it....I make a lot of friends there and, when I go back, I get to see them again....It's exquisite....you learn lots of stuff that kids there do...they treat us well...I liked the *Waterfire* best...they **REALLY** care about me... they made me feel great and they taught me that someone really cares about me...I learned to swim. I learned that people love me-a lot...when am I going back and who's going to pick me up?...thank you for the Harry potter books."

From Shirlee [as a representative of the parents]

"Although I've never seen an angel, I've truly been touched by them. As a struggling mother, I have a great appreciation for the care that has been provided for my son at your camp. It has been a blessing and a relief that my child has the opportunity to see a different way of life. What you have done is provided a different view of the world and for that I am immensely grateful."

An email from 'Mother Martha'

"Dear Sandy [Connor] and Al:

Yes, Edward White, Jr. did send his acceptance [for a summer (2011) Counselor-in-Training position] to ECC, and he is doing 'well' in school; so that looks like a go. *One life saved.*

In a true test of your mercy, Shirlee and Jeffrey would like to extend ECC for all three sessions for which he is eligible. [He is 13 and going into the 9th grade; so I believe he's eligible for music and creative arts, camper's choice and summer's end]. According to Shirlee [Jeffrey' Mom], the shelter where they are living has had to cancel all its summer youth programs because of budget cuts. Jeffery did get into the high school of his choice. *Another life saved.*"

Anthony Bonilla

Anthony, who was mentioned in *There Are Success Stories*, like Gladys Mercado, has moved himself beyond the negative impact of the inner-city and yet has chosen to remain in the South Bronx to help make a difference for others. Anthony attended the Bronx Leadership School and then-via an invitation-transferred to Cushing Academy. He is a 2004 graduate of Manhattanville College in upstate New York. Currently, he is on the administrative staff at St. Ann's and is usually the first person one encounters when walking through the door to the office area at St. Ann's or when telephoning the church. He has provided a much-needed assistance in the planning and facilitating of the mission trips. He is quietly courteous, helpful to all and is a very important part of the St. Ann's team; he is also a quietly spiritual person but, if you listen with your heart, you can easily hear him.

When Anthony was 13 years old he wrote: *"No violence will there be in heaven, no guns or drugs or IRS. If you still feel lonely in your heart, or bitterness, you'll know that you're not there. As for television, forget it! No one will look at you from the outside. People will see you from the inside. All the people from the street will be there. You'll recognize all the children who have died when they were very little. God will be there. He'll be happy that we have arrived."*

Chuck Morrison

On December 14, 2011, Chuck wrote this letter as a prelude to his reflections:

"I used to be a child who struggled with anger issues. That was, of course, until the summer of 2003 when I met a lady by the name of Jan Malcolm who realized I was an inner-city youth from the [South] Bronx who struggled with overcoming issues of defending my feelings with fighting rather than with words.

Our relationship started off rocky, with her trying to feel me out and me on the defensive. After starting several altercations with other church counselors, she decided to intervene. She sat me down and began to inquire about why I would resort to violence rather than talk it out? I responded that I was from a place in which talking just wasn't used to solve disagreements. And so it began-the long journey into myself where I learned to reflect on what my feelings were and how to better express that with others. She became like a mentor. After my six weeks at church camp, she invited me to spend a week at her house with her husband and two kids: Erin and Chris. There she and I had several talks about life in my world and how life in her world was not so different. After sharing stories, I began to realize that our lives were not so different-just different circumstances.......and then came a surprise to me. Jan believed that I might be suffering from ADD [Attention Deficit Disorder] which may or may not allow me to fully cope with my situation in different areas of life, which is why I just resort to a path of violence rather than take the time to weigh different ideas going on in my head. She handed me a book on the disorder and left me to my thoughts. Along the way listening to my feelings and letting me vent about the way certain things made me feel, then giving me advice on calm solutions to a teenager's everyday problems. Although I hadn't realized it, skeptical as I was, I couldn't see the values she had instilled in me.

After I stayed with Jan and her family for a week or so, it was time to say my goodbyes and although she told me we would see each other again, I didn't believe that we would. Back home I assumed my normal life and kept the book that Jan had given me, reading it now and then until it was finished. Weeks had passed when I was soon in an argument and all my natural feelings had come to the surface but before I gestured and positioned myself for a fight my brain kicked in and I thought about how I could defuse the situation before getting into a fight. Something I had never done before I met Jan and I couldn't believe how successful I was with the alternative.

And that's when I realized what Jan had done. The experience at church camp [ECC] had changed me forever. I no longer had only violence as my only way to deal with things. *I now had another way and it made me feel great!* I would never resort to violent behavior again. As a changed man I would talk about how I felt in every situation and it worked. To this day I have not had one fight with anyone. The quality of life to me has drastically improved due to those fine people in the smallest of the 50 states and my friend in Rhode Island."

I also had the opportunity to share some of Chuck's additional thoughts and reflections; they follow:

"Success is measured in different ways."

"I didn't want to fail at anything, I would rather quit."

"My life changed because I was able to express my feelings rather than shut down or walk away."

"I don't have to be violent to be decisive; I can express my views which usually lead to better outcome."

"St. Ann's was an enabling factor on my journey; without the Church, there can be no broadening of one's horizons."

"It is good to be school-wise but one must also be life-wise."

"There are South Bronx 'rules' and then there are Rhode Island 'rules'."

"There are not enough outlets for the children in the South Bronx; St. John's provided a huge outlet for the children and, for me, there was Incarnation Camp prior to my going to ECC summer camp."

"I will jump at every chance to leave the South Bronx and see and experience life outside of the South Bronx."

"The ministry efforts of St. John are wonderful, beautiful, commendable and St. Ann's isn't just a 'pit-stop' [as it is for others]; the people from St. John's always return. All of us here at St. Ann's feel good about that!"

"St. John's has helped create the foundation for being a better youth."

Carol Cushman

What's a Jewish Psychoanalyst, whose father was the President of her synagogue, and who was educated in a Quaker school doing in the middle of two Episcopalian churches? The story begins with a longstanding acquaintance with, Martha Overall, Esq. I spent some time with her brother, John, when he was ill. I had heard about and was so profoundly moved by a woman called Mrs. Wellington I vowed that I would go to St. Ann's to see if there was some way I could help.

I confess that it was with a certain fear and trembling I first took the short subway ride from my upper East Side home to the South Bronx. I have been in 'dangerous' locations more than once in my life, but prejudice and propaganda being what they are, I admit that until I got off the subway on 138th Street and, as the angel suggested to Hagar, opened my eyes., I was personally afraid. The first day I went to volunteer was Thanksgiving Day in 1997. This was a personally painful time in my life, which is why I was not where I usually had been for many of previous Thanksgivings.

Through no skill of my own, but only because Mother Martha vouched for me, I was introduced to Ms. Ruth Burrell and Ms. Bernice King and was permitted to work in the kitchen. That day, we served hundreds of people before taking a break. During the break (I later understood the English congregation is served after the first service at St. Ann's; there is a pause until the Spanish-speaking congregants come downstairs after their service).

During the break, the women who had been cooking, serving or cleaning the dishes took some food for themselves. As they put pieces of turkey on their paper plates, some said that they were taking turkey home for themselves or their children. I observed that many of those volunteering in the kitchen had little more than the people whom they were feeding. We then went back to work serving hundreds more hungry people.

The way it worked in those days was that the women cooked and served the food on paper plates and the men carried the plates out of the kitchen and served the people. Toward the end we ran out of various items that we had been serving. Just as we ran out of the last piece of turkey, the men came in and reported that there were still eight more people to be served and that was the end. Without missing a beat, all of the women who had put some food away for themselves immediately turned to their 'turkey stash' and divided it and offered it for the eight additional plates.

I knew at that moment that even if one were an atheist, God was for certain in St. Ann's kitchen. I knew at that moment that many of my investment banker or hedge fund patients, if they became aware that there were to be a shortage, would hoard. And I knew at that moment, that I wanted to come back to St. Ann's if these profoundly loving people would have me. Said in a humorous way, to misquote the old Levy's Rye bread ad, "You don't have to be Episcopalian to feel awe for the Holy Spirit."

I have come back virtually every Sunday for the past 15 years. At first I only worked in the kitchen, but pretty soon Cynthia Black outed me. My job was to serve the rice, which, because of my lack of culinary skills, often stuck to my serving spoon. One day, Cynthia bravely said, "Carol, if you want to get the rice off the spoon, 'bang' the spoon." I saw that whatever I did in the kitchen could be supplemented by some other skills and my middle class privilege. Thus, I began to help individuals with various health or social work issues. It is not that I gave up the pleasures of the kitchen camaraderie, it was just that I could do the sorts of things that I do more naturally as well. Also during these years, I thought it only right that I attend the church services before going to the kitchen.

In the course of my time at St. Ann's I heard about the good works of the people from Rhode Island. As I had spent many summers on Block Island, I was positively inclined in a general way toward anything Rhode Island. Then I began to hear and see the enormous positive and salubrious effect on the children who spent a week each summer in Rhode Island. The kids came back with as many, if not more, expanded memories and imaginings as those I experienced when, as a sophomore, I went to Italy. The stay in Rhode Island made the world became larger for one child after another. This I believe is of utmost importance because if we can expand what a person is able to imagine or dream, we are thereby offering that person the first steps to affecting that dream. Many spoke of people who cared for them, many of things heretofore unseen or experienced. Just about everyone wanted to go back year after year. And in allowing the kids to return year after year, St. John's offers the fidelity, consistency and benign teaching good parents and good shepherds provide.

As I became more aware of 'the people from Rhode Island', I knew that they were not just drop-in do-gooders. They were committed to St. Ann'; time after time they applied Edison's 99% perspiration as one St. Ann's room after another was improved by their work and sweat. First, they had a general name 'the people from St. John's'. Then, real names, as the kids spoke of the families they lived with and shared time and events. These families not only offered love, but, I believe, every bit as important, they offered the kids the gift of having the love they, the kids, offered to 'the people of St. John's, received and valued. This is an inestimable gift. Still, at this point, the 'people of St' John's' were, I knew, good people. But still, they were amorphous.

Only when some of the kids I had worked with for years, who were now living in Rhode Island, needed help did I learn how truly blessed we all are to have that character, intelligence, loving-kindness, practical know-how, dedication, energy and fidelity of the volunteers from St. John's sharing the road and the load. These kids in Rhode Island needed immediate help because of a housing and financial crisis. As my association with these volunteers became more frequent, I learned how absolutely unselfishly, year after year, they have been there every step of the way corporeally, spiritually and morally. Not just in this time of crisis, but all along. I learned in a way that is humbling how, when burdens are shared, the whole in infinitely greater than the sum of its parts. I learned what it means to have people whom I could trust, not only those who do what they said they would do, but who are competent, unselfish, resilient and generous, and all of this with their eyes wide open. Said simply, I am awed to observe and be a peripheral part of this joint community.

My favorite hymn is 'Here Am I lord'. The people of St. John's, most especially Al Colella, embody what always moves me to tears, whenever I hear it sung. 'Here am I Lord. It is I lord. I have heard you calling in the night. I will go lord, if you lead me. I will hold your children in my hand.'

So what's a Jewish psychoanalyst, who went to a Quaker school and regularly attending an Episcopalian church doing? The answer is respectfully having the time of my life and through the grace of God learning every step of the way

Janet Scott

In the winter of 2001, 2002, I worked part-time on call at a garden center in New Jersey for the holidays. As is the usual practice, I was let go Christmas Eve. I had applied for an ongoing job in the greenhouse for which I was later told was no longer available. This turn of events left me without the ability to garden for the winter. I called it the winter of my discontent.

To this day I have no idea why I attended a meeting at my church [St. James in NYC] sponsored by the community outreach committee. Perhaps, it was my restlessness. I found myself in a small audience listening to three clergy leaders of afterschool programs, who were basically asking for help with tutoring. Over and over in my head came the words "I am not a tutor.", "I am not interested in tutoring.", "I am lousy one on one with children." Then the idea of holding classes on houseplants occurred to me. I envisioned the usual spider plants and other easy, fun plants.

Until that meeting, I did not know any of these clergy but I asked each one if they would be interested in my doing classes. Two priests said "Yes." The third, Mother Martha, asked me if I knew Alice Waters. Because I heard Alice Waters speak at my daughter's commencement ceremony and, therefore, knew her story and philosophy [and I had eaten at her restaurant, Chez Panisse], I said "Yes." I also told Mother Martha I had designed an 1850 kitchen garden and would be thrilled to do another kitchen garden for the children at St. Ann's.

It turned out that in 2000, Hillary Clinton and Alice Waters had paid a visit to St. Ann's. In that meeting, Alice made the suggestion to Mother Martha that, perhaps, there could be an Edible Schoolyard at St. Ann's. Thinking Alice had plans for St. Ann's, Mother Martha said to write to Alice. I did. If you don't know about the Edible Schoolyard, it is a public school program in which middle school children garden, harvest and cook.

In April, 2001 Mona [a protégé' of Alice's], Susan Williams and I started a modified version of the Edible Schoolyard at St. Ann's Church of Morrisania. I thought my role would be that of head gardener and that Mona with Susan's help would do all the administrative work, find volunteers, organize the classes, etc. Then, in July, Mona left for a new job.

I was now the one with the time and 'expertise' to take on the roles for everything. *"Thank God for St. John's of Barrington, RI!"* With open hands and hearts, they gave me the help I needed with things which I could not do. They built a fence around what is now becoming a meditation garden and helped with any miscellaneous odd jobs. Most of all I cherish their 'weeding'. On one visit they actually rented a rototiller to attack the ragweed! Their warmth and encouragement were extremely helpful. I owe them many thanks.

Throughout the early years, the children's enthusiasm for the garden program remained strong. At first, it was a few teenagers and then about 5 years into The Garden at St. Ann's, I designed a new children's vegetable garden and began nutrition and garden classes for all 100 students in the afterschool program usually running from February through June 15 and then a harvest of potatoes in October. During the summer's freedom School, I organized classes for 5th and 6th graders and, later, 4th and 5th graders. Bout thirty of these children had also been in the spring's afterschool program.

These are a few quotes by the children from the garden classes:

"I did not think dirt was good for anything; it was just dirt." From a 13year old girl.

"I had no idea it took so long to grow carrots." From an 11 year old boy.

"Eeeeeeeee!" A 5th grade girl upon harvesting an ear of corn.

Then there are all the "I love the garden!" and "When do we have garden class?" comments and questions. I hear them all the time.

I have received more than I have given to these needy children. They are loving and lovable. [Author's note: more testimony to one of the continuing and growing outcomes of the ministry at St. Ann's, i.e., that *'Givers become receivers and receivers become givers!'*]

Ms. Daisy

'Ms. Daisy' is an octogenarian and has been at St. Ann's for more than twenty-five years; our first real introduction to this remarkable woman was during those mission trips that included the maintenance, rehabilitation and upgrades in the St. Ann's kitchen. The kitchen served meals for the children of the after-school program and the summer's Freedom School. It also serves as a base camp for the hungry of the community residents and for those who live on the streets; it is a very busy 'food pantry' as well as a 'meal-site' for the noontime meal. 'Ms. Daisy' is more than a member of the kitchen staff, she is really the Commander-in-Chief of the kitchen and valued, respected and cherished by all. She is a quiet epitome of a provider of service to those in need. We share both a common respect and admiration for each other; I once asked her what brings her to St. Ann's year after year after year. Her response was that "God directs us to where we should go!" With that simple but very powerful observation, the outreach members-over the years-achieved a more comprehensive understanding of what brings them to St. Ann's year after year after year.

Michael

Michael is the Sexton at St. Ann's and the bulk of the continuing maintenance and repair tasks at St. Ann's fall into his lap; the magnitude of these tasks is never matched by an equal amount of resources. He does well in the face of what appears to be a tidal wave of tasks. The Outreach membership interacts with Shelley on each and every visit to St. Ann's; his advice and guidance is crucial to whatever success is achieved. In that context, then, Michael is very appreciative of whatever assistance that is provided by the St. John's community. It was mentioned earlier that a collateral and continuing goal at St. Ann's is to maintain the Church buildings and grounds for the benefit and safety of the children. He must prepare both the buildings and grounds-inside and out- for the children; so all the painting, cleaning, kitchen work, library construction, garden work, etc. is especially acknowledged. Michael made it crystal clear that the cookouts brought to life at St. Ann's during the many mission trips are considered are very special events for the children and their families; Michael said the "The children love those cookouts!"

'Mother Martha'

Sermon by the Rev'd Dr. Martha Overall
  Second Sunday after the Epiphany, January 15, 2012
  St. Ann's Church, 295 St. Ann's Avenue, Bronx, NY
  "When Jesus spoke about angels ascending and descending, I don't think that he foresaw that he might be talking about the stretch of Interstate 95 between Rhode Island and New York. But, you see, many of our young people, when they go to Rhode Island, come back thinking that they have been to heaven.
  Some of our boys-excuse me-young men-have told me they are different people when they are in Rhode Island. When they are free of the stresses and the peer pressure of the South Bronx, they reveal the better angels of their nature. And that can change their whole lives.
  One little girl was *totally* convinced that Rhode Island is heaven. One

of the reasons that she was so sure was that when she went swimming in the waters there, the eczema that had plagued her, disappeared.

As a priest who particularly cares about children, I was delighted to have our children experience Rhode Island. But what I did *not* anticipate was that so many of them would then want to move there. And some of them actually did. Have you ever heard of runaway sheep?

Despite the fact that a *haven* is a refuge or a sanctuary, Mott *Haven* does not have a heavenly reputation. In fact, when the label 'South Bronx' began to be used with all its unpleasant suggestions, this area is where they were referring to.

Nobody wanted to be responsible for conditions in the South Bronx, so the politicians liked to pretend that we didn't exist. People were discouraged from coming here. The Gospel says "Can anything good come out of Nazareth?" but it might have said "Can anything good come out of the South Bronx?"

I actually had a supervisor in seminary who couldn't understand why I wanted to come here. He thought I must want to buy drugs. It used to be that if you looked as though you didn't belong here, they thought you were a teacher or a social worker. But these days, you could be a friend. Can anything good come out of the South Bronx, you bet it can.

Before Jonathan Kozol wrote *Amazing Grace*, people used to hide conditions in the South Bronx. The denial of reality was so extreme that on the abandoned buildings that people could see from the Bruckner Expressway, the city actually posted stickers of flowerpots in the windows so that commuters wouldn't find them so depressing. But conditions will never get better unless the truth is known.

And so *Amazing Grace* was published and people learned that conditions are very challenging here, but they also learned that there are a lot of good people that come out of the South Bronx.

In the Gospel, when Nathaniel heard that Jesus was from Nazareth, he reacted "Can anything good come out of Nazareth?" Scholars have observed that the closest thing we have to Nazareth is the South Bronx. Primarily they say that because so many people live in poverty. Mott Haven is still the poorest congressional district in the whole country. Most people in our neighborhood live in what's called extreme poverty, which means that their family income is less than one-half the poverty rate. That is what conditions were like in Nazareth where Jesus grew up.

Did anything good come out of Nazareth? *Does* anything good come out of the South Bronx?

There are more ways in which Mott Haven is like Nazareth. There is a strong sense of community among the people of the neighborhood, just as there was among the people of Nazareth. There is also a feeling of powerlessness, because what power we have is often not used.

But the way in which the South Bronx is most like Nazareth is the contrasting <u>economic</u> poverty and <u>spiritual</u> wealth. Because we live very close to the margins, most of us are extremely aware of how much we rely on God. As a result, there's a church on just about every block in this neighborhood. So, how can anyone question whether anything good can come out of a place like this?

My feeling is that it is more than likely that a <u>lot</u> of good will come out of places like this. You know the old saying: 'What doesn't kill you makes you stronger, and those that come out of Nazareth and Mott Haven are mighty strong.

But in addition to strength, growing up here gives many young people compassion-they really can feel other people's pain.

It also gives them a closeness to God. Even gang members wear rosaries around their necks and if you listen to rap, you'll hear a lot of God talk.

If you want immediate proof that something good can come out of a place like this, all you had to do was to look around here yesterday and today. You would see the results of angels ascending and descending along Interstate 95. The people of out two communities come together recognizing somehow that without each other we are not whole, that without each other we are not what God wants us to be.

And so a lot of good continues to come out of the South Bronx-and out of Barrington. We have a relationship that was born in <u>Amazing Grace</u> and nurtured by God. Those whom God has joined together let no one put asunder. Bringing communities together to reconcile this world to God was also the work of Martin Luther King, the work that we celebrate tomorrow. May we continue that work. Amen."

Chapter 16
Reflections From St. John's

As noted earlier more than several hundred individuals drawn from the parishioners and friends of St. John's have made the trek to the South Bronx since the inception of this ministry at St. Ann's. Some have made a single trip there, others have made several or more trips and, then, some have made this trip dozens of times. As the reflections and commentary of Gladys Mercado provided a meaningful entre' and context for the **Reflections from St. Ann's,** a St. John's parishioner, Steve Lippincott provides his unique reflections and commentary that **weave his thoughts of New York, the South Bronx, inner-city society, St. Ann's and** this ministry into a very special fabric with historical, social, spiritual and inspirational colors. With this context the reader will inevitably have a greater understanding and appreciation of the many stories of two very different communities with similar hearts and spirit.

Steven Lippincott

"Crossing the Connecticut State line into New York is not remarkable in that the highway becomes much wider. The Merritt Parkway is a beautiful, scenic parkway with magnificent Beaux's Arts and Art Deco bridges. Stately hardwoods in the dividing strip and on rolling hills cast mottled shadows across the winding tarmac road. Unfortunately it was designed with 45 miles per hour in a Packard in mind, but it breaks the monotony of an hour and a half on the better and more efficient interstate. More comforting is no trucks. There is little indication as I turn onto the Hutchinson River Parkway that we are leaving New England and moving closer to a city of eight million people. On

this trip I am riding with Peter, my co-pilot. Our passengers, Edward and Jeffrey, are on their way home. I am bringing them back from the ECC summer camp in Rhode Island to their home in the Mott Haven section of the South Bronx. As the highway meanders closer to the Hutchinson River, the urban outliers become more obvious; their journey is coming to an end. My landmark is an old brownstone railroad bridge, arching its way high across the highway. Beyond the bridge lay the grasslands, a flat landscape, one of many tidal estuaries of the Hudson River and Long Island Sound. It is one of the great wonders of our natural world. Sadly, it is also one of the most unappreciated. While beautiful in its natural beauty, it was overlooked, dismissed as real estate of no practical use, except as a garbage dump. I remember, as a child in the back seat with my sister, travelling through them in the family car, not appreciating their beauty because the stench of decomposition was unimaginable. Whether in New Jersey, the Queens, or here in Pelham Bay, our wishes were to have that leg of our journey over quickly. Now, the stench is gone, or at least diminished some, and, despite the broken concrete and a utilitarian lack of esthetic, their majesty is unmistakable, even with Co-op City breaking the horizon. Edward and Jeffrey see that and shout "The projects, we're home". They are happy. It is about 15 minutes from here to Motthaven, I am not so sanguine. I have made this journey often; I have known these boys since they were quite small. My emotions are mixed; personally, I am sad as this trip underscores the end of summer. I am worried for them over the challenges the ensuing year will present them as well. Mother Martha, into whose capable hands I will deliver Edward and Jeffrey, is a source of hope they will be cared for.

She is the Rector of St. Ann's parish that provides meals, instruction and, most importantly, a safe place for the families who have little in the way of options. She is a small woman. If she weighs 100 pounds, it is because she did not remove the ring of keys hanging from her neck when she got on the scale. Her clerics are threadbare. Yet she is not to be so easily dismissed. She has a law degree from Harvard University and is a member of the New York State Bar along with her theological degrees. When she walks the sidewalks surrounding her parish she walks with a purpose and drive; kings and princes stand aside. Everyone gives her deference and respect. Her church has the good fortune of being a national shrine; the patriot founders left her a legacy the City of New York feels worthy of preserving and its restoration is a product of this sentiment. This is a good thing since there is no money to keep it going. The programs of child literacy, after-school activities, the summer freedom School, soup kitchen, AA, NA, as well as normal church activity are run on a shoe string.

The summer began with my wife, Liz, and I bringing the boys up to Rhode Island. Edward got a job as a CIT {Counselor-in-Training} at ECC's summer camp.; Jeffrey [Edward's cousin] would attend camper for a couple of sessions, but spend the remainder of the summer at our home at his mother's request but also with a strong note of urgency from 'Mother' Martha. Motthaven is no place for a teenager in the summer, a fact that would be tragically demonstrated very soon. We hadn't been on the highway long before Edward said that he had 'things' to tell us. He had gotten into a scuffle with another teen resulting in Edward striking him, in full view of a NYPD officer. He would have to return to The Bronx to attend court to answer to an assault charge which we gladly [suppressing groans] agreed to facilitate.

Edward and Jeffrey are very different people; Jeffrey is brilliant and charismatic, insatiably curious and quite gregarious. He loves reading and loves school and libraries. He is very handsome. Edward, at first glance, seems none of this. The inner city is a world hostile to anyone breaking the social norm, especially when done in ways that are hard to understand. Pursuing intellectual achievement is definitely out of the social norm. It represents change. Not all that unusual in any Culture; consider an Amish child converting to Catholicism, think of any child showing the signs of homosexuality or. in my own case, when my sister's and my love interests looked outside the Nordic-Anglo-Saxon model of our clan, a factory worker who aspires to the arts or any high school child who would rather study for a chemistry exam instead of playing football. Change is threatening, change in a world where stability is already in peril present a challenge not quite understood. What is not understood poses a threat. Threats bring fear. In a densely populated ghetto where resources are greatly diminished and survival is always challenged, fear begets hostility leading easily to brutality. Brutality is the one quality that offers self-esteem as well as a measure of success to the ones who can pull it off. Severe consequences come to those who can't. It is pro-activity in a passive aggressive and acquiescent world. It is a flawed logic but not rare. Edward has the advantage of being quite large so presenting a menacing image comes easily. But he also is the reason why Jeffrey can pursue his heart. Jeffrey is almost as large as his cousin and athletic, which helps, but he remains in Edward's protective shadow. Edward, when here in New England, however, is another story. He possesses all the charm of his cousin. At summer camp he is peers with his summer camp mates. He is helpful and hard working, a great kid. With the weight of inner-city life off his shoulders he is quite handsome as well. He

171

stays in my home when not at camp and is known in my neighborhood as having all these qualities.

*In the Bronx, Criminal Court off The Grand Concourse feels like a bad airport [although cleaner than JFK]. No one is going on vacation here; the miscreants and misunderstood queue their way, serpentine through airport like x-ray scanners. Wallets, belts, bags, etc. are scrutinized; despair and despondency fill the air. It is a sprawling and grand complex, brightly lit by glass exterior walls. Clicks echo off the terrazzo floors as people with high heels scurry down wide hallways talking on their cell phones. Lawyers shuffle through papers, others just shuffle. In the courtroom I was struck by a young man standing beside me. He filled the stereotype of one associated with the gangs; he had tattoos on his neck, he wore a Yankees baseball hat sideways, he looked menacing. Yet, in his arms, was a 24 month old girl in a clean white pinafore dress. She had corn rows with ribbons and a necklace made of Cheerios. The corn rows are labor intensive to do and the necklace added to the unmistakable fact that this child was loved. The love this young man displayed in his protective demeanor led me to speculate on his capacity for deep love. Had Mother Martha reached him at a young age, how would his life been changed? Conversely, if Mother Martha not met Edward, or more to the point, if Edward's father had not taken him to church every Sunday where Mother Martha could reach him, how would **his** life be changed? This became one of three trips for this purpose; the last became combined with Edward bringing me to the wake of a young man, his friend, one of our summer campers from earlier trips. He was gunned down on the street while bringing his girl friend home. Jose' was one of the ones who were going to make it. Poor boy!*

New York City is in a way much like a great work bench. There are magnificent constructs displaying ingenious skills and talent sitting next to piles of unfinished and unlikely ever-to-be-finished projects. False starts and piles of trash the craftsman ignores lie everywhere. Co-op City is one example; it is a co-op; residents own their own home. One of the many projects of social engineering that is the legacy of Robert Moses. Moses' list of accomplishments is great and, for the most part, a product of good intentions. Jones beach, the Henry Hudson Parkway and the FDR Expressway have, indeed, made life better for all who live in and visit NYC. Moses' intention was to make the city car friendly and he made parkways that blended into natural landscape. All this is from a man who never drove a car. But sadly, the law of unintended consequences is at the heart of why life is so difficult for Edward, Jeffrey, Mother Martha and millions of others. The Cross Bronx Expressway, the Sheridan and other highways cut a deep trench between neighborhoods, isolating them and creating ghettos. One problem that has arisen is asthma; the truck traffic spews diesel exhaust, car brakes spew asbestos. The children have no place to escape the pollution.

The construction of the Cross Bronx Expressway hit the Grand Concourse, the cultural center of the South Bronx and home to Yankee Stadium, like a horrible plague. As a child in the 1950s I would visit relatives in that area. Been to a few Yankee games. The Concourse at that time was a city in itself, distinct from the other Boroughs and stood as a great city on its own-rivaling its neighbors. Sparkling windows in brownstones reflected a pride in place. Liveried doormen stood under awnings that went to the curb from grand apartment buildings.

Fixtures were brass and shined like fine gold. My grandmother thought nothing of sending my sister and me outside to play; there were abundant parks and she felt no cause to worry over our safety. It is true that the journey from our home in Newark, New Jersey was quite difficult if we went by car. Traffic was legendary in its problems. The solution seemed an easy one by Moses' logic. His logic, however, dismissed the real problem of cutting a limited access highway through an established community; people's homes stood in the way. The dominoes effect of condemning the buildings and leaving them abandoned invited crime and crushed the property values on the adjacent buildings. This, of course, created an exodus of the people living in them; consequently causing a crash of the municipal economy-which rendered the entire community uninhabitable. The irony of a great Jewish community forced into exodus by a man named Moses with a mind towards pharonic building is a painful one. But the area remained uninhabited. The poor and disenfranchised filled the void. Police, Fire and social services were overwhelmed. New York City, cynically seeing the area now isolated decided to abandon the area entirely and ignore the situation. With the exception of going to Yankee Stadium, one could easily ignore the concourse; you do not have to drive through it now.

One of the failed attempts to remedy the poverty and the resulting slums was in clearing them. Housing projects arose. Housing projects were another grand design that was doomed from the start. If you go down to Manhattan on The FDR Expressway to 23rd Street you will see peter Cooper Village and Peter Stuyvesant Town. It is a housing project that is very similar, architecturally, to those one finds in the South Bronx. One can see the intended design there. A cluster of huge apartment buildings, hundreds of them, gated and landscaped. Grand in their brick plainness. The apartments are large [by New York standards; the larger apartments being in Peter Cooper, with playgrounds, community centers and even its own post office. The hallways are tidy and painted in pastels. The elevators are reliable [by New York standards] and the lobbies sparkle with stone and terrazzo. The projects to which I will deliver Edward and Jeffrey are striking in their comparison; while attempts are made towards landscaping, the greater tide of indifference washes over all attempts; windows to the lobbies are rendered opaque by expanded metal screens and doors are battered by repeated attempts to defeat the locks. The halls are ceramic brick and everything is built with a mind towards mitigating vandalism. There are bullet holes. While at Peter Cooper there is a police presence, it is a reassuring one, as opposed to The Bronx where it reflects hostility, despair and, most of all, fear.

I am a descendant of immigrants; on my mother's side from 1909, my father's ancestors have been here since the 1960s. I suppose I have always had the belief that being American means I can do better. Certainly I can attest to it being my ancestor's belief, and that is their legacy. Although I cannot speak for my paternal immigrant ancestor, that page has been turned long ago, I did know my maternal grandmother. She came here from good circumstance; I have a picture of her on a ship with a bustled skirt, a large hat and, according to her, $5.00 in her pocket that was at a time that a shave and a haircut did cost two bits. But she came here because she thought she could do better. And she did and our family moved on. I don't see Edward and Jeffrey having that world view. In a sad irony, New York is their prison. Without support and guidance from beyond the pale their hope is severely limited. Isabelle Wilkerson wrote **A Warmth of Other Suns**, the story of the great migration of American citizens born in The South of Africa heritage. They are descendants of slaves who left the oppression of segregation in the Jim Crow South.

Segregation in the north is much different in that ghettoes are to some extent self selected; ethnic groups congregated around the immigrants of their homeland, continuing their culture and identifying themselves by their ancestry. They built societies creating cultural and religious institutions serving their individual needs. Children were raised with the expectation of continuing their individual mores and folkways and marrying within the culture. Martin Luther King said famously the most segregated institutions in America are the churches. Neighborhoods defined by Lithuanian, Polish, German, Italian, Scandinavian or Irish churches, Jewish temples to name a few, provided social services and welfare, had their own schools and hospitals and nursing homes. All of them served their specific cultures exclusively. They are proud of their *ghettoes. There are biases and antagonisms between these groups. Resources are limited; clans and tribes compete with others for their individual needs, and hegemony. Subsequent generations, however, have learned to identify with the land of their birth. New York is the melting pot, as is said, and in two or three generations ethnic restraints water down, legacies become more personal. As in my name, and some decorations in my home, especially on holidays, I do reflect a certain legacy [mostly Swedish] but they have no bearing on my relationships. They do give me a sense of history but solidarity I draw from the like-minded people, according to my interests, I prefer to seek an egalitarian meritocracy. Wilkerson told the sad story of a family who moved to Harlem with all the resolve to do better, only to find a malaise had come over their predecessors and, being country folk, they were not prepared for the evils despair can welcome there. The children fell prey to drugs and violence, and tragedy became the result of their idealism. But Harlem is not the Bronx. Despite the challenges the ghetto in Harlem presented, Harlem became a great and rich culture center. Columbia University sits in the core of the neighborhood. Riverside Church, a non-denominational church built by the Rockefellers is a great church built in the tradition of and equal to the great European cathedrals. The parish has many very well educated and affluent congregants who are people of color, people of Harlem. Harlem is a proud community. The Bronx is not so. The Bronx tries; Motthaven has made great efforts, the storied Fulton Fish Market has made a new home there, civic and grass roots groups and churches have created parks and gardens. Volunteer groups from all over the country have added their hands, hearts and money to assist. Abandoned and forlorn buildings became canvases for amazing muralists. Oddly, the Bronx is the only borough that is not on an island, yet with Westchester to the north and the Harlem River to the south, and Riverdale [part of the Bronx] to the west the South Bronx is more an island than any of her sisters.*

This is not an exclusively African-American issue. The ones of direct African-American heritage share the ghetto with Puerto Rican, Haitian, Jamaican, Dominican and all manner of South American immigrants from Africa and the Middle East. What resources are available must be shared. The same competition, antagonisms and heart-felt outreaches that have defined this region historically remain. However irrational it seems there is a grand design to history and we are following its course; the belief one is creating his or her own is being hubristic. Like the generations that preceded, the distinctions between clan and racial identities water down to a uniquely American identity, more to the point a uniquely New York identity. The good people of Motthaven and I share in common superficially, yet, if we visited Tuscaloosa or Phoenix together, we would be quickly identified as New Yorkers.

*138th Street now, the boys are home. And they are happy. For all its challenges and dangers, this is home. This is where the ones they love are. My hope is when they look down the dark stairs to the cavern that is the Brooke Street subway station they see a doorway to another world, or opportunity, as they are now aware there is another world out there. **More to the point those stairs lead to a world where they are welcomed and loved and possibilities`are as unlimited as their imaginations.**"*

Reflections from the Bus

On April 30th and May 1st of 2011, a mission trip was made to St. Ann's; this particular mission trip took on a very special characteristic: there had been a generational change at St. John's which meant an opportunity for a new cadre of volunteers for the ministry at St. Ann's. An early spring trip was planned and the response was, characteristically, very enthusiastic. More than 50 middle and high school students, young and older adults and some mission trip veterans signed up for the trip. At 6:30 AM on Saturday, April 30, these volunteers boarded a motor coach and departed for St. Ann's. Prior to departure, more than 2000 reading, literacy and English books and instructional 'flip-charts' [a donation arranged by Brian Cooper, parishioner] were loaded onto the bus. One of the tasks for the weekend was to build a series of bookshelves to convert a modest conference room into a robust library for the children and adults of the St. Ann's community. Arrangements and delivery to St. Ann's for the needed lumber et al had already been made. Without question, it was to be a remarkable trip as were the previous ones. On the return trip back to Rhode Island, the following [unedited] reflections were scripted and they, individually and collectively, speak for themselves:

"Before the trip, I was unsure of how the weekend would go. However, now I feel that it was a great weekend for both the St. John's community and the St. Ann's community. It was a great experience."

"What I loved?....The children….their simplicity, warmth and joy. What saddened me?....The lack of supplies, materials and $$. Ideas for the future?....A list of tasks for volunteers; a wish list from St. Ann's [ongoing]; bring more supplies, e.g., balls, chalk, bubbles, 'kids to read to kids'. Glad to be a part! Thank you!"

"*The trip was an incredible eye-opener and allowed me to make a connection with children who are just like me, except with a different economic status.*"

"*The one thing that I would like to see in the future is a prayer before every meal.*"

"*It was breath-taking to see all those beautiful brand new reading series books. When I saw the last shelf-which held the sixth grade books, I could only hope that these children would get that far. Then I realized that it should be part of our mission....like teaching a person how to fish.*"

"*This was a fabulous trip. Thank you so much for the opportunity to be involved. I would like to come back and see the kids again-I am sure it takes more than one visit to build relationships, trust, etc. I have two suggestions: OK-first suggestion is that we spend some time fixing up the inside of St. Ann's from painting and <u>cleaning</u> to continuing to work on the library, to fixing up bathrooms. Second-a little more organization around the explanation of the trip to the St. Ann's kids-we had some tears and very disappointed children who were not allowed to go. Nothing else....looking forward to the next trip.*"

"*The trip to St. Ann's was a great experience. In Barrington, RI we are used to more high class things and complain about everything; here the kids have nothing but still find little things to worship. The only thing I did not like was that every kid did not have a chance to go on the trip to Battery Park in lower Manhattan.*"

[Author's note: the motor coach only had 57 seats and those kids who did not go had a great time at St. Ann's with alternative activities. It was also an opportunity for one Barrington teen who chose to stay behind at St. Ann's with a child from St. Ann's with whom he had bonded. The teen's words to this child "Hey, if you cannot go then I'm not going either!" Very special! Very amazing!]

"*I had a great time coming to New York, bonding with kids and now we can help the kids and their community. Next time the trip should be longer.*"

"*I enjoyed that there was plenty of time to interact with the kids as they were the first priority.*"

"*Instead of hanging out at St. Ann's for awhile then going for a [field] trip, we should go to a park, or anywhere, for the whole day.*"

"*I wish the [church] service at St. John's was more like theirs. Great time.*

Loved the kids. The service was beautiful. Maybe a little more direction as to exactly what projects we'll be doing on the bus ride there."

"Hanging out with the kids at St. Ann's was great-I wished we had more to offer those who couldn't go on the [field] trip. Jack was great when his little guy couldn't go on the trip, he said he would stay with him."

"Trip was great, very rewarding, no negatives. Been on both day and overnite trips to St. Ann's and find that overnites get more done. Would love to go again."

"Good: getting to know the people and the kids and being able to visualize and see what they need, want, etc. Forming relationships: both with the St. Ann's people and with the St. John's people I didn't know. Could be both: more organized-I know this is hard to do. I'd love to have a project/goal and be able to work on it-I know it's needed-and not just something we're giving them."

"I learned so much from these kids and really connected with St. Ann's-look for me next year. I felt privileged and honored to help and make a difference-small or large."

"The 10:00 AM service was great! I loved meeting the kids and adults of St. Ann's."

"Great trip! Reflections and thoughts: humbling; inspiring/inspired about our young men and women; food for my soul; go with the flow experience; proud; grateful; indigent about inequality."

"Continue creating opportunities to bring groups to St. Ann's-be sure to give this group a follow-up opportunity. Keep the momentum going. Come up with a sustainable plan to create a simple program that people can look forward to and plan on. Follow-up questions: reuniting drives, hosts for this summer. There's an idea brewing to raise funds to provide a couple of tape players for the 'books on tape' that were in with the books we brought down."

"Praise & thanks. As enjoyable and rewarding as Saturday was spent with the children of St. Ann's, I was taken aback by the praise and thanks we received from Mother Martha's appreciation for the St. John's ministry was moving as she noted that the ministry has impacted and improved the life of St. Ann's parishioners."

"God's work-as an observer, it was amazing to watch how easily the Barrington young adults were able to bond and connect with the children of St. Ann's who soaked up the attention and compassion they received. It became evident that sometimes you simply need to show up and let God's work be done. It is truly amazing what can happen if you simply care and are willing to take the first step to make a difference."

"*The trip was very fun and exciting. I wish the trip lasted another day because not did it just change my view on life, but others of the Church of St. Ann's and the children.*"

"*I loved it and I don't have anything bad to say about it!*"

"*I had a magnificent time-spending time was getting to know the kids and I can't wait to go next year. The trip couldn't be improved.*"

"*It was really fun boarding the bus with all the kids on the trip and we made some great connections.*"

"*No downsides to this trip, great time all around. Wouldn't change a thing. Keep up the great work.*"

"*I had lots of fun bonding with the kids. I enjoyed going to Battery Park with them. They really wanted to go to the movies though I think the littler kids should be allowed to go next time.*"

"*It was a well organized and enjoyable trip. I would have added a little more variety to the food such as fruit and vegetables.*"

"*Many kids wanted to see a movie than go on the boat. Instead of the chaperones deciding what to do, why not let the kids vote. The trip we did, some kids were not included [**Author's note: limited to 57 seats; bus was full**]. We should do something everyone can do.*"

"*What a great experience to be a participant in that Sunday morning Eucharist; as I looked at a church that was full of individuals and families from both the St. Ann's and St. John's communities that had merged into a single congregation, a single family, a single community lifting the other to a very special place as the strains of* **'Amazing Grace'** *and* **'We shall break bread together....'** *filled the air.*

Absolutely moving and uplifting!"

Earlier it was pointed out that a question often posed to those who make the trip to St. Ann's from Rhode Island is "Why the South Bronx?" There were two answers provided; the first is brief and very much to the point: "Why not?" The second answer is really imbedded in the writings of this book: the aggregate reflections provided herein certainly provide a significant part of the second answer.

Photos

Group 2
Journey to St. Ann's; April 30, May 1, 2011

182

Some additional reflections about this particular journey:

"I still think a lot about that weekend and would like to be involved again in some way. One memory I will always have is of you getting your nails painted by the young girls and what utter joy they expressed. Although that moment was brief they will have that precious memory inside them forever." [**Martha Donovan** email to Al Colella]

"Thank you all very much for a beautiful time. I think that things went incredibly smoothly and that we figured out how to make them go even more smoothly. It has been suggested on this end that perhaps St. John's could help some of the Moms with their literacy. I would suggest that the teachers in your group could help them know how to do that. The Presiding Bishop has a very good project in which she and members of her staff [and people from some other Diocesan staffs, such as NY] are reading a book at the same time as a public school child, and the two are exchanging letters about the book. That has the advantage of helping writing as well as reading, and it can work long distance. Thank you again more than words can express." [**Mother Martha** email to Al Colella]

More reflections from St. John's:

"Thanks for the opportunity to get out of the bubble. I felt that I was part of a very important thing today. Al, your advice at the beginning of the day, that all might not go according to plan, was quite right. However, being concerned about being spot-on-time with no distractions is fortunately [for me] not my gift! I looked at it as I got a few minutes to read the paper with a cup of coffee and a piece of blueberry bread I lifted from Field Hall [at St. John's]!

Once in the South Bronx, having coffee with Mother Martha, Carol [Cushman] and Anthony [Bonilla] [and eating a meat pie] was a combination of a senate hearing, an executive board room, an analyst's office, and friends seeing each other again; all for others and for the gift of grace for ourselves as well!

When I arrived home, my guys had dinner in the oven and we were able to discuss the entire day. It turns out my son, Conant, has been to St. Ann's and it was the kind of dinner conversation we love. I know Ricky and Carlo's moms are happy to have them home and I'm happy to have been a small part of the community that made this happen." [**Donna Neville** who was a co-driver returning two boys to the South Bronx after their summer ECC camperships; the meeting mentioned took place at Raymond's at the corner of E. 138ᵗʰ Street and St. Ann's Avenue; Raymond's is a coffee shop/

restaurant/pizzeria that is a popular community gathering place but also the ministry's 'conference room' in the South Bronx.

"What you did for Edward, Jr. on Friday was truly heroic and tangible proof positive of how much he means. To put it in other words, it was a clear example of the incarnation of Jesus Christ in two of his disciples." **Mother Martha** to Steve Lippincott and the author who traveled to the South Bronx to support Edward in his court appearance.]

"In the spring of my sophomore year my mother forced me to go on a mission trip with my church to the Bronx, NY to make me realize how lucky I am to grow up in a town like Barrington, RI. Barrington is a wealthy town that is protected from the world around it.

When I arrived at the Bronx the atmosphere was much different from what I had adapted to living in Barrington. The streets were dirty and litter covered the sidewalks. The people dressed completely differently from the people in Barrington. They wore baggy and ragged clothing.

I stayed at a church in the middle of the Bronx that served as a daycare for kids whose parents were not home when they got home from school. The kids came to the church and had to do their homework first before they could play. I helped them with their homework and then played with them when they were done. We played tag, basketball and we played on the playground. These kids know how to have fun and play around without any video games or television.

Later on I realized that not only was I having fun with the kids but I was making a difference in their lives. I also began to realize how lucky I am to have two parents that love me and my brothers and are always there for us. I was also grateful for my possessions and I realized that I did not need all the things that I had to have fun. I had begun to realize everything that my mother wanted me to realize through this trip, and it was truly the biggest eye-opening experience of my life. When I got home I did not let my mother know that I had made all these realizations but she could tell by the way I acted. I began to look at life differently; I did not want as many things as I had in the past because I was so grateful and happy with what I had-I did not need anything more. Through this experience I realized that I have more as a teenager than some adults will ever have, but what you have does not matter in life, it is what you give to those that don't have as much that really matters." [An essay entitled ***Bronx Trip*** written by **Doug Newton** in support of his college applications.]

"I first met Reverend Overall [Mother Martha as she is more commonly

referred to] shortly after September 11, 2001 when I was part of a volunteers group from St. John's Episcopal Church sent to help out at St. Paul's Chapel near ground Zero.

We were met at the massive gates of St. Ann's by a small energetic woman who was so openly gracious and welcoming that I knew instantly she was Mother Martha. She is the Rector there and because of St. John's ongoing ministry with St. Ann's, we were invited to stay there at night during our time at Ground Zero in New York.

I had heard a lot about Mother Martha and her devotion and love for the children and families in her area and I had also read about these same disadvantaged children. I learned about her 'Freedom School', her after school program and the meals provided to them before they left for home. [For many, this was the only real meal that they had for the day.] I was so impressed by her work that I knew this would not be the only time I would be visiting St. Ann's and I also knew I wanted to do whatever I could do to help her with this wonderful ministry.

Over the next few years, I made several trips with other members of our Outreach team from St. John's church. On several occasions, my son, Tristan, and my husband, Bob, came along too. We spent a lot of time getting to know the children some other family members, and worshipping with them on a Sunday morning.

We also did a lot of work around the church, both inside and outside and many contributions were made to help Mother Martha with some things [like computers] that she might not otherwise be able to have available for these children. These children [and Mother Martha] have truly found a permanent place in my heart.

Summer camperships have been provided from our church to enable as many children as we can support to attend the rural camp at the Episcopal Conference Center [ECC]. On these trips that I have been a part of it has been wonderful getting to know these children even better. A simple stop at McDonald's along the way means so much to them. When they visit our homes it is really something to see. You realize instantly just how limited their own housing must be. The smallest things impress them. The summer camping experience has truly made a difference in the lives of many, both the children who attend and the people who had a hand in making camp possible.

I feel God's presence in this ministry and it is one that needs to and WILL continue. It may be by providing notebooks or other school supplies, clothing, games, textbooks or other basic needs. But, more importantly, it is the actual face-to-face contact with these children. Lifetime relationships have been formed and we have watched many of them grow up right before our eyes. Taking time to spend with them by playing basketball, reading, tutoring or simply talking about everyday things is so important to these children, and also extremely rewarding to the volunteer who is there with that child.

*My own personal experience with St. Ann's has been both humbling and heartwarming and truly an eye-opener. We tend to take so much for granted in our own lives. When we come face-to-face with those who are so deprived of the simple basics of everyday life we realize just how lucky we are. I also feel blessed to have been a part of this relationship over the years and honored to have gotten to know Mother Martha and the amazing woman she is. She has become the 'Mother Theresa' of the South Bronx and a guardian angel to all who are a part of her life. Truly '**Amazing Grace**', wouldn't you say?"* [**Judy Tavares**]

"I haven't gotten the experience you described out of my head-Edward couldn't have a better advocate than you or Steve-and I bet that he knows that, too! Teenage years are challenging for kids in much more stable environments than what these kids are dealing with-to have someone in his life who believes in him and is straightforward in dealing with his situation, and offers him alternatives to what he'd come up with on his own is such a blessing. You are saving his life-and giving him hope." [Email from **Sandy Connor** to Steve and Al.]

The reflection to follow is that of **Ainsley Judge**, a 2007 graduate of Barrington High School and a 2011 graduate of McCallister College. Her story is quite special because it captures the full essence of the ministry at St. Ann's. She had made the journey to St. Ann's as a sophomore and junior at Barrington High School. Her participation there was really enabled by Becky Gettel, the then Youth Director at St. John's. These are some of her thoughts:

"Life changing experience.", "Loved it!", "The walk around the St. Ann's neighborhood in the South Bronx was an 'eye-opener."

"In Barrington, I lived in a 'bubble', a very privileged environment, life was easy for me........when comparing this life to that of the South Bronx, it just didn't seem 'right'."

"The difference in schools and school efforts was huge.

"There is a significant distinction between 'reading' about St. Ann's and 'experiencing' it."

"**Informed volunteerism** is an individual's balance between 'reading' about an activity and 'doing it.'"

"This ministry is about seeing the humanity of the children at St. Ann's and having a role in the validation of these children as important human beings. It is about inter-cultural relationships."

"I remember a team of volunteers from St. John's and some from the South Bronx community painting a large wrought iron fence at St. Ann's; the 'real' activity was an entity beyond the painting, it was about 'togetherness'."

"I also remember a large pile of boxes and crates containing some well-worn fresh vegetables that would be thrown away in Barrington but, here in the South Bronx, they were considered 'gifts' for those hungry individuals and families and those who are homeless."

Ainsley also provides some interesting reflections about **The Politics of Urban Education**, a course she took at McCallister College; the context for her comments is her mind-set developed via her St. Ann's experience.

"It's one of the few different classes offered here that focus on urban education and inequalities in education. Most of what we focused on was the large political structure that created inequalities across school districts. We focused on national policy, state control, local level politics and school boards. I think if there's something useful for you out of this, it's that there is a strong and growing curriculum around school inequality issues, but it still needs more attention. What I took away from the class was a lot of frustration and confusion about how the political system works and doesn't work to support schools. Measuring success seems to be the culprit of many problems by the basic realization that there is no universal or accurate way to measure an individual's or a school's academic achievement, i.e., **No Child Left Behind** is a terrible policy."

"Maybe it's because I'm a geography major or maybe it's because my interest taking that course was inspired by working in the South Bronx, knowing the Brule family and having a greater understanding of the relevance of both academic and personal readings but it seems obvious that the injustice of the school system is geographical and, without the connection of neighborhood development with school development, the larger problems won't even be addressed….this is fairly obvious bit it seems policy doesn't always reflect that connection."

These are some added notes from the author: first, Ainsley is certainly a remarkable young individual whose maturity, ideals and social awareness are far beyond her years; she-and others like her, e.g., Ali Bulman-lend a greater faith in the younger generation and their roles as future leaders in their chosen endeavors. Secondly, it is important to note that Ainsley-and others like her-'just don't happen by accident'; she is a daughter of Joanne and Joseph Judge of Barrington and sister of her younger brothers, Joseph and Patrick, all of whom have been active and committed participants in the ministry at St. Ann's since 2005.

In her senior year at Barrington High School, Ainsley and Ali Bulman, now both veterans of the journey to St. Ann's, joined forces, so to speak, to do their required senior project in New Orleans as volunteers in the aftermath of Hurricane Katrina. Their experience at St. Ann's had inspired them to 'do a mission trip' to New Orleans. The planning and arrangements for this trip were, at best, challenging and even overwhelming to these two high school seniors; however, with their ideals and energy for fund-raising coupled with the advocacy and support of the Outreach team at St. John's, the trip reached fruition when thirty-two people were able to fly to New Orleans for a week.

Ali Bulman, also a 2007 graduate of Barrington High School and a 2011 engineering graduate of Tufts University, offers her thoughts about the St. Ann's experience:

"High school for me was mainly about 'book learning' and, for a while, I thought that my entire education consisted of factoring numbers and conjugating Spanish verbs. However, my experiences at St. Ann's Church in the South Bronx taught me that book learning was only one aspect of my education. The service trip allowed me to appreciate the steps necessary to effectuate change in a community."

Barrington is primarily made up of fairly affluent Caucasians-although, nominally, St. John's purpose in going to the South Bronx, was to provide volunteers for a valuable community service, I discovered that the unintended purpose was to show the 'book learned' people, like myself, what it means to form a community and just what positive change looks like.

I love St. Ann's because it is so unique. It is an old and truly beautiful church in New York-the wrought iron fence is gorgeous, especially to me because on one of my trips there Ainsley and I scraped and repainted the whole thing with a group of about 15 children. That was an amazing experience and, again, taught me important lessons about effectuating positive change in a community.

Mother Martha is so energetic and her ability to provide a fun educational and physical haven for children who might otherwise 'find mischief' is truly awe-inspiring. Bringing people together and taking little steps, like weeding a garden or painting a fence, can accomplish an even bigger goal.

My experience at St. Ann's absolutely drove me to the New Orleans project! It gave me a purpose and I wanted to help out other communities in the same way. The first time we went to New Orleans, Ainsley and I worked for a grassroots organization cooking meals for people in the lower Ninth Ward. The smallest tasks we were given, whether cooking sausage on a wok over a hand-made fire or washing out a tub of dried up refried beans, actually made a difference to the people there. The second time we went to New Orleans was the senior project we organized with about thirty people. We worked with Habitat for humanity in this case and worked on building two houses in the 'musicians village'. I don't think we would have had such a drive to fundraise and go on these trips if it weren't for our experiences at St. Ann's. So thank you for that."

Sandy Connor, one of the St. John's 'veterans' of the ministry at St. Ann's has provided her energy, commitment and consistency to the many efforts of the Outreach program at St. Ann's. She is especially involved in the facilitation of the summer campership program at ECC and remains a quiet and unassuming participant in the spectrum of ministry activities at St. Ann's. Her thoughts:

"Had a great trip bringing the boys to camp today; I have to admit, I'm exhausted-but, it's a good tired. Pat Judge and Eli Seltzer, both of whom made the' Journey to St. Ann's' in the Spring of 2011, were a big help and made the trip fun for the two young boys, Ricky and Carlos, and they were great co-pilots for me, too."

"The five boys came with no money, so I put $50.00 in the camp store so they could each have a $10.00 allowance for the week, to buy ice cream and snacks. These are five very polite, appreciative young men. Only one is a first-time camper. Jessie Pialesta has been here less than a year from the Dominican Republic. His ability to speak English is limited but he understands what others are saying with very little difficulty. Four of the five boys made the honor roll this year and camp is a good incentive for them to work hard at school. Two of the boys, Daniel and Shadrack Praza, have spent the past year living in a shelter with their Mom and 2 other brothers. They are about to move into a better situation. Jeffrey Goodwin and his cousin, Edward White, Jr., were the other two campers this week. They're all growing up with challenges-WAY more difficult than anything I've ever had to deal with. On the way up, they were talking about where they hope to go to college and the friends they hoped to see

at ECC again. I think because the boys know us pretty well now, they were very talkative and animated-at one point Edward started singing "If I had a hammer......" and the closer we got to camp, the more excited they got."

Sandy's expenses for that trip were: Mini-van rental: $100.51; gas: $45.71; McDonald's: $54.43; *: "Smiles on their faces: priceless."*

Becky Gettel, one of the outstanding Directors of the Youth ministry at St. John's [another being her equally outstanding predecessor, Eric McKnight] during the growth and development of the relationship between the two churches, recently spoke with me about the 'richness' therein.

Becky provides her reflection: "One of the most important aspects of the relationship between St. Ann's and St. John's that I was privileged to witness were the moments when there was a glimpse, or a moment, or an event of transformation for one of the youth group kids from St. John's. The transformation that I was watching for was the shift from I am doing service work *for* someone" to "I am building the kingdom of God *with* someone." It happened when our young adults were painting the big iron gates that surround St. Ann's and a man from the neighborhood, after observing them for a while, bought some thick paint gloves from the hardware store across the street and came over to show them how the gloves worked better than a brush for that particular job. It happened when the nine and ten year olds from St. Ann's helped our teenagers navigate the subway system, and it was to their credit and not ours that no one was lost or left behind. It happened when a lay minister at St. Ann's served each of us at the communion rail and called each of us 'sister' or 'brother' as he offered us the cup: "Sister, this is the blood of Christ, the cup of salvation." "

"Just wanted to drop an email to say 'hi' and I miss you. My freshman year is almost over and it feels amazing to know I came to college and tried my best. I just wanted to say 'thank you' because you helped me to where I am today." [**Liola Brule** in Spring, 2011; she earned an A in each of her courses during her first semester at Mitchell College in New London, Connecticut]

"Upon arriving at St. Ann's Church on a January morning, seventeen of us from St. John's descended the stairs to the cafeteria with armloads of goods and food. I remained upstairs talking with Mother Martha when a young man approached us. A strikingly handsome young man. He wore a Carhards Jump Suit like the ones many outside workers use. He carried a large duffel bag, he was far from home, if he, indeed, had one. After speaking briefly with Mother Martha, he went upstairs with us. The kids from St. John's and St. Ann's

had since gone upstairs to the gym for some lively and loud basketball while a small group remained behind making sandwiches for us all. He was well spoken, he made no sense whatsoever but he said it well. I tried to get him to eat some clementines we brought, drink some juice. When a plate of sandwiches was made, I gave those to him. He went on his way with the sandwiches and a cacophony of hungry teenagers filled the stairwell sounding somewhat like boulders in a cement mixer. I thought for a moment that I was a bit rude. We brought this food for our kids and I just grabbed some and gave it away without asking. Well, the food got devoured and, as we cleaned up, I couldn't help noticing, at the end of the table, what remained was a plate with the same amount of food I had given away." [**Steven Lippincott**]

"Al Colella and I were going to St. Ann's but took a wrong turn on the Hutchinson Parkway. He pulled into a parking lot and asked a security guard for directions. The guard was less than helpful. I wanted to get out of the car and tell the stupid ninny to get on his Motorola and be helpful or words to that effect. Al just smiled and thanked him for his lack of help. Either approach would have had the same result or lack of one. Al went on with his task of finding where we were supposed to go neither fazed nor frustrated. The security guard, I'll bet, experienced a rare moment of kindness and respect. I should have thought of kindness." [also Steve]

Jeff Taber is one of the more senior and equally respected parishioners of St. John's who has been a consistent advocate, supporter and participant of the ministry at St. Ann's. I first became aware of Jeff following one of the initial ministry announcements [at a Sunday Eucharist] about the forthcoming inaugural summer camperships; during this particular service, a gentleman unknown to me walked by my pew and simply and quietly handed me a check for the summer camperships at St. Ann's. Of course, I later learned that this gentleman was Jeff Taber. That initial donation was followed by an annual donation; it was also a prelude to a host of parishioners 'stepping up to the plate' to offer their time, treasure and talents over the years of this ministry. These are his thoughts:

"I remember Al making a ministry announcement at a Sunday service and then at a gathering in Field Hall after the service; my initial reaction was that 'something great is happening!'"

"I also remember meeting Al [we had never really met each other] at that service and we, without hesitation but with silent recognition, gave each other a 'high five' and smiled."

"What happened in this ministry was worth everyone's efforts; St.

Ann's coming to RI and RI going to St. Ann's gave to the people at St. Ann's a 'better grip' on life."

"St. John's was really very helpful; I would use the word 'extraordinary'."

"Al's leadership always 'hit the nail on the head' and both St. Ann's and St. John's are better for that leadership!"

"Finally, I have never forgotten my journey to St. Ann's."

Massa Family

Lou ['Dad']

"Originally, my objective was to be able to give back for the blessing of a wonderful family that I'm so fortunate to have. The first time that we went to St. Ann's, well, there is no preparing for what I was about to see. Just driving into what looks to be a very unsafe area and turning into the gates of St. Ann's was more than humbling. I took one look at the children and realized that at the same time my children walk home from their school in Barrington, these children are coming from their schools to what they feel is 'home'- this place called St. Ann's where their extended family lives. My memories are deep. I remember Mother Martha. I remember the faces of the children and the tattered and torn boxes of games that they would play. I remember the outdated computers that were donated to them, knowing how excited they were to have those.

But, most importantly, I remembered the day that I spent turning the soil of St. Ann's. I remember how hard the ground was, knowing that it had not been turned over in a hundred years. I was not going to let anything stop me from making this ground usable for the children the next day when they were to plant seeds for their first garden. I could only think that somehow God asked me to turn over his sacred ground, so the next day life could start anew. Knowing that I did it with my hands and a hoe. Just thinking about the plants that grew and how proud those children were of what they had accomplished."

Anne ['Mom']

"I have to say that my first visit to St. Ann's would affect me at a future, unexpected visit to NYC. That visit came shortly after 9/11 when I volunteered my time and efforts at St. Paul's Chapel adjacent to Ground Zero in lower Manhattan. Ironically, I continuously reflected on St. Ann's in some of those darker days at Ground Zero and it was the time at St. Ann's that gave me the push to volunteer at the site of the World Trade Towers."

Stephen

"St. Ann's made me understand perspective and diversity. Growing up in Barrington, my perspective was very limited and that limitation was directly impacted by a lack of diversity. What opened my eyes is the realization that the children of St. Ann's could have said the exact same thing themselves. It is only the result of going to St. Ann's that I truly understood how someone's perspective evolves."

"Visiting St. Ann's was a life changing experience. It was amazing to see the amount of good the ministry was doing not only for the children but for the volunteers as well."

"I went on to write my senior project at Barrington High School on the after-school program at St. Ann's. I was truly touched by this experience. Also, I believe that the experience gave me direction and pushed me to go to college in the City of Philadelphia where I now live."

Elizabeth

"I so remember the times that we went to St. Ann's. You cannot walk away without feeling fortunate for the love you have at home. The knowledge that you are able to be safe in your parents' arms every night. The St. Ann's kids were amazingly positive. We played games with them and they were so appreciative that someone would take the time to do that. They were all so upbeat. It's almost like they were safe in the arms of St. Ann's Church."

"I remember one of the times when we brought some candy with us to give to them. It is very impacting to watch another child eat candy, knowing that they either never had any before or that they didn't know when they ever would again. It wasn't just candy that would set the example. We brought every child a backpack, too. Another simple thing that we all have here [in Barrington] and yet, it was something that many never had if not for the generosity of St. John's donors. I was happy that I could see a true appreciation for the things we gave them."

Emily

"I remember playing games and helping my Dad clear the garden. The time seemed to go by so quickly when we were there. It felt so good to think that we made a difference in some of their lives while knowing that our lives were the richer for it."

"When I look back, I think the feeling of joy that I had continues to push me to a profession of teaching. I want to give back. I want to know that I can touch someone and change their life. St. Ann's will always be an inspiration for that passion."

Medeiros Family

The Medeiros family is the second of three families that provided their respective reflections about their experiences at St. Ann's. Their reflections are very much in concert with the totality of reflections from both the St. Ann's and St. John's communities. Specifically, their experiences enhanced their understanding and attitudes of *humanity* and provided a sound foundation for integrating that understanding and attitude into their daily lives-especially the children whose embracing of ministry principles and spirit became a 'fuel' and genesis for follow-on ministries.

Tricia ['Mom'], David ['Dad'] and daughters Samantha, Emily and Christina are examples of those who came to St. Ann's to serve and to make a difference. Their experience at St. Ann's was a natural extension-a very special extension-and a reinforcement of their innate commitment to outreach and community service. It was Tricia and David who 'stepped up to the plate' to provide an SUV for the Brules for the price of $1.00 when the Brules were without transportation in their early years in Rhode Island. The entire family had also been long involved in a variety of outreach and community service efforts, e.g., making sandwiches for the homeless of the greater Providence area, conducting birthday parties for all the children at a family shelter, using their spending money to purchase the very valued *composition notebooks and school supplies for the children at St. Ann's, etc.* In fact, it was Emily who had a summer assignment at her middle school to research a community service project as a candidate for action in the forthcoming school year. Emily submitted a proposal for additional birthday parties at the family shelter. Her proposal was accepted by her entire class; her class was divided into three teams and, during the academic year, there were three more birthday parties with pizza, cold drinks, cookies, ice cream, a sheet birthday cake and, of course, gifts for each of the thirty or so children based on their age and gender.

Samantha [16 years old]

"By having the experience at St. Ann's, my eyes were opened to a new world with very different economic and social challenges. However, we were able to overcome these differences and relate to each other as young adults. All it took were some kids and a soccer ball."

Emily [14 years old]

"On the way to St. Ann's, my family traveled through the rough end of the Bronx, called the South Bronx. I saw litter everywhere, windows shattered, buildings boarded up, metal pasted on every window and people walking around on the streets and giving me looks which made me feel uncomfortable and scared. Later, I remember when it was 7:00 PM, we were not allowed to venture out on the streets because it was risky to do so. This came as a dramatic surprise because I never had to worry about my safety in Barrington. However, part of my learning process was to understand the realities of life in both communities. This truly opened my eyes [and my mind] about life in the South Bronx. It made me grateful for what I had. I then tried to put myself 'in the shoes' of those living near St. Ann's. I would be so frightened about my safety in my home and on the streets. I don't think that I could ever be peaceful but the people in the St. Ann's neighborhood are so brave. When I had conversations with them, I realized that they were just like us; I thought they were really wonderful people.

I then realized that people living in a difficult environment have a goodness about them and simply make the best out of what they have. You have to be grateful for what you have. I couldn't believe how much I complained over the littlest things that the people in the South Bronx would be overjoyed to have. Here's a tip: whenever you get mad because you didn't get what you wanted just think about how the kids at St. Ann's would react. It will change your mind! St. Ann's changed me as a person and encouraged me to do more community service to help those in need. I am so glad for the time and experience at St. Ann's. So, "Thank you, St. Ann's, you made me a better person and the giving person that I am today. I love you all!

Christina [10 years old]

"My experience at St. Ann's also made me open *my* eyes! I used to complain to my Mom that I need more shirts, skirts, pants and/or shoes. Once I arrived at St. Ann's I saw how little the children there have. I now look back and wonder to myself...'Why did I ever complain?' "

Judge Family

My first encounter with the Judge family was nearly a decade ago when I met Joanne ['Mom'] and Ainsley [whom the readers met in *Reflections* and is now a college graduate] after a Sunday service at St. John's. Ainsley was then 'about' thirteen years of age and a member of the Youth Group at St. John's. Our conversation was generally about outreach and community service; the feelings and passion of our mutual commitment to a ministry addressed to serving those in need quickly surfaced. How can I best describe that scene? Respectfully submitted, it was like discovering soul mates of ministry! I had not yet met Joe ['Dad'] nor Joseph, Jr. or Patrick [Ainsley's younger brothers]-all of whom eventually became very active in the ministry at St. Ann's. The Judges, indeed, were a family of soul mates. I also recall mentioning to Joanne ['Mom'] at that same meeting that young adults like Ainsley just don't happen by accident; I can safely say that about the entire Judge family as well as the Massa and Medeiros families and so many of the individuals and families that have chosen to serve at St. Ann's over the last decade.

I sat down with Joanne and Joe on January 21, 2012 and they shared their reflections with me at the Coffee Depot in Warren, Rhode Island which, over the years, had become the unofficial off-site conference room for the Outreach team of St. John's. Their reflections follow:

"We wanted to plant a seed in our children, Ainsley, Joe, Jr. and Patrick about not only shaping their lives but, as a humanitarian responsibility, helping to shape the lives of other children as we have strived to shape theirs."

"The plight of the children at St. Ann's was disturbing and mind-bothering and such an injustice, it motivated each of us, all of us into *ministry action*. The journey to St. Ann's over the years has been a long but exceptionally fruitful one for all those involved in both communities."

"We thought about the ministry at St. Ann's and said '*If not me, if not us, who will?*'; our initial involvement has led the family to return to St. Ann's again and again. This ten year journey to St. Ann's continues today."

"One of the more rewarding aspects of this ministry is that '*One person can make a difference.*'

"One of the reasons for the unbounded success of this ministry is that it was truly a 'people-to-people' process. Whenever the St. John's contingent arrived, the children from St. Ann's were quick to ask about those who were unable to make that particular trip and the inquiries would follow: 'Where are the Judges?', 'Where is Steve and Liz?', 'Where's Al?' and so on!"

"The continuity of mission trips directly enabled the feelings of familial bonds, trust and credibility. Priceless commodities in the humanity market!"

"There were no expectations of just what the experience would bring to the two communities; the experience is still quite difficult to articulate. However, the experience was an *enrichment* for all involved; it was a *spiritual uplifting* as well; it was, in fact, a *transformation*."

"The ministry also provided a sense of brotherly love with the white kids going to New York and the black kids going to Rhode Island."

"Patrick has made a number of trips to St. Ann's but his commitment and leadership skills were very much in evidence during the annual [2011] Shrove Tuesday pancake dinner. Patrick was there with five of his friends and the topic of the upcoming 'Journey to St. Ann's' was mentioned. Initially, the response was sort of measured and really lukewarm but, after a few minutes of persuasion by Patrick, his band of brothers had signed onto this mission trip."

"Ainsley clearly remembers that coffee cup given to her by Jan Malcolm with a quote from Gandhi: *Be the change in the world you want it to be!*"

"Ainsley leveraged her experience at St. Ann's into 'paying it forward' as she [and Ali Bulman] subsequently led a team of thirty-two on a relief mission trip to New Orleans following Hurricane Katrina. She also embraced the principle inferred by the title of this book by facilitating a bike-riding program for some inner-city middle school kids in Minneapolis. Her parents explained that this program was modeled after her St. Ann's experience and really 'more than bike-riding'; it was about the empowerment of children."

"One of the richer aspects of the ministry was the 'home stays' by the children of St. Ann's within the summer camperships program at ECC. A number of families had opened their hearts and homes to some of the girls and boys from the South Bronx. However, the Judge family and Liz Hallenbeck and Steve Lippincott deserve a note of acknowledgement for their 'home stays' year after year after year. Their commitment enabled the participation by other families of the Barrington community. The bonding that took place within the first five or ten minutes of their initial 'homestay' mirrored the bonding that took place during the mission trips to St. Ann's. The bonding was instantaneous, sincere, moving and enduring over the years. The experience as members of their extended families in Barrington gave the children a unique view of family living, family values and some lasting insight into life beyond that which they knew in the South Bronx. There were the usual pool-centered activities, bike rides, basketball games, etc. and even neighborhood walks when the children from St. Ann's would ask about the narrowness of the Barrington sidewalks. The children would also walk on the street side of these sidewalks because they felt safer there. They would also leave the house lights on in their quest for safety and security; they exhibited [temporarily] a fear of noises and wooded areas. They were in a very different place but this place also gave them a very different view of life."

"Probably the more meaningful barometer of the intrinsic value of these 'home stays' was the individual validation and shaping of the minds and lives of the children from St. Ann's and St. John's. It was an opportunity to ponder the contrasting difference of life in the two communities, to dream of 'what could be' and, to wonder "Why am I here and why are you there?" A more tangible measurement was that the time of departure bringing the 'home stays' to a close always came much too soon."

CHAPTER 17
Potpourri

Why 'Start with the children'?

Always an interesting question and one that certainly has application well beyond this book. The residents of the inner cities of America have obviously been the focus of this book but the 'children' have emphatically been the focal point. The inner cities of America present a living environment that is not healthy for the minds, bodies, emotions, wholeness and, most importantly, the humanity of most residents there. These inner cities are also learning environments that offer a curriculum far different from most of those environments beyond the inner cities. A representative inner city curriculum *of vulnerability* includes strategies, schemes and means of survival from one day to the next; other items in this curriculum could include safety issues, exposure to and/or participation in the drugs marketplace, health risks, abuse and neglect, continuing unemployment, educational shortfalls and rampant poverty which directly enables another host of issues, concerns and life-long risks for the inner city residents.

There have been references within this book that those many well-intentioned efforts of the last six decades have not really provided significant and lasting relief from the spectrum of innate disadvantages of inner city residency. This continuing issue of the impact of inner city life upon all of its residents may even be perceived by many who have the authority and resources-but insufficient political will-as a very imposing challenge beyond their available authority and resources. Additionally, a situation that has developed over several centuries and persisted for decades cannot be neither addressed nor alleviated in a time frame significantly less than that time it took to develop, foster and become an organic entity and a self-sustaining culture.

There are, inevitably, many meetings, commissions, study groups et al with much verbiage about the sadness, unwanted social impact and misfortune of any one of a number of intimidating inner city situations. However, there have also been some irrefutable voices of warning over the years. This certainly was the case for the landmark efforts and writings of Daniel Patrick Moynihan and others since the 1960s. Their efforts had the outcome of raising the awareness of the plight of inner city residency. However, issues, problems, concerns et al that are imposing, threatening and intimidating may also serve to deter and defer motivations, efforts and attempts to address the situation in its entirety or even a single issue, problem or concern despite the awareness and knowledge of an issue. However, history has demonstrated that a starting point is to identify a specific arena of need and 'make the choice' to 'make a difference' within that arena regardless of its size. This could apply to a specific segment of the population, a geographical region or area, ..., a family or even an individual! History has also demonstrated that each solution and success has its genesis in a positive mindset that embraces the goal and the commitment to achieve that goal. In the absence of this mindset, it is usually inevitable that the feasibility of success diminishes over time. Transforming the fear of the enormity of the total need into denial and/ or inaction is then a disservice to and a denial of freedom and wholeness to some. Fortunately for society and humanity, there are those who do 'step up to the plate' with such a mindset. In doing so, those individuals in the particular arena of need do acquire their freedom from that need. This is the principle embodied within *Let's Start With the Children*, i.e., despite the great need that permeates the entire age spectrum of inner city residents, it is the 'children' who haven't had their youthful innocence, enthusiasm, hope and dreams irrevocably impacted and diluted by the inner city environment. There is still a relative wholeness upon which to build. Conversely, as the years of inner city residency increase, it seems that the residents' multi-faceted vulnerability also increases and their measure of wholeness diminishes.

Clearly, there is a consensus that education was, is and shall always be an integral part of the wholeness, quality of life and success of an individual as well as a nation. This consensus has served to enable an extremely wide spectrum of efforts to provide, improve and sustain the quality of education. Too many of these well-intentioned efforts become experimental in nature and, inevitably, move on to the the valley of unproductive efforts. However, there doesn't seem to be a clear consensus about 'what to do' and a methodology for doing 'what must be done'. I have previously provided *A Note on the Educational Arena* that is my perspective in this regard; the message here is to do 'what must be done' but do it earlier.

Recently, I heard an interview of a nationally recognized individual in the educational arena on public radio addressed to the educational needs of children-young children- in particular. The point being emphasized is that those required educational needs of young children are, essentially, irrecoverable if these needs are not met by the end of the 3rd grade. Rephrasing that same statement, one can also infer that those resources applied beyond the 3rd grade to those early educational deficiencies of children have a rapidly diminishing return, i.e., they have little impact on countering the deficiencies. These lasting 'deficiencies', then, only serve to take away from the wholeness, quality of life and success of the children and, with some extrapolation, from the entire nation.

Coincidentally [if you still believe in 'coincidences'], a few weeks later, I heard another interview on public radio about a product of the inner city who did receive the benefits of an education; he attended Princeton and Harvard Universities and now is on the academic staff at Harvard. Nothing less than an admirable and truly outstanding achievement! The topic of discussion was *Affirmative Action* and its 'pros and cons'. This scholarly gentleman pointed out the flaw embedded in achieving diversity in the academic world by having an admissions policy based on race rather than being judiciously tempered with merit. It certainly appears that opportunities became more available than ever before to products of the inner city. The question was raised concerning the fairness and logic of the placement of an individual in a competitive academic environment *in which most other participants have been adequately prepared throughout their pre-college education*. Again, let me again mention that America loves the 'quick solution' strategy but, as the interviewee pointed out, it simply was a flaw within the program of *Affirmative Action* in which there **are** some. success stories. What does this tell us? Is there an alternate strategy that offers the roadmap to wholeness, quality of life and success enjoyed by so many Americans for so many years? Hopefully, the reader is now thinking: *Let's Start with the Children.*

With that perspective, there may be a greater appreciation for the philosophy, principles and practices of schools similar to the after school and summer Freedom School programs at St. Ann's in the South Bronx, the San Miguel School in Providence, RI and so many others in the unrecognized and unheralded trenches of education throughout America.

If the area of education was the only outstanding need for a school system's pre-K, 1st, 2nd and 3rd grades beyond the inner city, the feasibility of overcoming any educational deficiencies becomes quite reasonable. However, within the inner city, in particular, the collateral impact of poverty, health, safety, etc. challenges that feasibility.

Although Rhode Island is the smallest state in geographical size, it's compactness and diversity offers a ready-to-use model, a laboratory, if you will, for an integrated and comprehensive analysis and understanding of the factors and dynamics that directly impact the wholeness, quality of life and success of children! Since 1995, **Rhode Island Kids Count** has given life and meaning to this model in a most comprehensive fashion; its functions and activities have a wide but very understandable spectrum. '**Rhode Island Kids Count** provides independent, credible and comprehensive information on Rhode Island's children and engages in information-based advocacy to affect public policies and programs for the improvement of children's lives.' The efforts and activities of **Rhode Island Kids Count** are very well-documented and, collectively, provide a veritable Encyclopedia Britannica equivalent answer to '*Why start with the children?*' One example of this relevant reservoir of documentation is the '*2012 Rhode Island Kids Count Factbook*' which addresses five areas: family and community, economic well-being, health, safety and education. It is a powerful and required primer for those who are active in the arena of child advocacy especially for the disadvantaged children of poverty and inner city residence. It is a powerful, relevant and comprehensive data base. It is also that data base that is integral to the overall solution methodology and process, i.e., the journey from 'requirements' to 'making a difference'.

I met with the **Rhode Island Kids Count** Executive Director, Elizabeth Burke Bryant, in October of 2012. Two realizations followed: [1] there is a strong resonance between the motivation, goals, spirit and thrust of **Rhode Island Kids Count** and '*Let's Start with the Children...*' although there is an obvious enormous difference of scale and [2] words are hardly sufficient to truly characterize and acknowledge the accomplishments of this organization and the efforts of its leadership, e.g., Elizabeth Burke

Bryant, and the entire organizational staff. There is an overview and very relevant and informative excerpts from some of the documentation developed and published by Rhode Island KIDS COUNT as well as some additional information in Appendix D.

This resonance, then, serves to reinforce the prime reason that *Let's Start with the Children* became a reality for this author!

I also met with Representative Grace Diaz of the Rhode Island General Assembly several times-the most recent meeting was on October 12, 2012. She is both a resident of and the State Representative from District 11 which encompasses the inner city of Providence. Representative Diaz is active in many areas of advocacy for the people of her district and Rhode Island. She is particularly concerned with the status, education and the overall well-being of the children there.

She is more-much more-than an activist and advocate for the people; she is an individual that has leveraged her commitment to children, her sense of public service, her awareness of people in need and an inner passion to 'make a difference' in her life and in the lives of others throughout her life's not-so-easy journey. I have often referred to the 'voices' throughout the years that have given a 'voice' to those individuals and populations that have little, if any, 'voice'. There are so many: high-profile individuals like William Wilburforce, Abraham Lincoln, Daniel Patrick Moynihan, Martin Luther King, Jr., Nelson Mandela…. and, lest we forget, those myriad individuals and groups who have been quietly diligent, but mostly unacknowledged, in the trenches of humanity-all of whom have given 'voice' to those in need and to their humanity. Grace Diaz is such an individual. There are many such individuals throughout the State of Rhode Island [and elsewhere] who are committed advocates for children-especially, the younger children.

Representative Diaz has always had education on her personal agenda although her path to an education wasn't direct and easy. She received her high school diploma in 1977 and, 31 years later, she was awarded the the baccalaureate degree in *Human Services* [2008]. She followed that by earning her grauate degree in *Human Services and Management* [2010]. Without question, but with commendation, Reprentative Diaz is another such 'voice' for the people!

She was elected to Rhode Island's General Assembly on November 2, 2004. From 2005 until the present day, there have been nearly fifty press releases addressed to her wide spectrum of activities as a State Representative.

These activities include tax relief, health care jobs, health care advocacy, a prime mover in community organizations, e.g., the Elmwood Community Center in her district, mortgage foreclosure issues, reduction of school drop out rates, raising the required stay-in-school age from seventeen and, then to eighteen......and, most importantly at this point, *education* and children advocacy.

She is a deserving recipient of awards and acknowledgement for her efforts, e.g., the Extraordinary Woman award [2006] and the Dorcas Place Government Service Award [2006]. Dorcas Place is an adult education agency with a thirty year legacy and service to adult learners. Dorcas Place has a history of and a significant role to play with respect to the continuous and persistent need for adult education and workforce education in Rhode Island.

Currently, Representative Grace Diaz is the *Vice Chair* of the House Health, Education and Welfare Commission, *Secretary* of the House Rules Committee, *Member* of the House Oversight Committee, *Chair of the* Permanent Legislative Commission on Child Care and a *Member* of the House Commission to Study Public Higher Education Affordability.

Her 'voice' has been always active and often heard within the various arenas of advocacy within Rhode Island's government and private sector network addressing the issues, concerns and advocacy for children. The government network-like most political, government and administrative networks-is somewhat complicated and is difficult to accurately capture in an organizational chart. However, like most similar networks, there are those many entities [commissions, groups, positions, etc.] that also have an inevitable and intangible dynamic characteristic. It is really within this dynamic environment that both progress and, sometimes, hindrance to progress co-exist! *It is important to note that the 'voices' of Representative Diaz [and others] are very active in [1] the facilitation of those efforts for the educational welfare of the children and [2] overseeing the relevance and relationships between those entities that are organizationally distinct but linked together and working on the same children-oriented educational issues.* For example, an important part of the latter activity is to monitor those requirements for and the development of regulations, e.g., licensing, related to the educational welfare of children. Representative Diaz-together with some of her colleagues-serve as an informal and respected 'watchdog' group; their activities are proactive and preemptive rather than reactive to relevant events. Such a protocol allows constructive input in the early stages of the legislative and executive processes.

It is really to Rhode Island's credit and its growing commitment to the education of children that it has spawned/enabled/supported a wide network of government and private sector efforts and agencies-Rhode Island KIDS COUNT is one-that, collectively, provide a credible foundation for the continuing commitment and improvement to the safety of, services for and education of its children. Some insight into this complex network follows:

Within the state government sector, there are both executive and legislative authorities. There is formal linkage between the two as well as the inevitable and intangible dynamics. On the legislative side, there is the *Permanent Legislative Commission on Child care in Rhode Island*. It's **Vision** is 'All Rhode Island children and youth will be safe, healthy, well-educated, employable and valued contributors to their communities'. It's **Mission Statement** is 'to advise the Governor and Legislature on the issues, problems, and solutions related to affordable, quality child care in Rhode Island and to advocate for the availability of safe, quality and affordable child care'. Representative Diaz is the Chair and Senator Elizabeth Crowley is the Vice-Chair. The remaining diverse membership is drawn from the following organizations: Office of the Child Advocate, Rhode Island KIDS COUNT, Prevent Child Abusr RI, Department of Health, RI School-Age Association, RI Association for Education of Young Children, Department of Health, Retardation & Hospitals, Family/Youth RI Information Netwok, Head Start, The Poverty Institute, RI Alliance of Boys and Girls Clubs, Ready 2 Learn of Providence, Department of Children, Youth and Families, RI Economic Development, Chamber of Commerce, Lt. Governor's Office, Family Child Care Homes of RI, State Alliance of YMCA, RICCDA Academy for Little Children, RI Afterschool Plus Alliance, RI Department of Education, Department of Human Services, Childspan, Local Initiative Support Corp/Child Care and the Family Child Providers Union. This diverse membership is essential to listening to [and hearing] the 'voices' of varying perspectives. Their 'voices', collectively, provide a necessary and meaningful context for progress.

On the executive side there is the Executive Office of Health and Human Services [EOHHS] which was created to-taken directly from its website-'facilitate cooperation and coordination among the five state departments that administer Rhode Island's health and social service programs-the Department of Children, Youth and Families [DCYF], the Department of Human Services [DHS] including the Divisions of Elderly and Veterans Affairs, the Department of Health [HEALTH] and the Department of Behavorial Healthcare, Developmental Disabilities and Hospitals [BHDDH].'

'Together, these departments affect the lives of vitually all Rhode Islanders, providing direct services and benefits to over 300,000 citizens while working to protect the overall health, safety and independence of all Rhode Islanders.'

Within this executive 'umbrella', there are three very relevant organizations that play extremely important roles in the safety, services and education of children. They are the Department of Education, the Department of Children, Youth and Families [DCYF] and the Department of Human Services [DHS]. The DCYF *mission* in a single word could be 'safety' for the children; however-taken directly from the DCYF website-its *mission* is 'to assist families with their primary responsibility to raise their children to become productive members of society. We recognize our obligations to promote, safeguard and protect the overall well-being of culturally diverse children, youth and families and the communities in which they live through a partnership with families, communities and government. As active members of the community, it is the DCYF *vision* that all children, youth and families reach their full potential in a safe and nurturing environment.' Simply put, DCYF is the 'back-up' function for families in need.

The Department of Human Services [DHS] –via its available budget-provides direct medical and financial aid, food stamps and social services to those Rhode Islanders who just don't have access to those resources necessary to sustain life and its quality as other Rhode Islanders do as a matter of course and continuity. It is important to note that state budgets are developed based on their immediate history as well as projected need and requirements, reviewed for relevance and validity and usually, if not always, face the threat and reality of reduction because of budgetary constraints. Reductions are usually made in an 'across-the-board' manner probably because this strategy is perceived as 'fair'. In this light, then, those budgetary items related to the safety, security and overall well-being of the children are reviewed as 'budget items'. The author believes-as it has been mentioned in my previous treatment of 'life-cycle costs'- that children 'costs' are really not just budget items but they are, without question, *investments-very unique investments-* for Rhode Island as well as the lives of the children as they transition through life.

It is a matter of incurring those 'costs' in the early stages of the lives of children that will result in a significant reduction in those costs for children, youth and families over their lives. Conversely, the unavailability of funding for the children in their early lives is an example of 'kicking the proverbial budget can' down the road for future generations not to mention the human cost to children, adults and families. It is a matter of 'paying now' or 'paying more-much more-later.'

I have reviewed the power point presentation considered by the Permanent Legislative Commission on Child Care at its meeting on October 15, 2012. It is an informative report; the highlights follow: [1] it is addressed to increasing the number of children with *high needs*, ages birth to K entry, who have access to high-quality early learning programs [author' note: clearly, consistent with the message of *Let's Start with the Children'*] and its derivative requirements to improve both access and quality. Currently, only 18.6% of Rhode Island infants and toddlers are known to be in early learning programs. For preschoolers is just over 30%. [2] *affordability* for child care needs is a very real issue [while the United States levels of child care assistance is increasing, Rhode Island levels are decreasing-the overall trend is a decreasing one]. [3] Whereas the *quality* of preschool and infant-toddler centers is, essentially, acceptable, the quality of nearly 2/3 of family child care is less than acceptable. [4] The incoming limit for child care eligibility and the exit limit for Rhode Island are identical whereas those limits [as measured by per cent of the Federal poverty level] for the other New England states have reasonable margins [aka *range*]. The zero range or margin for Rhode Island represents *financial instability and direct risk* to families receiving child care assistance.

Under the executive umbrella, there is also the Department of Education with its programs, e.g., *Bright Stars,* and the *Rhode Island Early Learning Council.* The goal of the latter group-formed in 2010- 'is to ensure that Rhode Island children from **birth to school entry** have access to high quality early learning experiences in a variety of settings.The appointment of a Early Learning Council is a provision of the Federal 2007 *Head Start Reauthorization Act.'* The current co-chairs are Deborah Gist, Commissioner, Rhode Island department of Elementary and Secondary Education and Elizabeth Burke Bryant, Executive Director, Rhode Island KIDS COUNT.

There is a third equally important component complementing the legislative and executive efforts; it is the important role of the many community efforts of child advocacy, child care, day care operations, after school programs, supportive families, etc.

The Permanent Legislative Commission on Child care and the Rhode Island Early Learning Council are two of the four major entities concerned with early learning. The third is the *Bright Stars* program which helps child care providers learn about best practices in early learning and to apply them to the care children receive, recognizes program quality and gives parents information to make [positive] choices about their children's care and education. The fourth is the *Successful Start Steering Committee* which ensures that state agencies have consistent, comprehensive and gap-free administrative and funding policies.

Complementing this early learning network are those Rhode Island entities concerned with extended learning. These entities include *Bright Stars*, the Providence After School Alliance, the Rhode Island After School Alliance, Rhode Island's 21st Century Community Learning Centers Initiative [RI 21st CCLC] and the School Aged Care Alliance which is the liaison between the issues and concerns of school age children and the Rhode Island Legislature as well as related regional and national programs.

Summarily, there are five points to be made:

[1]   Within the State of Rhode Island, there is a symphony of 'voices' for the children and families of Rhode Island.

[2]   *Let's Start with the Children*, although an independent effort, is really another 'voice' for the children-especially, the young children.

[3]   The issues and challenges are many for achieving quality education and providing the required learning environments and supportive services. It is a challenge that must be embraced by all.

[4]   Rhode Island is probably a reflection of similar efforts across America.

[5]   The needs for quality education and quality of life are significantly greater in an inner city environment.

My Knitting Neighbor

From the nucleus of this ministry came a spectrum of supportive efforts by individuals and organizations; one of these individual efforts that truly reflects the **enabling effect** of the ministry. One of my neighbors, Ann Beekley, had made a neighborly inquiry about the experiences at St. Ann's. She and her husband, John, do their own share and style of community service via St. Michael's Episcopal Church and they do their frequent traveling by car. Ann inquired about just how she could "do something for the children at St. Ann's." Coincidentally, Ann is a passionate knitter and knits while John drives. She then asked about the possible need of knitted hats for the children at St. Ann's; in accordance with Outreach protocol, Mother Martha was asked that same question. Her response was that the children **always** need a warm hat during the colder months of the year. Having said that, Ann has knitted-and she continues to do so-more than several hundred multi-colored knitted hats for the boys and girls at St. Ann's. At the risk of repeating myself, I ask the now proverbial question: "Could this be just another *amazing* coincidence?"

The Consortium of Endowed Episcopal Parishes [2005]

It was the 4th year of the ECC summer camperships component of Outreach ministry efforts at St. Ann's, the Spring and Fall mission trips there had also became a ministry fixture, the *miracle of the backpacks* was added to the growing litany of *coincidences*; in general, the overall Outreach activity and especially the one at St. Ann's continued to grow and surge forward. The number and spirit of the parishioners and friends of St. John's who participated did likewise!

St. John's was and is also fortunate enough to be a member of *The Consortium of Endowed Episcopal Parishes [CEEP]*. This consortium was founded in1985 as a way of having a network of peers where endowed parishes could learn to manage their endowments more efficiently and effectively and **to explore opportunities for greater outreach and ministry through their use.** The membership includes those parishes with endowments of one million dollars or more. The annual conferences provide a unique opportunity for individuals from similar parishes-mostly large, mostly urban, mostly old and well-established-to meet, interact and share ideas for enhanced outreach. St. John's certainly fits this profile with the exception that it is a suburban parish. The annual conference provides the attendees to meet creative people and new ideas for outreach and to think 'outside of the proverbial box'; the program of sessions, seminars and workshops are specifically shaped to this end. These gatherings typically include a spectrum of participant-oriented interests and experiences that are both practical and theological. Topics include stewardship, grant making and acquisition ideas, mission-based investing, globalization and human development, AIDS ministry, sexuality, inclusive leadership, ***models of community ministry***, diversity and multiculturalism, volunteerism and the role of the Anglican community. The 20th Annual Conference in 2005 was convened in New York City.

One of the major themes of the 2005 CEEP conference was outreach and community service; six members of the outreach Ministry at St. John's were in attendance at this conference. We were invited to a dinner at the Riverside Drive residence [overlooking Riverside Park] of one of the clergy but also a member of the conference directorship. There were about ten tables arranged so that all those Outreach individuals attending could be comfortably accommodated. The only protocol requested was that no more than one individual from any particular parish was to be seated at any table; the obvious goal here was to encourage and maximize the interaction and the exchange of Outreach experiences and information amongst the parish representatives. The evening was a most meaningful, spirited and even moving affair; as stories were related amongst the guests, it certainly seemed that the St. John's ministry at St. Ann's became a prevalent topic of interest and information. Whenever a St. John's representative would share his/her experience at St. Ann's, it was described through the lens of his/her spirituality, passion and commitment to Outreach; these experiences attracted a lot of interest and a litany of questions and inquiries about the genesis of the ministry at St. Ann's. Inevitably, the discussions would focus upon the Outreach procedures and methodology that were employed in the *development* of the St. John's Outreach Model which is described in greater detail in Appendix H. There was a similar reaction at the *Presiding Bishop's Summit On Domestic Poverty in May of 2008*. Although the explicit focus of this conference was not outreach and community service, this topic was imbedded in the discussion on poverty and candidate collaborative programs and efforts by parishes, dioceses, Episcopal social services and relief agencies that could potentially alleviate the tragedy of increasing poverty. It is relevant to note today [December 21, 2011] that [about] 50% of Americans are either 'poor' or 'living in poverty'.

In those informal gatherings that arise at most conferences, St. John's outreach experiences and model, again, became a topic of interest amongst many of the attendees; there were numerous 'sidebars' throughout the conference and the opportunity to distribute the information of Appendix H.

For those members of the St. John's Outreach ministry, the reaction of others both within the Episcopal family and beyond was an enormously encouraging, empowering and validation that they were 'doing the right thing' and doing it well. In the days that immediately followed the 2005 CEEP conference, an invitation was extended to the St. John's outreach ministry to conduct one of the workshops at the 2006 CEEP conference in Alexandria, Virginia.

The Consortium of Endowed Episcopal Parishes [2006]

In keeping with the meaningful, informative and interesting workshops offered at the annual meetings of past Consortium gatherings, this Consortium included the following workshop:

A5: Amazing Grace-Based Outreach: Modeling Shared Ministry

Presenters: Al Colella, Liz Crawley & Jan Malcolm of St. John's, Barrington, RI; Reverend Martha Overall, Rector, St. Ann's, Bronx, NY

This workshop will address the genesis, development and progress of the Outreach ministry efforts of St. John's, Barrington, RI with St. Ann's in the South Bronx. The reality-based model used in this successful ministry will be shared as we take you through a clear, user-friendly sequence of steps that can be shaped to fit the profile of any individual church and challenging ministry. You will leave with a methodology that facilitates the development of successful outreach ministries within any parish environment and beyond.

This workshop was one of the best-attended workshops; there was a standing-room-only attendance which reflected the interest and commitment of so many of the Conference attendees to faith-based outreach efforts that effectively and efficiently serve those in need *without exception*. The essence of this workshop is provided via the power-point presentation included in Appendix K. Some interesting notes of the workshop follow.

One of the many questions submitted to the presenters was "What per cent of St. John's budget is committed to outreach?" An interesting question because the usual outreach budget as a parish line item was eliminated in 2001 and the outreach membership was simply told that its expenditures were limited to whatever could be realized via its own fund-raising. This was a most disappointing mandate dictated by the new rector. The 'drums' of Amazing Grace were still beyond the horizon but their sound levels were growing louder. In time, though, this initially disappointing edict turned out to be an enabling and motivating factor to realize via outreach fund-raising an amount of dollars committed to outreach far beyond that provided in earlier Church budgets. This being true, then how was one to respond to the aforementioned question within this context? Hmmmmm! One always has a choice and the one here is 'to take the high road or the low road'; a principle that is integral to all ministry efforts, i.e., 'doing the right thing *always* and which inevitably yield positive outcomes'! My truth-based response was that the parishioners of St. John's are uniquely generous and practitioners of *faith in action* and, therefore, assistance [albeit previously eliminated] wasn't really necessary! I have always noted that an event, e.g., the elimination of direct support from the Church budget, is an event but one must 'keep their eyes on the ball', e.g., the process that follows the event. That process that followed includes a spectrum of successful outreach efforts and, most certainly and emphatically, includes the one at St. Ann's.

It is important and relevant to note that in the 1990s, St. John's was very fortunate to have had the Reverend Darryl Stahl as its Rector. He was somewhat unique within the Episcopal Church because he truly and pragmatically valued the Vestry there as well as the parishioners. His gifts clearly included his ability to empower, to enable and to equip the parishioners and their individual ministry journeys. His array of gifts not only included his ability to encourage, suggest but also, and most importantly, ***to delegate both responsibility <u>and</u> authority*** for a particular ministry effort and, then, of even greater importance to 'get out of the way'. He both valued and trusted the parishioners. It was his leadership that was a major contributor to the foundation upon which the outreach Ministry became almost a legacy in the Rhode Island community. This idea of encouragement and having a value for the parishioners and their many gifts-as did the Reverend Darryl Stahl-is a crucial component for any successful ministry and/or outreach endeavor. Conversely, as

219

it shall be discussed in the *Summary and Conclusions*, another crucial factor for successful ministry and/or outreach endeavors is that intangible characteristic of persistence and faith in the face of the inevitable overt and covert fear-fueled measures of doubt, resistance and reluctance that arise whenever *another road is taken* albeit the 'high road'.

Another barometer of the impact of this particular CEEP 2006 workshop upon these fear-based measures was brought to our attention by an individual who had attended our workshop but had subsequently also attended another workshop addressed to new ideas and initiatives for outreach efforts. She had listened to the usual notes of fear, e.g., "It's never been done before!", "It's too far!", "It will cost too much!", etc. Well, this woman, God bless her!, who was from a church in Texas, had the courage and inspiration to offer in her Texas drawl: "Well, I just attended the workshop on *Amazing Faith-Based Outreach* by a small church in little old Rhode Island and, by golly, if they can do it, I'm sure that we in Texas can also do it!"

Chapter 18
South Bronx Today

In 2012, as the veteran members of the Outreach ministry approach St. Ann's, it is difficult for them to see any significant differences in the South Bronx environment. Everything seems to be the quite the same as it was in 2001: the people and their street activities, the traffic and the many forms of creative on-street parking, the urban sounds and noises, the scattered litter, children everywhere, etc. The South Bronx environment around 138th Street certainly looked and even 'felt' very much unchanged. The neighborhood environment still includes those multi-floored apartment buildings better known as 'the projects' in which are located unique communities of residents doing whatever they can to cope with the realities, risks and challenges of life within and around the 'projects'. *The process of survival remains very much in evidence* It is also clear that the ugly heads of unemployment, poverty, crime, guns and drugs are still there with the collateral social, health and economic challenges.

One experiences a sense of amazement and appreciation that the neighborhood has managed to maintain some sort of 'status quo'; perhaps, even that is considered a measure of progress that the neighborhood and its residents have not fallen further behind in their individual and collective journeys of life. Survival also remains a basic measure of 'success'.

However, there are differences; for example, the people are very much the same and still represent a resource of life, energy and commitment to make a difference as best as they can. There is a network of community efforts that have banded together to advocate for better housing, schools, safer and cleaner streets and a host of city and social services that seem to be commonplace beyond the South Bronx. There is also an absence of a more 'systemic' [comprehensive] effort significantly alter the character of the South Bronx, i.e., to address, minimize and, hopefully, eliminate those long-standing inherent disadvantages of inner-city life. As pointed out earlier, the cost of such an effort is probably astronomical but the cost of not embracing such an effort is far beyond astronomical with costs to humanity well beyond dollars.

Some additional succinct observations are aptly provided by Steve Lippincott, veteran New Yorker and veteran participant in the ministry efforts at St. Ann's:

"Motthaven, a section of the South Bronx has been for ten years a focus and perhaps an obsession. I come from not far away; I grew up in Newark, New Jersey; I had relatives all over the five boroughs and came to know the Bronx in my very early years. Consequently, my perspective of the Bronx covers nearly sixty years. I lean towards optimism as a default. Believing one can make the world better comes with a vision of what better would look like. One looks for signs that this is so. I haven't found many. I have found some, but only on an individual level. Some of the children I have watched grow up have seized opportunity and are doing incredibly well; some are just now blossoming and we are quite hopeful. But life on 138th Street and St. Ann's Avenue does not seem to have changed dramatically. St. Ann's Church seems to be quite healthy but the credit lies with the Rector and her staff doing an excellent job and not in events surrounding the parish having improved by any measure. The 'successes' that we have celebrated all took a tremendous amount of time, work and no small expense from a large distributed network of people. The area is heavily dependent on a crumbling, truncated and sometimes uninspired social services network and the sheer number of people in distress is overwhelming even in a mega-city. But the Bronx is full of remarkable people; they provide optimism and hope and they provide me with a vision of what good would like. At least we have something to work with.

My traditional approach to Motthaven comes with taking the 138th Street exit from the elevated Bruckner Expressway. The exit itself is a combination of iron workers' masterpiece and an antique carnival ride descending perilously to a four lane service road. The pavement is a patchwork of broken asphalt, patched pot holes and remnants of the cobbles from the original surface poking through; here one must traverse to the outside lane before approaching a concrete divider that will lead the left lanes South, the right lanes North. The secret of driving in New York

City is in knowing what lane one must be in. Upon making the correct choice one must quickly cross through heavy traffic, car service Lincoln Town cars, gypsy cabs [no city cabs in the South Bronx] and the occasional meandering pedestrian; all [except the pedestrians] in a frenetic exercise of multitasking. When I began this ministry ten years ago, one would, upon reaching Bruckner Avenue, see the burned out remnants of the Faber Ware cookware factory, various small businesses, a bustling lumber yard, neighborhood men waiting at the corners to be selected for a day of labor for a day of wages, and,, upon reaching 138th Street, the burned out remnants of a gas station. On 138th Street is a giant Catholic church. Beside it is a foundation, dug decades ago but abandoned, possibly the evidence of a more optimistic time for the church but also an enduring sign of that optimism shattered.

Now, the road surface hasn't changed but the factory is gone, replaced by a modern reproduction of a classic brownstone. However, there remains no sign of life there. The gas station has been recently rebuilt and looking smart and one with a sense of architectural style. The expressway above is showing a fresh coat of light green paint. The church on 138th Street still shadows the empty cavernous foundation but its towers are covered with scaffolding; workers at cement mixers bear evidence that the seeming lost optimism has been reborn. At St. Ann's Avenue, Ray's always busy corner restaurant, the unofficial boardroom for St. Ann's Church and the Outreach teams from St. John's, is also decked out in scaffolding. The burned apartment house next door to St. Ann's Church has been renovated as are some of the other surrounding buildings. Some storefronts are still quite grimy but others bear bright new signage and a lot of foot traffic; there are people everywhere. The streets of the South Bronx are always busy! Bordering St. Ann's is a community garden, its Japanese foot bridges and meandering paths done with volunteer labor remain a loving work in progress. Across the street on 139th Street-and elsewhere-are new and modern town houses with cars in the driveways and well kept tiny front yards behind heavy steel gates.

Perhaps these are signs of transition; a glimpse of what Motthaven could be what that would look like. But progress depends on the perilous state of the greater national and regional economies improving in a sustainable way as well. The children I see who are happiest, healthiest and least threatening are wearing uniforms of parochial schools. Churches seem to have the greatest share of the burden in social welfare and child advocacy. These, too, are subject to the whims of the greater economy. They are swimming against the tide of a greater multigenerational apathy.

I can effortlessly count off a dozen names of St. Ann's people we at St. John's Episcopal Church in Barrington, RI have impacted for the better. Some have made it out of the Bronx and are pursuing the American dream. Some have remained and are 'fighting the good fight'. So many more are on the line and I cannot accurately predict the future they will greet and encounter. I *am* hopeful, but hopefulness comes out of having no other option. **But we have more to work with!**"

Chapter 19
St. Ann's Today

From Steve Lippincott:
My first experience of St. Ann's is not out of a mission for their benefit. It was the good folk of St. Ann's being host to us, as a base camp, for our volunteer work at Ground Zero in 2001. A number of parishioners from St. John's in Barrington, Rhode Island had volunteered for shifts at St. Paul's Chapel [directly adjacent to ground Zero] distributing food, water, socks and basic necessities needed by the workers on the 'pile' across the street. By the spring of 2002 the pile was significantly diminished. The cemetery behind St. Paul's looked, at first glance, to be covered by a gentle snow, already dirtied as it naturally would be in a busy city. The 'pile' by this time resembled a pile of rusted iron in a scrap yard, a common sight to anyone of the greater metropolitan area. At the end of our shift, we were privileged to join some of the first-responders on a tour of the 'pile'. We descended in a golf cart to the bottom level of the 'pit' on a roadway that had been created with the rubble. At the bottom one could look up [more than eight stories to ground level] and see the surviving garage levels. At this point the resemblance to typical industrial waste remained-reinforced perhaps. Then, amongst the twisted I beams and crushed sheet metal, there was the remnants of a water cooler and crushed office furniture. And, no, that wasn't snow in the cemetery but a very fine dust from pulverized concrete that had blanketed much of the area around Ground Zero and those who worked on the 'pile' and the many volunteers at St. Paul's Chapel.

We arrived at St. Ann's, as what would become routine in the future, by going down 138th Street from the Bruckner Avenue off-ramp. New York was in mourning. The fire station on 138th Street, which got hit particularly hard, was festooned with memorials. The avenue is lined with magnificent 19th century building of five or six stories. Under the grime of neglect, one can see that they are adorned with brownstone, iron, copper and tin ornamentation accenting equally laid brickwork. They look down on broken and stained sidewalks with litter and people shuffling or loitering. Some are pushing shopping carts overflowing with nothing of value or utility; some are pushing baby carriages. Some of the baby carriages actually have babies in them; many do not. Turning onto St. Ann's Avenue there are various businesses and store fronts with torn and grubby awnings. Some storefronts are blackened holes; some looked dubious as to their function. St. Ann's Church looked similarly forlorn. Built in the 19th century, it sits on a hill above an early graveyard and it is surrounded by 19th century wrought impressive iron gates and fence. There is the familiar but shaded shield stating 'The Episcopal Church Welcomes You'. The church is made of stone. A battered copper steeple sits on its gable with peeling paint and its cross listing noticeably. Its gutters were sagging, its doors were distressed. Mother Martha's ebullient greeting, however, brought into focus that we were in a very much alive place. *This was a place of hope!*

Subsequent visits have seen dramatic changes; the State granted funds to restore the historic building. Mission trips from St. John's as well as other churches resulted in flower gardens, vegetable gardens and a contemplative garden. The church sits once again on her copse with a new steeple, gutters doors and a fresh coat of paint. Mother Martha's hope hasn't diminished a bit. There are changes for the good in the appearance of the neighborhood but it still seems that the need has remained the same. People's lives are also dramatically changed for the good but the line of people needing the most basic of needs still queue in a line that does not diminish; at times, the lines seem to have grown in length. Some children are malnourished; children come to church in freezing weather without coats. Substance abuse support groups are larger than communicants attending church services.

It is fitting that this journey began with such an unthinkable tragedy. Now the mourning has run its course; there is an emerging generation having no living memory of the events of that sad day of September 11, 2001. A more permanent memorial has been placed on the fire house on 138th Street. The view east from St. Paul's Chapel looks upon a typical New York City building project. Nothing is remarkable about either.

The tragedy that is the South Bronx, however, did not occur with a

226

dramatic moment where, on a single day, these beautiful buildings looking down on a borough full of hope and a bright future crashed and became what we see today. Though the tragedy in lower Manhattan has moved on, the tragedy in the South Bronx continues. 9/11 was a call to work, a call for enthusiasm and energy towards making a horrible wrong right again. St. Ann's remains a base camp for the end of suffering. The 'pile' at Ground Zero was overwhelming in its size. No one looked at it and declared it beyond one's ability to clear and rebuild. People simply jumped on the 'pile' and joined bucket brigades. Contractors brought their equipment even before their offices could draw up contracts. Ground Zero became a magnet for the vast goodness of America as volunteers, craftsmen, firemen, emergency personnel, medical experience and expertise, chefs, donations of all types and thousands of volunteers poured into lower Manhattan from every corner of the country.

Mother Martha and the St. Ann's community have similarly enabled and encouraged many to simply jump in and do whatever they can and, in the process, discover what gifts an individual has to uniquely offer.

From the author:

As Steve has written, there are some differences within the South Bronx community and, yet, there are persistent disadvantages that still remain for so many of its inner-city residents.

Someone had once referred to St. Ann's as a 'candle' in the South Bronx; this 'candle' has assumed huge dimensions and, today, provides warmth, light and hope for an increasingly expanding number of people: for adults, families, the hungry, the homeless, ..., but *especially for the children!* This book certainly details many of the changes that have taken place at St. Ann's since 2011. Perhaps a more succinct description of *'St. Ann's today'* can be had by recalling that I have written that one of the motivations for this ministry has been to provide a view, a vision for the children that there is life beyond that which they have in the South Bronx and, then, to enable and encourage them on their journey to that view, that vision.

Without question but with gratitude it is safe to say that *'There are success stories.'*, that *'There are success stories in the making.'*, that *'More and more children have seen and experienced life beyond the walls of the South Bronx.'*, that *'The children do have a significantly greater self-expectation.'*, that *'An enduring difference has been made for the children at St. Ann's'!*

Chapter 20
Summary and Conclusions

This book will end just as it began, i.e., a reminder that the 'story' of the book is really a litany of 'stories' of human kindness and goodness, individual and collective spiritual journeys, the belief that life itself is a unique gift, a sharing of a myriad gifts of this life with those in need, a collateral passion, thanksgiving, a perseverance of character that inevitably overcomes unsought and undeserved disadvantages, faith in a greater power [aka *Amazing Grace*],........, it is a love story, it is another 'voice' in a series of 'voices', e.g., Abraham Lincoln, John Fitzgerald Kennedy, Daniel Patrick Moynihan, Nelson Mandela and a host of civil rights activists, author-activists, myriad quiet under-the-radar committed individuals and groups, etc., crying out and putting their faith into action that a respect and value for humanity is the ultimate barometer of an individual's life as well as the character of local, national and global societies and, therefore, it can also serve as a moral, ethical and spiritual compass for 'those who follow' as it has for so many from the St. Ann's and St. John's communities!

It is precisely this latter consideration that was the prime motivation for putting into print the 'story' of this book, i.e., to provide a foundation and direction and inspirational fuel for the lives of 'those who follow' as well as a roadmap where there are few, if any, roadmaps. As our faith, commitment to action and *Amazing Grace* have been the inspirational fuels for the ministry at St. Ann's......as the impact of this ministry upon the lives of so many of the children, teens and more than a few adults from St. Ann's and St. John's was witnessed, experienced and grew over time...... as the 'voices' of the past have enabled the 'passing of the torch' to the then current and future generations......as the aggregate of advocacy and

228

supportive ministry efforts, of which St. John's was one, at St. Ann's have clearly and emphatically 'made a difference, a sustained difference'......as this ministry like the unheralded tens of thousands ministries that also exist throughout America offer models for the betterment of humanity, then it is hoped that this book will follow suit and provide a single step in that same direction. For every story told herein-and elsewhere-there are countless untold stories! It is safe to say that in each of those stories-told and untold-that 'Givers have become receivers and receivers have become givers!' *Life simply doesn't get any better than that!*

It is worthwhile to revisit the 'costs' of society's blindness to the humanity of an individual, a community and, yes, even a nation. The experienced financial cost of America's blindness to disadvantaged inner-city residents-**especially the children**-is simply staggering and overwhelming. It is true that there are costs for the spectrum of programs that have and still do address the inner-city situation and it is equally true that they do 'make **some** difference' in the lives of **some** of the children. However, it is also true that the disadvantages of inner-city residence have persisted-and even worsened-over the decades of the 20th century and into the 21st century. It has been mentioned earlier in this book that the required resources, i.e., funding, advocacy, mentoring, tutoring, education, a vision of the availability and experience of life beyond the inner-city, etc., to overcome the disadvantages of the inner-city environment and make a difference in the path of life for one child are enormous. The enormity of required resources is enhanced when one considers that these resources need to be provided over a timeline of years, many years **to myriad individuals**! The cost of resources required to bring the promise of America to all of its inner-cities is almost beyond one's imagination. It is not unlike the 'dream' of going to the moon which required enormous national resources; however, there is one significant difference, i.e., the national commitment to, in fact, go to the moon also had a sustained political will! The bottom line, as the world knows, is that the 'dream' became a 'reality'. Could the dream of erasing the disadvantages of inner-city residence also become a reality? If it is to be, it is absolutely critical that the 'voices of advocacy' of the past and present be continued into the future. Hopefully, a chorus of 'voices' will provide a symphonic awakening for the aggregate political and moral will of responsible individuals including those in school and city administrations, local, state and national governments.

It is fundamentally critical to realize that the dollar costs of a comprehensive solution to the inner-city poverty-driven culture are probably beyond anyone's comprehension or imagination; this perspective remains unchanged even in the light of [1] the continuing and increasing enormous costs to humanity, [2] the likelihood that the 'solution costs' will-in time-be far less than the spectrum of dollar costs of 'doing business as usual' and [3] the failure to see that "there are no shortcuts!". Consider the following:

Collateral to these cost requirements for the *sustained replacement* of 'band-aid' solutions with a sustained and sufficient local and national effort is an awareness of the litany of **life cycle costs** that are imbedded in these 'band-aid' solutions with benefits that diminish with time and that probably far exceed those required for the long and much needed local and national integrated initiative. There are four components to the entire spectrum of life cycle costs which the sad history of the inner-cities of America has placed into evidence.

First, there is the growing menu of costs for those 'band-aid' solutions which admittedly do have some level of effectiveness but also an effectiveness that fades with the passage of time. Secondly, there are the unavoidable and undeniable long-term costs [that steadily *increase* with the passage of time] that become necessary but hardly sufficient to address the derivative costs of the disadvantages of inner-city residence. These tangible long-term costs are medical, mental health, social service, homeless and housing, unemployment, law enforcement, imprisonment, rehabilitation, vocational, education et al.

The third and fourth components of life cycle costs are intangible and just cannot be quantified with a dollar cost! There are the immeasurable but very real costs in the overall quality of life for most inner-city residents: lack of opportunity, lack of education, unemployment, loss of self-esteem, depression, loss of one's intrinsic value, damage to family wholeness and functionality, a life span significantly less than that enjoyed by non- inner-city residents, lack of a roadmap out of the morass of the debilitating environment of the inner-cities and, also, the ultimate human cost of the loss of hope. Finally, there is the second intangible and immeasurable cost of the forever-lost and foregone contributions of inner-city residents to the local and national reservoir of gifts, expertise, creativity, intelligence and skills spectrum simply because they have been –for the most part-excluded from participating in the American dream.

One of the more devastating residues of the inner-city environment is the wide age range [or spectrum] of those disadvantaged for life: young children, youth, young adults, older adults and even senior citizens. Recall that earlier in this book, it was offered that the inner-city situation, i.e., the overall living environment there, took many years-even decades-to be in the state that has both existed and persisted for so many of those years. It is the author's pragmatic belief that an increasing time of residence [and increasing age] for most inner-city residents directly impacts two factors.

First, the development of a way of living characterized by habits, protocols, procedures et al that are essentially necessary for a day-to-day existence and not that personal and family growth enjoyed by most other Americans. Secondly, the challenge and the associated required resources-including time-to 'turn this trend around' is simply overwhelming. The real question then becomes *"What can be done?"* What can be done by the individual, the community, the leaders of society or by the governing bodies of the nation is a more complete question. The question that then surfaces and which must be confronted is the exact same issue posed by Daniel Patrick Moynihan nearly a half-century ago. He is best remembered not for saying "This is what we must do!" but rather inferring that something needs to be done. There does not exist a master plan, a methodology or a roadmap for 'doing that something that must be done'. Individuals, communities, society's leadership and even the governing bodies of the cities, states and nation-in their own ways-have waged a continuum of skirmishes and losing battles with the disadvantages of the inner-cities.

A very credible starting point is that reservoir of writings that have reviewed, summarized, analyzed, criticized, praised and offered both relevant and sometimes less-than-relevant commentary about *The Moynihan Report*. Individually and collectively, there is an abundance of attention to the longstanding inner city 'problem' in terms of criticisms, reviews, analyses and some relevant and not-so-relevant commentary. However, there is also a scarcity of really any efforts addressing any candidate *comprehensive* solutions as compared to those that focus upon a real 'piece' of the problem. This limited focusing does not take into consideration the functional and dynamic linkage amongst the many 'pieces' of the inner-city situation that have, at least, persisted since 1965 and, perhaps, worsened by almost any humanitarian measure. It certainly makes the author think that the 'problem', i.e., the aggregate dynamics of these many pieces-some of which are known and, perhaps, some are not-is so longstanding, organic, complex and vast that they present too much of a challenge for most individuals and/or organizations.

Also, from my perspective I understand that the American culture gravitates toward quick-fix solutions and that the protocols of funding and political variations at the national level discourage and even prohibit long-term funding for candidate solutions. However, one must also remember that America has successfully solved complex and challenging problems over a duration of years and, more importantly, the solution to the inner city 'problem' will probably take a continuity of effort for decades. Having said that, I am suggesting that the initial step in the solution process is the development of both a methodology and credible model of the inner city dynamic factors. The comprehensive solution must include all known relevant factors [existing national data bases make this possible], have an imbedded time-based *adaptive* capability that accommodates the inevitable variations in funding, the operational environment, political leanings and the continuing assessment-for purposes of accountability [a most difficult and always unattractive task] and relevance- of performance [or non-performance] of those factors within the solution process. Simply put, the solution process has an organic 'fine-tuning' capability driven by a goal-oriented requirement. Given that this model can be developed, funded and initiated, it is imperative that the national, social and humanitarian will of the nation be continually present!

This very ambitious effort is an inevitable topic at another time!

However, today, there is something that every individual and group can do to make a difference for the children and that is simply to make the choice to, in fact, do something just as there are many that have made the choice to light a candle somewhere. For the reasons and rationale stated herein, the St. John's community made the choice to join the efforts of those at St. Ann's in the South Bronx and focused upon the plight of the children there and, therefore, directed our ministry efforts there. Sometimes situations, crises and issues are so vast and imposing that it is understandably difficult-very difficult-to determine just where does an individual or a group start. *The title and thesis of this book suggest 'Let's Start with the Children!'* ....and the sooner the better! Some readers may be asking themselves "Why start with the children?" Simply put the inner-city situation of so many children disadvantaged for life is probably the most fertile and promising area for progress. Support, mentoring, advocacy, guidance and a quality education in their early years can provide the shaping of their mindset, their moral and ethical compass, their self-expectations and, most importantly, their hope and humanity. Hopefully, this book provides a measure of reinforcement for this thesis. It is also important to remember that ***all children are important:*** those in our families, our schools, our communities,……, our nation and beyond!

The spectrum of choices is literally endless: as the Outreach team at St. John's made their choice to make the journey to St. Ann's in the South Bronx for more than a decade, so can an individual or a group make the choice to ***start with the children*** and create their own journey. Certainly, there are children who are within one's family circle, their community, the school systems, family shelters, soup kitchens, the social service networks, literacy programs, Big Sisters, Big Brothers, organizations and 'homes' for young children and teens without families,………***there are children in need everywhere***………..one can even look beyond America's shores.

How does one get to the moon? One step at a time! How does a sports team turn a losing cause into a victory? One point at a time, one yard at a time, one play at a time, etc. How could a difference in the lives of so many children be made? Perhaps, one child at a time…………...and then another and another and…………!

Now go make a difference…..in their lives and yours!

"Step up to the plate!" Be a 'moral and humanitarian compass' for a child! Rekindle the gift of 'hope' in their hearts, minds and lives.

Remember those individuals upon shoulders you have stood in your own journey! Pay back by paying forward! For every child that is motivated, guided, encouraged and enabled onto a meaningful life's journey, there will be another crack in the disadvantaged bondage of the past. Therefore there will a greater hope for that child's future….and that of their children…. and their children's children….ad infinitum.

It is again important to acknowledge those many, perhaps thousands, of ministry and volunteer efforts directed to making a difference in the lives of children locally, nationally and globally. Perhaps, just perhaps, these efforts represent a model for a more comprehensive and sustained political will and action! Another very relevant model can be found in the wisdom, forethought and humanitarian lens of America's forefathers when they created the Constitution of the United States and, subsequently, all of its amendments for 'those who followed'.

There are no ministries without the inevitable challenges, trials and tribulations; ministry success is critically dependent upon patience, the ability to 'keep your eye on the ball', i.e., the goal of the ministry, and, in this case, the will to persevere for the sake of those children in need. It is also more than helpful to embrace your faith in *Amazing Grace*. Amongst these challenges are those who represent the antithesis of those 'voices' who do recognize the situation through their humanitarian and moral lens and, then, their call for action. History is replete with those individuals and groups, local and globally, who resort to gross denial to avoid reality and postpone humanitarian progress. They become expert in creating distractions and irrelevant issues to de-energize the ministry. As it was in the past and will surely occur in the future, there are those 'not in the arena', the inevitable 'doubters', 'inhibitors' and 'naysayers' that will cast doubt and criticism upon any efforts to assist those in need. Individually and collectively, these individuals have *chosen* to be part of the problem and not contributors to the solution. Their acts of denial, doubt and criticism assume overt, covert, adversarial and subtle forms. For example consider the recent article by Gene Marks in Forbes Magazine. He wrote:

If I was a poor black kid I would first and most importantly work to make sure I got the best grades possible. I would make it my #1 priority to be able to read sufficiently. I wouldn't care if I was a student at the worst public middle school in the worst inner city. Even the worst have their best. And the very best students, even at the worst schools, have more opportunities. Getting good grades is the key to having more options. With good grades you can choose different, better paths. If you do poorly in school, particularly in a lousy school, you're severely limiting the limited opportunities you have.

And I would use the technology available to me as a student. I know a few school teachers and they tell me that many inner city parents usually have or can afford cheap computers and internet service nowadays. That because [and sadly] it's oftentimes a necessary thing to keep their kids safe at home then on the streets. And libraries and schools have computers available too. Computers can be purchased cheaply at outlets like TigerDirect and Dell's outlet. Professional organizations like accountants and architects often offer used computers from their members, sometimes at no cost at all.

How does one respond to this vile, naïve, irrelevant and ignorant-of-the-facts article? Rather than writing a treatise of Mr. Marks' article, I'll just provide a few of many blistering observations from the World Wide Web. First, from Imani Gandy's *'If I Were a Poor Black Kid': Really, Forbes?',* "The white privilege wafting from this article is so thick it's practically choking me."..... "Privilege and racism are imbedded in the system, and grand statements like 'Try harder! Get a computer [which a poor black kid likely can't afford in the first instance]! Get into a private school!' are offensive in their banality.".....So Mr. Marks, the next time you want to opine about life as a poor black kid, just stop. You know nothing of growing up black. You know nothing of growing up poor. You know nothing of the systemic problems in education that result in many black kids, poor or otherwise, being left behind. It's not a matter of just "trying super hard and really wanting to succeed." Your assumptions are faulty, and frankly, you sound like a jackass. A well-meaning jackass, perhaps, but a jackass all the same.

There are many internet postings and 'counterattacks' that are available but they are far less gracious than the one above!

A word of encouragement for those who choose to be a 'voice', to serve and to 'make a difference': successful ministry requires patience and perseverance especially in light of the inevitable 'obstacles' that arise in opposition to humanitarian progress. In Appendix G, *Rules of Life [aka 'Keys' of Life]* there is a rule/key called *Understand Process* which states that 'sometimes an event takes place that is difficult to understand and to deal with'-call this event a 'snapshot'. In reality it is the first 'snapshot' within a series of 'snapshots'. The subsequent series of 'snapshots', however, provides a more meaningful context in which to understand the 'process' that is taking place before your very eyes; but you only see a single 'snapshot' and you inevitably want to respond to that first snapshot [which is only one piece of the puzzle].

Obstacles are also unwanted 'snapshots' and are sometimes viewed as crises; but these perceived crises are also *potential opportunities for enhancing/ improving the ministry efforts*. For example, recall that in the early years of the ministry at St. Ann's, there was a unilateral clergy decision to reduce the St. John's Outreach budget of the church to zero. This decision was viewed by many parishioners as being harsh, entirely unwarranted, irrational and against the spiritual principles of the Episcopal Church not to mention the teachings and guidance of the New Testament. In effect, the message was that 'If Outreach wants to continue, and then they can only spend whatever they achieve via fund-raising.' This is the point where patience, perseverance and faith come into play; indeed, the Outreach team did not only raise enough funds to replace that amount usually earmarked in the annual budget but exceeded that amount by a factor of 400%. The ability to raise funds not only serves to highlight the validity and success of the ministry efforts at St. Ann's since 2001 but the generosity and commitment of the parishioners.

Remember the Forbes article by Gary Marks in December, 2011? That article is a classic example of 'noise' and distraction by an uninformed individual who, at first glance, really contributes to the problem and not the solution. However, his article, albeit irrelevant, did actually provide the opportunity for others to respond in a more meaningful and factual manner. These responses, then, were part of that much-needed chorus of 'voices' of advocacy and support for children disadvantaged. So the 'crisis' of his absurd article is the first 'snapshot' of a process that provided numerous positive responses that far outweighed that single 'snapshot'.

Then there is another example of 'noise' and distraction, this time from a well meaning-although misinformed and, therefore, misguided-clergy. The St. John's Outreach ministry had enjoyed an unparalleled resurgence of interest, participation and commitment to this ministry during the mission trip to St. Ann's in the spring of 2011. Planning was in process for a 2012 trip to join St. Ann's in celebrating the life of Dr. Martin Luther King, Jr. on the holiday in his honor as was done in 2011. The new rector of St. John's became alarmed at our methods. St. John's had by this time had been through seven rectors and the team, out of necessity, was in the necessary habit of operating without consistent clergy advocacy or leadership but always with its own sense of responsibility and direction. This new rector, probably feeling somewhat like a commander finding that his troops were initiating missions without his knowledge or authority, called some members of the mission team together. The team members received an email inviting them to a meeting without any warning, explanation or preparation or even an agenda. The meeting was opened with prayer and the good Reverend expressed his thoughts that began with "All ministries run their course........" What an interesting and surprising opening for a ministry that had enjoyed a continuing and growing success with unprecedented parish-wide support for more than a decade. What a discouraging 'snapshot' for a ministry that [1] had been uniquely successful for more than a decade, [2] had made significant-even dramatic-differences in the lives of so many who served as well as those being served and [3] had received national recognition and exposure thereby being a catalyst for additional ministries. To make a long story short, it became immediately evident that the Outreach ministry at St. Ann's was in danger of being curtailed or even eliminated for reasons that were puzzling, blatantly erroneous, unknown and well beyond the borders of reality and reason. This 'snapshot' had all the earmarks of a crisis and a disaster for the community at St. Ann's in the South Bronx and that of St. John's in Barrington. One Outreach member then provided a very moving, gentle and spiritual rebuttal about the life-changing impact of the ministry upon so many lives both at St. Ann's and at St. John's. Following this eloquent rebuttal, it became extraordinarily obvious for the real and rational world that the topic of this ministry having run its course should have been put aside and the meeting adjourned. It was now time for 'process' to take place: there was additional comments and dissertations provided by other Outreach members supporting the continuity of the ministry. The 'snapshot' of canceling the ministry efforts at St. Ann's soon faded-as it should have-and plans for an additional mission trip on the MLK weekend were resumed. I am sure that the mission trip will be as successful as those of the past; interestingly enough, the good Reverend will finally be making his initial trip to St. Ann's after his litany of inexplicable excuses for not making his initial 'journey to St. Ann's'! It was a time to put fear aside and place our faith in *Amazing Grace*!

As a post-trip note, it is reassuring and interesting to note that the MLK weekend trip, like all that had come before, was successful and even inspirational for a follow-up trip now being planned for the spring of 2012. ***Most importantly, this last trip provided a unique and very timely opportunity for Mother Martha to accurately and spiritually describe the on-going collaborative ministry by the St. Ann's and St. John's communities. She chose the Church service of 1/15/2012, attended by members of both communities, to provide this description in the form of her sermon.*** [Her sermon is included in its entirety in ***Reflections from St. Ann's***]. Her sermon is probably the most appropriate response to the doubters, naysayers, inhibitors and those who are 'not in the arena'! Not only the arena of the South Bronx but everywhere!

In the mind of the author, the thoughts were something like *"Perhaps, just perhaps, following his initial mission trip, this rector's mislead feelings of resistance and thoughts of shutting down the ministry at St. Ann's were undergoing a transformation of an individual discovering where his people were headed so that he could lead them there!" And just perhaps, he may have discovered 'why' so many parishioners have been making that trip for nearly a decade.* Could this be just another coincidence in the growing litany of ministry coincidences? His transformation continues! Only time will tell!

It seems to be a mystery of sorts as to the reason for placing denials, delays and obstacles along the roads of ministry; especially inexplicable and even bewildering when it occurs in the paths of those ministries that are uniquely successful in terms of making a difference in the lives of many! Could it be fear, envy, arrogance, insecurity, territorial imperatives, a need for 'control', lack of faith, lack of trust in those who are very capable within the ministry or any number of intangible entities-any of which are really symptoms of a greater malaise? Hmmmm! Could these symptoms just be another form of blindness to humanity?

Most authors-including yours truly-struggle with their books' closing statement; it is usually a search for a powerful, profound, earth-shaking or prophetic statement. Mine is quite simple: "Having said what has been written, I wonder if the future will be characterized by a 'business as usual' mindset [and heartset].... or..... will ***Amazing Grace*** 'show us the way home? Having had the experience of the collaborative ministry at St. Ann', like so many others, I emphatically have faith in the latter!

Acknowledgements

When it comes to acknowledging the spectrum of contributions made by individuals there is always the inevitable risk of unintentionally omitting individuals who should have been included. One obvious option is to include a sweeping [albeit convenient] acknowledgement, e.g., "Thanks to all those who made this book possible!"; this option is just neither acceptable nor appropriate for this book for several reasons. First, it is not consistent with one of the goals of this book, i.e., to provide a reference point for outreach ministry for 'those who follow'. A list of contributors [albeit *almost complete*] would allow them to provide a reference point for their involvement for future generations. It would be an opportunity and natural entry point to address and explore ministry efforts, outreach and community service; one could say "I was part of that outreach team at St. John's!", "I was there!", "I helped make a difference!" or "You can also make a difference in someone's life!" Secondly, this option would preclude a view of the magnitude of participation by the families and friends of the St. John's community; on the contrary a list of acknowledgements may just provide a model for the possibility of a greater participation in ministry, outreach and community service.

The preferred option is to make every attempt to include all those individuals who have contributed in some way to the genesis, development and continuing success of St. John's ministry efforts at St. Ann's; each and every contribution has had a role in the success of this ministry with respect to *having made a difference*. It is recognized that there will be the inevitable omissions but those who did and do serve do so because their faith has guided them to serve because it was the right thing to do and not for the recognition. There were so many: those who made the 'journey to

St. Ann's', the drivers, those who made their vans and SUVs available for transportation, those who opened their homes and lives to the children from St. Ann's, those who donated food, clothes, toys, games, books, computers, backpacks, a ton of school supplies, composition notebooks, those who provided food and cookies for the many trips to the South Bronx, those who wrote letters and Christmas cards over the years, those who raised this ministry in prayer, etc. In their hearts, minds and spirit, there will always reside the knowledge that they were part of the team and there is great peace in that knowledge. Their individual roles, knowledge and peace are simply priceless!

Having said that the acknowledgements follow:

Reverend Darryl Stahl for his enabling gifts; those many voices and authors who provided the inspiration, impetus and foundation for *the* genesis *of the Outreach ministry;* Reverend Shirley Andrews for bringing *Amazing Grace* to the attention of the parishioners of St. John; Hana Andersen-Earley; Kim Anderson; Noreen Andreoli; Jean Audette; Curtis Barton; Paul Barroso; Ann Beekley; Shirley Berriman-Rutter; Felice Billups; Becky [Gettel] Binns. Youth Director; Mars and Prudence Bishop; Adrian Boney; Ali Bulman; Julie Cardente; Reverend Susan Carpenter; Donna Casanova; Zin Chiulli; Lyn, Brendan and Carolyn Cleary; Mike Coken; Marion Colella; Gus Colella; Linda Colella; Matt Collins; Sandy Connor; Brian Cooper; Cassidy Costa; Tammy Costa; Carol Cushman; Liz, Adam and Bethany Crawley; Addie Crenson; Monica and Rick Daniels; Rik and Kelly Deering; Robin and Davis Dewey; Martha Donovan; Tom Duarte; Pat Dubois; Michelle and Gary Dupont; ECC staff over the years; ECW; Pam and Bob Faulkner; Emily Faxon; Leslie, Meredith and Mckenzie Ferland; Martha Fish; Dee and Tom Fredericks; Betty Genetti; Sharah Gharib; Mary Glenn; 'Mar', Todd and Lindsay Glosson; Kim and Mia Goyette; Cliff Goldsborough; Liana and Larson Gunness; Liz Hallenbeck; Nick Hallenbeck; Timothy Hallenbeck; Martha and Porter Halyburton; Jeanne and Jere Hawkins; Susan Henthorne, ECC Director; Sloane Hetterick; Beth Holmes; Emma Holmes; Mary Hood; Lib Huston; Cindy Isherwood; Kate Isherwood; Denise, Mike and Alison Javery; Joanne, Joe, Ainsley, Joseph, Jr. and Patrick Judge; Peter Kanarian; Cheryl and Richard King; Steve Lippincott; Cindy Lomas; Jan, Bob, Erin and Chris Malcolm; Joyce and Carmine Marabello; Robert Marshall; John Martin, Headmaster, St. Andrews School; Dallas Mashburn; Laine Mashburn; Anne, Lou, Stephen, Elizabeth and Emily Massa; Kelly McCormick;

Dorothy and Sandy McCulloch; Eric McKnight, Youth Director; Tricia, David, Samantha, Emily and Christina Medeiros; Sheyna Medina; Rick Meers; Donna Neville; Sally and Doug Newton; Donna Nicholson; Mary, Anne, Catherine and Laura Nixon; Helen Oliver; Deryl Pace; Martha and Jim Peters; Greg Piper; Julia Piper; Marilyn and David Renner; Cam Roy; Kate Roy; Benjamin Rubin; Barbara Sage; Judy Schantz; Nancy and Richard Silva; Julia Soares; Travis Soares; Bonnie Soper; Audrey and Robert Sprague; Jeff Taber; Judy, Bob and Tristan Tavares; Ruthie Tavares and Family; Amy and Peter Tomasi; Jim Tracy; Nancy Tripp; Charlie Vanier, Jack Vanier; Sam Vetromile; Joan Warren; Stuart Weeman; Bobbi, Bob, Kevin, Gregg and Lisa Wexler; Kristyn Whitney; Oscar Wilkerson; Eli Zeltzer.

These are the individuals identified via memories, conversations, reflections, etc. as well as a thorough search and review of correspondence, emails, articles in local newspapers, journals and church bulletins. It is probably a conservative list because for every individual included there is more than likely an individual not included.

Finally, I would be gravely remiss in my responsibility if two 'group acknowledgements' were omitted; without question, the entire St. John's parish provided an abundance of advocacy, support and for 'stepping up to the plate' again and again and again........! Those deserving an equal measure of appreciation and acknowledgement are the parishioners of St. Ann's who provided that much-needed guidance and advice in the South Bronx environment and who also became our comrades-in-arms.

Appendix A
William Wilberforce

There has been much written about this historical and pivotal individual and his consistent and effective efforts as an abolitionist. One could develop a career addressed to the study, analysis and assessment of this wealth of literature. However, I have selected a single reference for relevance and paraphrasing, i.e., [http://en.wikipedia.org/wiki/William_Wilberforce]; this comprehensive, information-laden and stand-alone document, in my opinion, essentially captures the spirit and content of the available literature. This particular reference, however, contains 248 supportive 'notes' to documents whose dates of origin range from 1817 to 2007 and 22 bibliographic references that span the years from 1807 to 1980. It's interesting that the referenced 'notes' enjoyed a flurry of activity in the first decade of the 21st century; this seems to indicate a renewed interest in slave trade related events and individuals.

William Wilberforce was born on August 24, 1759; he became active in the political arena at the young age of 21. Being a native of Kingston upon Hull, Yorkshire, he became the independent Member of Parliament for Yorkshire from 1784 to 1812. Parallel to his role as a Member of Parliament, he became an evangelical Christian following a conversion experience in 1785 in his second year in Parliament. Several years later in 1787 his political future was taking shape via his relationship with a group of anti-slave-trade activities, e.g., Hannah More, Charles Middleton and Granville Sharp. Their influence motivated William Wilberforce to become an activist for the abolition of slavery; presumably, based upon Christian principles. Nearly three decades after his entry into Britain's political arena, he facilitated the parliamentary campaign to abolish the British slave trade; through his efforts and leadership, the Slave Trade Act became a reality in 1807.

It's quite relevant to note that the seeds for the abolition for slavery in America were really planted in England and planted by William Wilberforce et al.

He believed in the integration of religion, morality and education into the British mainstream. Although the Slave Trade Act was passed in 1807, he continued the struggle to completely outlaw slavery; his efforts continued through 1826 until his failing health necessitated his resignation from Parliament. His efforts paved the way for the Slavery Abolition Act of 1833 which abolished slavery throughout most of the British Empire. William Wilberforce passed away on July 29, 1833 just a few days after this Act received official passage through Parliament.

Although born into a traditional and supportive family and school environment, he was sent to live with an uncle and aunt after the death of his father in 1768. This residency also introduced Wilberforce to evangelical Christianity at an early age. He was brought back to live with his mother and grandfather in 1771 because of their perceived threat of the nonconformist ways of evangelicalism. Wilberforce wasn't too pleased with this move and moved into the social arena as his religious interest faded. In October 1776, he went to St. John's College in Cambridge where he continued his social wanderings and experiences until being awarded the B.A. in 1781. It was at St. John's College where he met William Pitt [eventually, the Prime Minister in 1783] who befriended Wilberforce and encouraged him to take a Parliament seat. He was elected a Member of Parliament in 1780 and, because of his financial resources, assumed a position as an independent man. In the 1784 General Election, he returned to Parliament as the MP for Yorkshire. A direct quote from the central reference for William Wilberforce accurately captures the story of his conversion and self-enlightenment: *'Wilberforce's spiritual journey is thought to have begun [in 1784]. He started to rise early to read the Bible and pray and kept a private journal. He underwent an evangelical conversion, regretting his past life and resolving to commit his future life and work to the service of God. His conversion changed some of his habits but not his nature: he remained outwardly cheerful, interested, and respectful, tactfully urging others toward his new faith. Inwardly, he underwent an agonizing struggle and became relentlessly self-critical, harshly judging his spirituality, use of time, vanity, self-control, and relationships with others.'*

Not unexpectedly then nor in contemporary times, his religious enthusiasm was seen as contrary to the established social mores. As an early advocate and practitioner of 'thinking outside the box', Wilberforce- and others like him-were viewed as 'radicals' and became targets of doubt and ridicule. With support and advocacy from friends, including William Pitt, he chose to remain in the political arena.

Britain was an active and dominant participant in the slave trade since the 16th century; the growing economy of the slave trade has been addressed earlier in this book. It is sufficient to say that [1] the triad of slave trade economics represented 80% of Great Britain's foreign income and [2] an estimated 11 million Africans were transported into slavery and about 1.4 million of those died horrible deaths during the trans-Atlantic crossing.

Within the context of this book, it's important to note that there were other 'voices' during the years of the slave trade beside that of William Wilberforce. For example, the Rev. James Ramsay, a ship's surgeon and clergyman, and an acquaintance of Wilberforce, wrote *an essay on the treatment and conversion of African slaves in the British colonies*; this essay was exceptionally critical of the horrendous treatment of slaves. Another early 'voice' was that of Thomas Clarkson who was a fellow graduate of St. John's College; he, too, was convinced that the abolition of slavery was a necessary journey. It was Thomas Clarkson who provided Wilberforce with accurate information and evidence of the slave trade malaise. Clarkson convinced Wilberforce to advocate for the abolition of slavery in the House of Commons. There was a series of meetings and conversations to develop support for such an effort but it was a conversation with William Pitt and the future Prime Minister William Grenville that in 1787 that was the pivotal turning point for Wilberforce's commitment to action. His reason and rationale for involvement in the abolition tide was based upon his increasingly less dormant need to put his Christian faith into action and to serve God. One of Wilberforce's 1787 journal entries was entitled '*God Almighty has set before me two great objects, the suppression of the Slave Trade and the Reformation of manners [moral values]'*.

The strategy for success focused upon the condemnation of the Slave Trade but not slavery, per se; their belief was that the abolition of slavery would be an inevitable consequence of the abolition of the Slave Trade.

There was a steadily growing awareness both within the public, private and political arenas that the final days of the Slave Trade, and, perhaps, slavery itself, were numbered. The abolition team included William Wilberforce, William Pitt, Thomas Clarkson and others. The political arena-then and now-is a complex and convoluted process that consumes enormous amounts of time and inevitably results in angers, frustrations, disappointments and challenges. Wilberforce introduced the first parliamentary bill to abolish the Slave trade in 1791. Recalling the 'blindness to humanity' theme put forth earlier in this book, one can only view the claims by pro-slavery advocates that enslaved Africans were lesser human beings who benefited from their bondage as being misinformed and misguided-tragically so!

In 1792, Wilberforce brought a bill calling for the abolition of the Slave Trade but was confronted with a compromise arrangement for a dubious 'gradual abolition'. Such a compromise was a typical political strategy to simply slow down the abolition movement to a point of ineffectiveness, at best, and perhaps to an indefinite delay. In 1793, another vote to abolish the Slave Trade failed passage by only eight votes. In 1793 and 1794, Wilberforce sponsored parliamentary bills to outlaw British ships from transporting slaves to foreign colonies. Both bills were unsuccessful!

There were other events, e.g., as the French Revolution, that eroded the public consciousness and support for the abolition movement. However, Wilberforce continued to bring forth parliamentary bills for abolition during the 1790s. As the turn of the century took place, there was a growing public interest in abolition. In 1804, Wilberforce's bill to abolish the Slave Trade passed through the House of Commons but not the House of Lords because of insufficient time. His persistence and perseverance were admirable and remarkable through this political process; in 1805, he introduced the bill once again but it was defeated. A reminder that this early version of the 'lack of political will' carried the day-***then and now***

In 1806, Wilberforce authored *A Letter on the Abolition of the Slave Trade* which provided a comprehensive restatement of the case for abolition; in reality, his 'letter' was a 400-page book which set the stage for the forthcoming final campaign. Lord Grenville, advocate for abolition and now the Prime Minister, decided to introduce the bill in the House of Lords where it had not previously had a successful passage and then to the House of Commons. The Abolition Bill received a successful passage by a large margin and then, on February 23, 1807, the bill was passed in the House of Commons by an overwhelming 283 to 16 vote. The long but successful journey was completed and still stands as a model for *political will.*

The Wikipedia reference provides additional insight into political and social reform, evangelical Christianity, moral reform, the emancipation of enslaved Africans and the last years, funeral and legacy of William Wilberforce. The text of the emancipation of enslaved Africans raises two points: [1] the British determination to enforce the Slave Trade Act following its passage in the House of Lords and the House of Commons and the subsequent Royal Assent in March of 1807 and [2] the United States mirrored the abolition efforts of Britain by abolishing the slave trade in 1808 [*55 years prior to Lincoln's Emancipation Proclamation*]. However, Wilberforce lobbied/prodded the American government to also mirror Britain's enforcement of the slave trade prohibition. The prohibition of the slave trade was clearly a pre-requisite for the abolition of slavery, per se.

Appendix B

Moynihan's Message

Source: Providence Journal [June 27, 2010]
Title: *Moynihan's Message*
Author: Paul Davis, Journal Staff Writer

PROVIDENCE. – Forty-five years ago, Daniel Patrick Moynihan shook the nation with a government report that painted a bleak portrait of lower-class black life in America.

Called "The Negro Family: The Case for National Action", it urged the government to go beyond recent civil rights legislation and provide blacks with the same opportunities as whites.

President Lyndon Johnson drew on Moynihan's report for a 1965 speech. In it, Johnson called for more jobs, health care, education and social programs for struggling blacks.

It was considered one of the most far-reaching civil rights agendas in U.S. history.

It never happened.

James T. Patterson, a professor emeritus at Brown University, explains why in his fascinating new book, "Freedom Is Not Enough: The Moynihan Report and America's Struggle over Black Family life from LBJ to Obama."

Patterson spends a chapter looking at Moynihan's past, but the book is not a biography. Instead, the acclaimed historian, who lives on Providence's East side, examines the impact of his report on the civil rights movement and race relations in American politics.

Moynihan, who served with four presidents before becoming a U.S. senator in 1976, was not a typical politician, says Patterson.

He grew up, in part, in Depression-era New York City and worked on the docks and shined shoes in Times Square. His father, an alcoholic and gambler, abandoned the family when Moynihan was 10. The fact that he grew up without a father helped him identify with families living through hard times, Patterson says.

(Moynihan, who sometimes exaggerated his family privation, also went to Tufts University, Harvard and the London School of Economics and Political Science, where he developed a taste for fine cheeses, wines and well-cut clothes.)

As LBJ's assistant secretary of labor, Moynihan was convinced that the government had to act quickly to combat years of racism and other ills harming black Americans.

His timing was good.

A wave of optimism swept America in 1965. In stark contrast to today's political gridlock, Johnson and a sympathetic Congress passed far-reaching measures, including the Elementary and Secondary Education Act, clean air and water acts, immigration reform, the creation of the national Endowment for the Arts and more money for the war on Poverty.

Johnson, who would later proclaim, "These are the most hopeful times since Christ was born," asked Moynihan to help him write a speech for a June 4, 1965, commencement ceremony at Howard University. In it, he outlined a bold new plan. Congress had enacted the civil Rights Act of 1964, but it was not enough.

"You do not wipe away the scars of centuries by saying: Now you are free to go where you want, do as you desire, and choose the leaders you want." Johnson said. It was unfair to think blacks would enjoy the same privileges and prosperity as their white counterparts because of new laws, he said.

Eager to take charge of the civil rights movement, Johnson promised to improve black employment, health care, housing, education and social programs to help black families stay together.

It was an essentially "an affirmative action notion," says Patterson.

Soon after, however, Johnson stepped up U.S. involvement in Vietnam "and alienated many in the liberal coalition," says Patterson.

Then, in August, blacks – frustrated by a lack of jobs – rioted in los Angeles and other cities.

The nation recoiled from the violence. Blacks, who burned more than 600 buildings in Watts, "lost the high ground," says Patterson. They were no longer the Christ-like sufferers of the non-violence movement. "They were also angry, nasty looters."

The civil rights movement splintered, and militant blacks stopped working with whites. "They wanted to control their own movement," says Patterson. Against this backdrop, the message of Moynihan's report, leaked to the public, was distorted and misinterpreted, he says.

"Then along comes this white Irish guy" who offers a "very negative report on the black family. It made it seem as if it was a festering problem," although many of Moynihan's ideas came from other scholars. Some charged Moynihan – who focused on out-of-wedlock births and fatherless families – with racism. Moynihan blamed the victim, his critics said. Others called his report overly simplistic.

"People started savaging him," says Patterson. "Blacks closed ranks against the report, and argued that the only thing wrong with black families was white racism."

During the summer and fall of 1965, a pivotal time in modern U.S. political history, the exuberant liberal mood of the nation dissipated.

"Johnson," Patterson says, "consigned the report to oblivion."

Patterson, who taught at Brown for 30 years before retiring in 2002, won the Bancroft Prize for his sweeping history, "Grand Expectations: The United States, 1945-1974." Patterson also authored "Restless Giant: The United States from Watergate to 9/11."

Other books have focused more narrowly on topics and events, including "Brown v. Board of Education: A Civil Rights Milestone and Its troubled legacy," and "America's Struggle Against Poverty in the Twentieth Century."

A former reporter for the Hartford courant, the 78-year old historian became interested in Moynihan while working on other books. "His name came up and it was always in the back of my mind. I wanted to know more about this man."

Patterson says he admires Moynihan for raising the issue. "He did not say, 'This is what we must do.' He didn't really know what the government should do, but he knew we had to do something."

Many of Moynihan's concerns remain.

In 2004, Bill Cosby raised the issue of out-of-wedlock births and single-parent households at an NAACP conference in Washington.

As Patterson notes in his book, president Obama – who grew up in a fatherless house – has called for a number of educational reforms that could help poor black families. Obama favors an expensive program that has helped poor students earn good grades in Harlem.

But so far, the president has been preoccupied with other concerns, he says, including the ailing economy, health care reform, wars in Iraq and Afghanistan, ongoing terrorist threats and the Middle East.

"Coping with the distress of black families in the ghettos – as ever a complicated matter to address – continues to be a relatively low priority among politicians." He writes in "Freedom Is Not Enough."

But something must be done, he says. If not, he said in a recent New York Times editorial, the "tangle of pathology" described by Moynihan in 1965 – now much worse – will be impossible to unravel, and America will become "more deeply divided than ever along class and racial lines."

Appendix C

Amazing Grace

Source: http://www.texasfasola.org/biographies/johnnewton [This internet article was reprinted from the July-August 1996 issue of *Away Here in Texas*]
Title: Amazing Grace: The Story of John Newton
Author: Al Rogers

"Amazing grace, how sweet the sound..." So begins one of the most beloved hymns of all times, a staple in the hymnals of many denominations, *New Britain* or "45 on the top" in Sacred Harp. The author of the words was John Newton, the self-proclaimed wretch who once was lost but then was found, saved by amazing grace.

Newton was born in London July 24, 1725, the son of a commander of a merchant ship which sailed the Mediterranean. When John was eleven, he went to sea with his father and made six voyages with him before the elder Newton retired. In 1744 John was impressed into service on a man-of-war, the H.M.S. Harwich. Finding conditions on board intolerable, he deserted but was soon recaptured and publicly flogged and demoted from midshipman to common seaman.

Finally at his own request he was exchanged into service on a slave ship, which took him to the coast of Sierra Leone. He then became the servant of a slave trader and was brutally abused. Early in 1748 he was rescued by a sea captain who had known John's father. John Newton ultimately became captain of his own ship, one which plied the slave trade.

Although he had had some early religious instruction from his mother, who had died when he was a child, he had long since given up any religious convictions. However, on a homeward voyage, while he was attempting to steer the ship through a violent storm, he experienced what he was to refer to later as his "great deliverance." He recorded in his journal that when all seemed lost and the ship would surely sink, he exclaimed, "Lord, have mercy upon us." Later in his cabin he reflected on what he had said and began to believe that God had addressed him through the storm and that grace had begun to work for him.

For the rest of his life he observed the anniversary of May 10, 1748 as the day of his conversion, a day of humiliation in which he subjected his will to a higher power. "Thro' many dangers, toils and snares, I have already come; 'tis grace has broth me safe thus far, and grace will lead me home." He continued in the slave trade for a time after his conversion; however, he saw to it that the slaves under his care were treated humanely.

In 1750 he married Mary Catlett, with whom he had been in love for many rears. By 1755, after a serious illness, he had given up seafaring forever. During his days as a sailor he had begun to educate himself, teaching himself Latin, among other subjects. From 1755 to 1760 Newton was a surveyor of tides at Liverpool, where he became known to George Whitefield, deacon in the Church of England, evangelistic preacher, and leader of the Calvinistic Methodist Church. Newton became Whitefield's enthusiastic disciple. During this period Newton also met and came to admire John Wesley, founder of Methodism. Newton's self-education continued and he learned Greek and Hebrew.

He decided to become a minister and applied to the Archbishop of York for ordination. The Archbishop refused his request, But Newton persisted in his goal, and he was subsequently ordained by the Bishop of Lincoln and accepted the curacy of Olney, Buckinghamshire. Newton's church became so crowded during services that it had to be enlarged. He preached not only in Olney but in other parts of the country. In 1767 the poet William Cowper settled at Olney, and he and Newton became friends.

Among Newton's contributions which are still loved and sung today are *"How Sweet the Name of Jesus Sounds"* and "Glorious Things of Thee Are Spoken" as well as *Amazing Grace."* Composed probably between 1760 and 1770 in Olney, *"Amazing Grace"* was probably one of the hymns written for a weekly service. Through the years other writers have composed additional verses to the hymn which came to be known as *"Amazing Grace"* (it was thus entitled in *Olney Hymns*), and possibly verses from other Newton hymns have been added. However, these are the six stanzas that appeared, with minor spelling variations, in both the first edition in 1779 and the 1808 edition, the one nearest the date of Newton's death. It appeared under the heading of *Faith's Review and Expectations* along with a reference to First Chronicles, chapter 17, verses 16 and 17.

Amazing Grace! (how sweet the sound)
That sav'd a wretch like me!
I once was lost, but now am found,
Was blind, but now I see.

'Twas grace that taught my heart to fear,
And grace my fears reliev'd;
How precious did that grace appear,
The hour I first believ'd!

Thro' many dangers, toils and snares,
I have already come;
'Tis grace has brought me safe thus far,
And grace will lead me home.
The Lord has promis'd good to me,
His word my hope secures;
He will my shield and portion be,
As long as life endures.

Yes, when this flesh and heart shall fail,
And mortal life shall cease;
I shall possess, within the veil,
A life of joy and peace.

The earth shall soon dissolve like snow,
The sun forbear to shine;
But God who call'd me here below,
Will be forever mine.

I can provide two footnotes to this appendix: [1] As set forth in Appendix A, William Wilberforce had also embarked on his own spiritual journey in an evangelical conversion quite similar to Newton's. Wilberforce, along with his friend and political colleague, Prime Minister William Pitt, and guidance and mentoring from John Newton, decided to remain in the political arena. This decision eventually led Wilberforce to the cause of humanitarian reform and the advocacy for the abolition of slavery in England. [2] A reference, and meaningful commentary, on the historical context is the movie, *Amazing Grace*.

Appendix D
Rhode Island Kids Count

The documentation provided by Rhode Island KIDS COUNT is [1] meaningful and relevant in substance and content, [2] absolutely comprehensive in its integration of the many factors from multiple sources, [3] totally relevant to the overall well-being of children, [4] presented in clear and concise fashion both in text and graphics and [5] complete with references that ensure its factual credibility. *One observation by this author is that, collectively, these documents provide 'linkages' amongst the many factors from multiple sources. These 'linkages' provide a foundation for the child advocate to envision the 'bigger picture' about the overall status and well-being of the children of Rhode Island.* A visit to its website, <u>www.rikidscount.org</u>, will reflect these comments and a review of the available literature from **Rhode Island Kids Count** will provide an abundance of confirmation for these comments. It borders on irresponsibility for any child advocate to forego this unique opportunity.

I have selected three documents as representative of the entirety of the available documentation.

2012 Rhode Island Kids Count Factbook

This annual publication is 'an important tool for planning <u>*and*</u> action by community leaders, policy makers, [child] advocates, [educational professionals] and others working toward changes that will improve the wholeness, quality of life and success for all children. This document provides a quantitative foundation for analysis and assessment; it provides a meaningful statistical portrait of the multi-faceted status of Rhode Island's children. It pays particular attention to four core cities in which the highest percentage of children are living in poverty. The multi-faceted status of children becomes self-evident with the focus upon sixty-seven indicators in those five areas that affect the lives of children: Family and Community, Economic Well-Being, Health, Safety and Education. Each of these five areas is made up of indicators [7, 10, 16, 12 and 22, respectively] with definitive text, data and graphics. The relevance of each indicator is clearly established via a *definition* and *significance.*This user-friendly documentation enjoys additional clarity with the readers' review of the *methodology* employed and the *references* [pp. 158-175].

The following ten pages provide excerpts directly from the **2012 Rhode Island Kids Count Factbook**:

- Table of Contents [p. 3]
- Children in Poverty [pp. 36, 37]
- 4th Grade Reader Skills [pp. 136, 137]
- All Indicators, www.RhodeKIDSCOUNT, Data-Indicators
- Compilation of Child Care and Early Learning Indicators
- Compilation of Educational Indicator

Table of Contents

DEFINITION

Children in poverty is the percentage of children under age 18 who are living in households with incomes below the poverty threshold, as defined by the U.S. Census Bureau. Poverty is determined based on income received during the year prior to the Census.

SIGNIFICANCE

Poverty is related to every KIDS COUNT indicator. Children in poverty, especially those who experience poverty in early childhood and for extended periods, are more likely to have health and behavioral problems, difficulty in school, become teen parents and earn less or be unemployed as adults.[1,2] Children in poverty are less likely to be enrolled in a preschool, more likely to attend schools that lack resources and rigor, and have fewer opportunities to participate in extracurricular activities.[3,4,5]

Nationally and in Rhode Island, minority children are more likely to grow up poor than White children. Children under age six, who have single parents, whose parents have low educational levels, or whose parents work part-time or are unemployed are at increased risk of living in poverty.[6]

In 2011, the federal poverty threshold was $18,123 for a family of three with two children and $22,811 for a family of four with two children.[7] The official

poverty measure does not reflect the effects of key government policies and programs that support families living in poverty, does not take into account variations in the cost of transportation, child care, housing and medical care, and does not consider geographic variations in the cost of living. To address these limitations, in 2011, the U.S. Census Bureau began releasing a Supplemental Poverty Measure. This measure does not replace the official measure, but will provide policy makers with a new way to evaluate the effects of anti-poverty policies.[10]

According to the *2010 Rhode Island Standard of Need*, a single-parent family with two children would need $48,576 a year to meet its basic needs, far short of the federal poverty level for a family of three. Work supports, such as subsidized child care, health care (RIte Care), food assistance and tax credits, can help families with incomes below the federal poverty threshold meet their basic needs.[11]

Children in Poverty

	2007	2008	2009	2010
RI	17.5%	15.5%	16.9%	19.0%
US*	18.0%	18.2%	20.0%	21.6%
National Rank*				22nd
New England Rank**				6th

*1st is best; 50th is worst
**1st is best; 6th is worst

Source: U.S. Census Bureau, American Community Survey, 2007-2010, Table R1704.

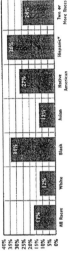

Children in Poverty, by Race and Ethnicity, Rhode Island, 2008-2010

*Source: U.S. Census Bureau, American Community Survey, 2008-2010, Tables B17001, B17001, B17020A, B17020B, B17020C, B17020D, B17020G and B17020L. *Hispanic children may be included in any race category.*

◆ Between 2008 and 2010, 17.4% (38,733) of Rhode Island's 223,170 children under age 18 with known poverty status lived in households with incomes below the federal poverty threshold.[12]

◆ In Rhode Island as well as in the United States as a whole, Hispanic, Black and Native American children are more likely than White and Asian children to live in families with incomes below the federal poverty threshold. Between 2008 and 2010, 36% of Hispanic, 34% of Black and 27% of Native American children in Rhode Island lived in poverty, compared to 12% of Asian children and 12% of White children.[13]

◆ While Native American and Black children in Rhode Island are more likely to experience poverty than White children, children from these groups represent less than one-fifth (17%) of all children living in poverty in Rhode Island. Between 2008 and 2010, of all children living in poverty in Rhode Island, half (50%) were White, 16% were Black, 2% were Asian, 1% were Native American, 24% were Some other race and 7% were Two or more races.[14]

◆ Between 2008 and 2010, 41% of Rhode Island's poor children were Hispanic. Hispanic children may be included in any race category. The Census Bureau asks about race separately from ethnicity, and the majority of families who identify as Some other race also identify as Hispanic.[15]

Children in Poverty

Child Poverty Concentrated in Four Core Cities, Rhode Island, 2006-2010

City/Town	Number in Poverty	Percentage in Poverty	Number in Extreme Poverty	Percentage in Extreme Poverty
Central Falls	1,975	35.8%	741	13.4%
Pawtucket	4,505	27.3%	1,703	10.3%
Providence	14,921	35.6%	7,054	16.8%
Woonsocket	3,581	34.9%	1,714	16.7%
Rhode Island	37,925	16.7%	16,711	7.4%

Source: Population Reference Bureau analysis of 2006-2010 American Community Survey data.

❖ Between 2006 and 2010, two-thirds (66%) of Rhode Island's children living in poverty lived in just four cities. These cities, termed core cities, include Central Falls, Pawtucket, Providence and Woonsocket, all communities where more than one in four (25%) children live below the poverty threshold. The four core cities also have substantial numbers of children living in extreme poverty, defined as families with incomes below 50% of the federal poverty threshold, $9,062 for a family of three with two children and $11,406 for a family of four with two children in 2011.[427]

Young Children Under Age Six in Poverty, Four Core Cities and Rhode Island, 2006-2010

City/Town	Number	Percentage
Central Falls	897	38.1%
Pawtucket	1,769	30.9%
Providence	5,022	35.4%
Woonsocket	1,408	35.7%
Rhode Island	12,915	18.5%

Source: Population Reference Bureau analysis of 2006-2010 American Community Survey data.

❖ Between 2006 and 2010, 18.5% (12,915) of Rhode Island children under age six lived below the poverty threshold.[428] Children under age six are at higher risk of living in poverty than any other age group.[429] Increased exposure to environmental toxins, exposure to risk factors associated with poverty, including inadequate nutrition, crowded and unstable housing, maternal depression, trauma and abuse, lower quality child care and parental substance abuse interferes with young children's emotional and intellectual development.[430][431]

Rhode Island's Poor Children, 2008-2010

By Age

33%	Ages 5 and Younger
31%	Ages 6 to 11
17%	Ages 12 to 14
19%	Ages 15 to 17

n = 38,733

By Race*

50%	White
16%	Black
2%	Asian
1%	Native American
24%	Some Other Race
7%	Two or More Races
<1%	Unknown

n = 38,733

Hispanic children may be included in any race category. Between 2008 and 2010, 15,688 (41%) of Rhode Island's 38,733 poor children were Hispanic.

By Family Structure

23%	Married Couple Family
6%	Unmarried Male Householder
68%	Unmarried Female Householder
3%	Not in Related-Family Households

n = 38,733

Source: U.S. Census Bureau, American Community Survey, 2008-2010. Tables B17001, B17006, B17020A, B17020B, B17020C, B17020D, B17020D, B17020F, B17020G & B17020H. Population includes children for whom poverty status was determined. Percentages may not sum to 100% due to rounding.

Fourth-Grade Reading Skills

DEFINITION

Fourth-grade reading skills is the percentage of fourth-grade students who scored at or above the proficiency level for reading on the *New England Common Assessment Program (NECAP)* test.

SIGNIFICANCE

Reading proficiency is fundamental to the development of academic competencies and basic life skills. Students with poor reading skills will experience difficulty completing academic coursework and graduating from high school and can experience difficulty finding and maintaining employment later in life.[1]

Literacy begins long before children encounter formal school instruction in writing and reading. Enhanced vocabulary, comprehension and cognitive development can be seen in children under three years of age who are read to daily.[2] Literacy-rich home environments (including reading and telling stories to children) contribute to advanced literacy development and reading achievement.[3]

Participation in high-quality preschool and Pre-K programs can boost language and literacy skills by providing early literacy experiences including storybook reading, discussions about books, dramatic play, listening comprehension and writing activities.[4] Children who participate in high-quality Pre-K score higher on reading test scores at the third and fifth grade levels and develop stronger cognitive skills.[5]

When students continue to have difficulty reading beyond third grade, they often need intensive interventions in order to read proficiently.[6] Once they fall behind, most children never catch up to their grade-level peers.[7]

Literacy development in the elementary grades can be enhanced through the prioritization of literacy development, early warning systems that identify students who are falling behind and provide intervention services as early as possible, individualized teaching strategies and materials designed to meet diverse student needs, high-quality teacher training and parent involvement.[8]

4th Grade NAEP Reading Proficiency

	2002	2011
RI	32%	35%
US	30%[a]	32%[a]
National Rank[*]		15th
New England Rank[**]		5th

[*]*1st is best; 50th is worst*
[**]*1st is best; 6th is worst*

Source: The Annie E. Casey Foundation, KIDS COUNT Data Center. datacenter.kidscount.org

The *National Assessment of Educational Progress (NAEP)* measures proficiency nationally and uses scores every other year.

Fourth-Grade NECAP Reading Proficiency Rates, by Income Status, Rhode Island, 2005-2011

Source: Rhode Island Department of Elementary and Secondary Education. *New England Common Assessment Program (NECAP)* October 2005–October 2011. Low-income status is determined by eligibility for the free or reduced-price lunch program.

◆ In October 2011, 71% of Rhode Island fourth graders scored at or above proficiency for reading on the *New England Common Assessment Program (NECAP)*, up from 60% in 2005.[9]

◆ In Rhode Island between 2005 and 2011, the percentage of higher-income fourth graders achieving at or above the proficient level on the *NECAP* was consistently higher than that of low-income fourth graders. In 2011, 56% of low-income fourth graders scored at or above the proficient level, compared with 83% of higher-income fourth graders.[10]

◆ In Rhode Island in 2011, 27% of fourth graders with disabilities achieved reading proficiency, compared with 77% of non-disabled fourth graders.[11]

◆ National data indicate a significant gap between the reading skills of English Language Learners and their native English-speaking peers.[12] On the October 2011 *NECAP*, 20% of Rhode Island's fourth grade English Language Learners scored at or above proficiency in reading, compared to 74% of non-ELL students.[13]

◆ Seventy-nine percent of White and 75% of Asian fourth graders in Rhode Island were proficient on the October 2011 *NECAP*, compared with 50% of Hispanic students, 57% of Black students, 54% of Native American and 65% of students of Two or more races.[14]

262

Fourth-Grade Reading Skills

Table 43.

Fourth-Grade Reading Proficiency, Rhode Island, 2005 & 2011

SCHOOL DISTRICT	COMMUNITY CONTEXT			OCTOBER 2005		OCTOBER 2011	
	% MOTHERS COMPLETING HIGH SCHOOL	% LOW INCOME STUDENTS	% ENGLISH LANGUAGE LEARNERS	# OF 4TH GRADE TEST TAKERS	% AT OR ABOVE THE PROFICIENCY LEVEL	# OF 4TH GRADE TEST TAKERS	% AT OR ABOVE THE PROFICIENCY LEVEL
Barrington	96%	6%	1%	248	89%	282	90%
Bristol Warren	89%	34%	3%	268	69%	249	74%
Burrillville	88%	33%	<1%	164	63%	208	73%
Central Falls	55%	86%	24%	253	40%	217	45%
Chariho	90%	19%	0%	269	73%	246	93%
Coventry	88%	29%	<1%	405	68%	388	86%
Cranston	86%	34%	5%	801	71%	861	73%
Cumberland	91%	23%	2%	410	74%	390	85%
East Greenwich	94%	6%	<1%	201	86%	165	92%
East Providence	84%	45%	6%	415	59%	391	65%
Exeter-West Greenwich	94%	13%	1%	162	74%	130	82%
Foster	88%	19%	0%	66	69%	44	82%
Glocester	91%	17%	0%	124	77%	104	73%
Jamestown	96%	7%	0%	42	83%	60	88%
Johnston	88%	36%	3%	276	58%	255	69%
Lincoln	89%	27%	1%	267	72%	236	79%
Little Compton	94%	15%	0%	37	73%	41	88%
Middletown	91%	27%	2%	195	68%	194	77%
Narragansett	90%	7%	<1%	122	81%	79	91%
New Shoreham	90%	9%	5%	14	100%	12	92%
Newport	81%	56%	3%	178	46%	153	58%
North Kingstown	90%	20%	1%	337	79%	340	83%
North Providence	87%	39%	2%	250	64%	254	72%
North Smithfield	92%	15%	1%	128	77%	137	83%
Pawtucket	72%	76%	13%	703	48%	671	60%
Portsmouth	95%	16%	<1%	236	75%	193	87%
Providence	64%	81%	17%	1,487	31%	1,804	46%
Scituate	93%	16%	0%	141	72%	116	82%
Smithfield	93%	13%	<1%	219	79%	181	89%
South Kingstown	91%	18%	1%	249	76%	236	90%
Tiverton	91%	24%	1%	354	77%	148	83%
Warwick	87%	31%	1%	853	71%	724	77%
West Warwick	81%	50%	2%	295	55%	253	74%
Westerly	90%	34%	2%	255	69%	198	82%
Woonsocket	69%	70%	7%	489	46%	450	59%
Charter Schools	*NA*	*66%*	*14%*	*159*	*43%*	*248*	*70%*
Four Core Cities	*65%*	*79%*	*15%*	*3,332*	*37%*	*3,142*	*51%*
Remainder of State	*88%*	*28%*	*2%*	*7,781*	*71%*	*7,268*	*79%*
Rhode Island	*79%*	*44%*	*6%*	*11,272*	*60%*	*10,658*	*71%*

Source of Data for Table/Methodology

Data are from the Rhode Island Department of Elementary and Secondary Education, *New England Common Assessment Program (NECAP)*, October 2005 and October 2011.

Due to the adoption of a new assessment tool by RIDE, *Fourth Grade Reading Skills* cannot be compared with Factbooks prior to 2007, when the *NECAP* data were first presented.

% at or above the proficiency level are the fourth grade students who received proficient or proficient with distinction scores on the reading section of the *NECAP*. Only students who actually took the test are counted in the denominator for the district and school proficiency rates. All enrolled students are eligible unless their Individualized Education Program (IEP) specifically exempts them or unless they are beginning English Language Learners.

% mothers completing high school is from the Rhode Island Department of Health, Center for Health Data and Analysis, Hospital Discharge Database. 2006-2010. Data for 2010 are provisional. Data are self-reported and reported by the mother's place of residence, not the place of the infant's birth. Between 2006 and 2010, maternal education levels were unknown for 3,280 births (6%).

% of low-income students is the percentage of students eligible for the free or reduced-price lunch program on October 1, 2011, from RIDE.

% ELL is the percentage of all public school children (including preschoolers) who are receiving ELL services or bilingual education services in Rhode Island public schools and is from RIDE for the 2011-2012 school year.

2011 *NECAP* data for independent charter schools include The Compass School, Highlander Charter School, International Charter School, Kingston Hill Academy, The Learning Community and Paul Cuffee Charter School. Charter schools are not included in the core city and remainder of state calculations. NA indicates that the school district does not serve students at that grade level or that the number of students is too small to report.

Core cities are Central Falls, Pawtucket, Providence and Woonsocket.

See Methodology Section for more information.

(continued on page 174)

Rhode Island KIDS COUNT: Data - Indicators

FAMILY AND COMMUNITY SECTION
- Child Population
- Children in Single Parent Families
- Grandparents Caring for Grandchildren
- Infants Born at Highest Risk
- Mother's Education Level
- Racial and Ethnic Disparities
- Racial and Ethnic Diversity

ECONOMIC WELL-BEING SECTION
- Children in Families Receiving Cash Assistance
- Children in Poverty
- Children Participating in School Breakfast
- Children Receiving Child Support
- Children Receiving SNAP Benefits
- Cost of Housing
- Homeless Children
- Median Family Income
- Secure Parental Employment
- Women and Children Receiving WIC

HEALTH SECTION
- Access to Dental Care
- Alcohol, Drug, and Cigarette Use by Teens
- Births to Teens
- Breastfeeding
- Childhood Immunizations
- Childhood Obesity
- Children with Asthma
- Children with Lead Poisoning
- Children with Special Needs
- Children's Health Insurance
- Children's Mental Health
- Housing and Health
- Infant Mortality
- Low Birthweight Infants
- Preterm Births
- Women with Delayed Prenatal Care

SAFETY SECTION
- Child Abuse and Neglect
- Child Deaths
- Children in Out-of-Home Placement
- Children of Incarcerated Parents
- Children Witnessing Domestic Violence
- Disconnected Youth
- Homeless Youth and Runaway Youth
- Juveniles at the Training School
- Juveniles Referred to Family Court
- Permanency for Children in DCYF Care
- Teen Deaths
- Youth Violence

EDUCATION SECTION
- Children Enrolled in Head Start
- Children Enrolled in Special Education
- Children Receiving Child Care Subsidies
- Chronic Early Absence
- College Preparation and Access
- Early Head Start
- Early Intervention
- Eighth-Grade Reading Skills
- English Language Learners
- Fourth-Grade Reading Skills
- Full-Day Kindergarten
- High School Graduation Rate
- Licensed Capacity of Early Learning Programs
- Math Skills
- Out-of-School Time
- Public School Enrollment and Demographics
- Quality Early Care and Education
- School Attendance
- Schools Making Insufficient Progress
- Student Mobility
- Suspensions
- Teens Not in School and Not Working

Summaries and Highlights
- Child Care and Early Learning Indicators
- Child Welfare Indicators
- Economic Well-Being Indicators
- Education Indicators
- Health Indicators
- Youth Indicators
- New England Rankings

Methodology, Committees and Acknowledgements

2012 Rhode Island Kids Count Factbook: Child Care and Early Learning Indicators

Licensed Early Learning Programs

- In December 2011, there were 309 licensed early learning centers (serving children from 6 weeks through age 5) in Rhode Island. Of these, 37 (12%) were participating in BrightStars, Rhode Island's Quality Rating and Improvement System for child care and early learning programs.

- In December 2011, there were 639 family child care homes licensed by DCYF in Rhode Island. Of these, 75 (12%) were participating in BrightStars, Rhode Island's Quality Rating and Improvement System for child care and early learning programs.

- In December 2011, there were 5,771 infant/toddler slots (ages 6 weeks to 3) and 13,056 preschool slots (ages 3 to 5) in licensed early learning centers in Rhode Island. There were 4,274 licensed slots in family child care homes (ages 6 weeks and up).

- In December 2011, there were 11,061 licensed school-age child care slots in Rhode Island.

Head Start and Early Head Start

- In October 2011, there were 519 children under age three and 16 pregnant women receiving Early Head Start services in Rhode Island.

- Rhode Island KIDS COUNT estimates that there are approximately 8,008 children income-eligible for Early Head Start in Rhode Island. Approximately 6.5% of the income-eligible population was receiving Early Head Start services in October 2011.

- In October 2011, there were 2,432 children ages 3-5 enrolled in Head Start in Rhode Island.

- Rhode Island KIDS COUNT estimates that there are 5,607 children income-eligible for Head Start in Rhode Island. In October 2011, approximately 43% of the income-eligible population of children was enrolled in Head Start.

Early Childhood Special Education

- During 2011, there were 3,883 children under age 3 who received Early Intervention services under *Part C* of the *Individuals with Disabilities Act (IDEA)* in Rhode Island. This is 11% of the population of children under age 3. Of these children, 77% were eligible because of a significant developmental delay, 16% due to a single established condition, and 7% due to multiple established conditions.

- During the 2010-2011 school year, there were 2,838 preschool students (age 3 to kindergarten entry) who received special education services under *Part B* of *IDEA* in Rhode Island. Of these children, 52% had a speech disorder, 37% had a developmental delay, 6% had an autism spectrum disorder and 4% had other disabilities.

2012 Rhode Island Kids Count Factbook:
Child Care and Early Learning Indicators

Children Receiving Child Care Subsidies

- ◆ In December 2011, there were 7,708 child care subsidies for children in Rhode Island, up slightly from 2010 but down from the peak of 14,333 in 2003.

- ◆ Of the 7,708 child care subsidies, 1,888 (24%) were for children under age three, 2,916 (38%) were for children ages three to five and 2,904 (38%) were for children ages six to twelve.

- ◆ In 2011 in Rhode Island, 72% of child care subsidies were for care in a licensed child care center, 27% were for care in a licensed family child care home and 1% were served by a non-licensed relative, friend or neighbor.

- ◆ In December 2011, 80% of all child care subsidies in Rhode Island were being used by low-income working families not receiving cash assistance and 13% were used by families enrolled in the Rhode Island Works program who were engaged in employment activities, and another 8% were used for children in the care of DCYF.

Child Care Subsidies, Rhode Island, 1996-2011

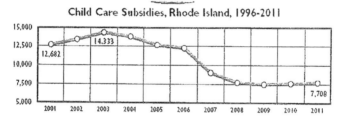

Source: Rhode Island Department of Human Services. December 2001 – December 2011.

Full-Day Kindergarten

- ◆ During the 2011-2012 school year, 64% of the children enrolled in public kindergarten in Rhode Island were in a full-day program.

- ◆ 86% of the public school kindergarten children in the four core cities attend full-day programs while 50% of the public school kindergarten children in the remainder of the state attend full-day programs.

2012 Rhode Island Kids Count Factbook:
Education Indicators

Public School Enrollment and Demographics

♦ On October 1, 2011, there were 142,854 students enrolled in Rhode Island public schools in grades pre-K through 12, a decrease of 9.7% from 158,218 on October 1, 2001.

♦ Almost one-third (29% or 40,986) of Rhode Island public school students on October 1, 2011 were attending schools in the four core cities (communities with the highest percentages of children living in poverty), 67% (96,414) were attending schools in the remaining districts and 4% (5,454) attended charter schools, state-operated schools or the Urban Collaborative Accelerated Program (UCAP).

♦ In October 2011, 64% of Rhode Island public school students were non-Hispanic White, 22% were Hispanic, 8% were Black, 3% were Asian/Pacific Islander and 1% were Native American.

♦ In October 2011, 44% of students in Rhode Island were low-income (students who qualified for the free or reduced-price lunch program).

Full-Day Kindergarten

♦ During the 2011-2012 school year, 64% of the children enrolled in public kindergarten in Rhode Island were in a full-day program (a kindergarten operating for at least 6 hours per day).

♦ Eighty-six percent of the public school kindergarten children in the four core cities attend full-day programs while 50% of the public school kindergarten children in the remainder of the state attend full-day programs. All of the independent charter schools in Rhode Island that offer kindergarten run full-day programs.

English Language Learner Students

♦ In the 2010-2011 school year, 6% (8,307) of students in Rhode Island public schools were receiving English as a Second Language or bilingual education services.

Students Receiving Special Education Services

♦ In the 2010-2011 school year, there were 25,652 students enrolled in special education in Rhode Island (not including parentally-placed students in private schools), making up 18% of the preschool-12 public school students in the state.

♦ In Rhode Island, students with disabilities achieve at lower levels than non-disabled students on the state assessments. In 2011, 45% of special education students in fourth grade were substantially below proficient in reading, compared to 7% of regular education students.

Student Mobility

♦ The overall school mobility rate for Rhode Island was 14% for the 2010-2011 school year. There was significant variation across school districts, from a high of 25% in Providence to a low of 3% in Barrington. The four core cities have a significantly higher mobility rate (23%) than districts in the remainder of the state (10%).

267

2012 Rhode Island Kids Count Factbook:
Education Indicators

School Mobility and Education Outcomes in Rhode Island,
2010-2011 School Year

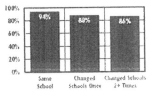
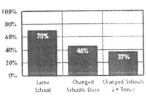

Source: Rhode Island Department of Elementary and Secondary Education, Data Warehouse, 2010-2011 school year

Reading Skills
♦ In 2011, 71% of Rhode Island 4th graders achieved proficiency in reading on the state assessment exam (NECAP), up from 60% in 2005. Although low-income students continue to have lower reading proficiency rates than higher-income students (56% versus 83%), the reading proficiency rate among low-income students has improved from 40% to 56% from 2005 to 2011.

♦ In 2011, 77% of Rhode Island 8th graders achieved proficiency in reading on the state assessment exam (NECAP), up from 56% in 2005.

Math Skills
♦ In 2011, 65% of Rhode Island 4th graders achieved proficiency in math on the state assessment exam (NECAP), up from 52% in 2005. In Rhode Island in 2011, 49% of low-income 4th grade students were proficient in math compared to 78% of higher-income 4th grade students.

♦ In 2011, 58% of Rhode Island 8th graders achieved proficiency in math on the state assessment exam. Forty-one percent of low-income 8th grade students were proficient in math compared to 72% of higher-income 8th grade students.

Schools Making Insufficient Progress
♦ In 2011, 41 schools in Rhode Island were classified as making insufficient progress under *No Child Left Behind*, making up 14% of schools in the state. Thirty-four percent of schools in the four core cities received this classification, compared with 6% in the remainder of the state.

Chronic Early Absence
♦ During the 2010-2011 school year, about one in eight (12%) Rhode Island students in kindergarten through 3rd grade were chronically absent (i.e., missed at least 10% of the school year or more, including excused and unexcused absences.) More than a quarter (26%) of kindergarten through 3rd graders missed 12 or more school days during the 2010-2011 school year.

Getting Ready [Findings from the National School Readiness Indicators Initiative, A 17 state Partnership, February 2005]

Two of the opening statements in this document are: 'The first five years of life are critical to a child's lifelong development. Young children's earliest experiences and environments set the stage for future development and success in school and life.' There are probably no other words that can convey the strong resonance with *Let's start with the Children*'. Two additional supporting statements are *'We know what works to support early learning and improve school readiness.'* and *'We can't wait. Success in school begins before a child enters a classroom.'*

I am sure that this belief is shared by many, if not all; however, *Getting Ready* provides a special insight into the world of 'readiness' as it applies to children and their well-being. This insight is expressed in *The Ready Child Equation* which tells us that the **readiness** of children for school is a functional summation of [1] *ready families,* [2] *ready communities,* [3] *ready services* and [4] *ready schools.* In this sense, then, education takes on a much broader meaning and platform than the curricula at various schools. For example, there is an established belief and experience that police departments enjoy a 'multiplying factor' brought about by their presence within a neighborhood. In similar fashion, the educational process has a multiplying factor whenever the presence of families is integrated into the overall educational process. One can recall that a traditional component of educational success in decades gone by was family advocacy, support and sincere interest in the education of their children. Simply put, families took some ownership in their children's education. Without doubt, this ownership provides a 'multiplying factor' for the necessary ingredients of the overall educational process.

The *Getting Ready* program has three objectives:

- To create a set of measurable indicators related to and defining school readiness that can be tracked regularly over time at the state and local levels.
- To have states and local governments adopt this indicators-based definition of school readiness, fill in the gaps in data availability, track data over time and report findings to their citizens.
- To stimulate policy, program and other actions to improve the ability of all children to read at grade level by the end of third grade.

The following two pages provide the *Core Indicators at a Glance*; it is an excerpt from *Getting Ready*.

Core Indicators at a Glance

The following chart summarizes the core set of common indicators agreed upon by the 17 states involved in the National School Readiness Indicators Initiative. This core set of common indicators is based on the national research and informed by the state experiences in selecting measurable indicators relating to and defining school readiness.

In the section of the report that follows, the core indicators are explained more fully and accompanied by a list of emerging indicators. Emerging indicators are critically important to the school readiness of young children but are currently difficult to measure and track at the state level.

Ready Children

Physical Well-Being and Motor Development
% of children with age-appropriate fine motor skills

Social and Emotional Development
% of children who often or very often exhibit positive social behaviors when interacting with their peers

Approaches to Learning
% of kindergarten students with moderate to serious difficulty following directions

Language Development
% of children almost always recognizing the relationships between letters and sounds at kindergarten entry

Cognition and General Knowledge
% of children recognizing basic shapes at kindergarten entry

Ready Families

Mother's Education Level
% of births to mothers with less than a 12th grade education

Births to Teens
# of births to teens ages 15-17 per 1,000 girls

Child Abuse and Neglect
Rate of substantiated child abuse and neglect among children birth to age 6

Children in Foster Care
% of children birth to age 6 in out-of-home placement (foster care) who have no more than two placements in a 24-month period

Ready Communities

Young Children in Poverty
% of children under age 6 living in families with income below the federal poverty threshold

Supports for Families with Infants and Toddlers
% of infants and toddlers in poverty who are enrolled in Early Head Start

Lead Poisoning
% of children under age 6 with blood lead levels at or above 10 micrograms per deciliter

Ready Services – Health

Health Insurance
% of children under age 6 without health insurance

Low Birthweight Infants
% of infants born weighing under 2,500 grams (5.5 pounds)

Access to Prenatal Care
% of births to women who receive late or no prenatal care

Immunizations
% of children ages 19-35 months who have been fully immunized

Ready Services – Early Care and Education

Children Enrolled in an Early Education Program
% of 3- and 4-year-olds enrolled in a center-based early childhood care and education program (including child care centers, nursery schools, preschool programs, Head Start programs, and pre-kindergarten programs)

Early Education Teacher Credentials
% of early childhood teachers with a bachelor's degree and specialized training in early childhood

Accredited Child Care Centers
% of child care centers accredited by the National Association for the Education of Young Children (NAEYC)

Accredited Family Child Care Homes
% of family child care homes accredited by the National Association for Family Child Care (NAFCC)

Access to Child Care Subsidies
% of eligible children under age 6 receiving child care subsidies

Ready Schools

Class Size
Average teacher/child ratio in K-1 classrooms

Fourth Grade Reading Scores
% of children with reading proficiency in fourth grade as measured by the state's proficiency tests

Rhode Island KIDS COUNT Issue Brief Series

This is the third member of the publication triad; from 1996 through 2000, there were two publications per year; from 2001 through the current year, there were from three to five publications per year. Each publication-as are all of those by Rhode Island Kids Count-have a 'stand alone' quality built on research and references. However, the intrinsic value of each publication rises significantly via the process of synergism. If I were to include a representative sample, it would be the August, 2011 publication entitled *Reading By The End Of the Third grade Matters*. However, it is an eleven page document that is rich in data, rationale, factors related to academic achievement gaps, critical components of effective education systems, birth through grade three, effective instruction guidelines for various student populations, language development from infancy to preschool, developing strong readers: kindergarten through grade 3, the Rhode Island preK—12 literacy policy and recommendations and supportive references.

In short, this particular series publication is a self-contained reading curriculum planner, a basis for class and lesson plans and a roadmap to a comprehensive understanding of a sound literacy policy. Each publication of the series exhibits these characteristics; the complete series publications follow:

Al Colella

PUBLICATIONS & REPORTS

Publications and Reports > Issue Brief Series

Issue Brief Series

This Issue Brief Series provides an in-depth analysis of current issues affecting children. The Issue Brief series is made possible through the generous support of Hasbro Children's Fund.

JOIN OUR MAILING LIST   Go

RI KIDS COUNT FACTBOOK

2010 CENSUS

Publications & Reports

- **New Releases**
- **Census Briefs**
- **Child Care Snapshots**
- **City/Town Fact Sheets**
- **Factbook**
- **Issue Brief Series**
- **Legislative Wrap-Ups**
- **Special Reports**
- **Archives**
- **Order Here**

Rhode Island Children in Immigrant Families, Updated August 2012, Issue Brief #50

Disparities in Children's Health, February 2012, Issue Brief #49

Safety, Permanency and Well-being for Children in the Care of DCYF, November 2011, Issue Brief #48

Access to Oral Health Care for Children in Rhode Island, September 2011, Issue Brief #47

Reading by the End of Third Grade Matters, Updated August 2011, Issue Brief #46

Improving High School Graduation Rates in Rhode Island, June 2011, Issue Brief #45

Reading by the End of Third Grade Matters, December 2010, Issue Brief #44

Rhode Island Children Living in Immigrant Families, Updated May 2010, Issue Brief #43

Children's Behavioral Health: Psychiatric Hospitalizations and the Continuum of Care,

January 2010, Issue Brief #42

Improving High School Graduation Rates in Rhode Island, Updated October 2009, Issue Brief #41

Access to Early Learning Programs in Rhode Island, October 2009, Issue Brief #40

Juvenile Justice in Rhode Island, July 2009, Issue Brief #39

Effective Public Education Policies: Lessons from Massachusetts and New Jersey, July 2009, Issue Brief #38

2008 Supplement Child Poverty in Rhode Island: A Statistical Profile, September 2008

Rhode Island Children with Autism Spectrum Disorders Issue Brief, August 2008, Issue Brief #37

2008 Supplement with New High School Graduation Rates, June 2008

Achieving Permanency for Children and YouthS in Foster Care, May 2008, Issue Brief #36

Health Insurance for Children and Families in Rhode Island, May 2008, Issue Brief #35

Rhode Island Children in Immigrant Families, January 2008, Issue Brief #34

Quality Child Care and Early Learning in Rhode Island, December 2007, Issue Brief #33

Child Poverty in Rhode Island, September 2007, Issue Brief #32

Preterm Births in Rhode Island, June 2007, Issue Brief #31

Teen Pregnancy and Parenting in Rhode Island, December 2006. Issue Brief #30

Improving Graduation Rates in Rhode Island Issue Brief, November 2006, Issue Brief #29

Preventing Childhood Obesity in Rhode Island Issue Brief, May 2006, Issue Brief #28

Al Colella

Building Better Lives for Youth Leaving Foster Care, May 2006, Issue Brief #27 🔁

Child Poverty in Rhode Island: A Statistical Profile, January 2006, Issue Brief #26 🔁

Food Stamps: A Comprehensive Food Assistance Program, November 2005, Issue Brief #25 🔁

Parenting and Family Support, July 2005, Issue Brief #24 🔁

Grandparents and Other Relative Caregivers in Rhode Island, May 2005, Issue Brief #23 🔁

Safety, Permanency, and Well-Being for Children in State Care, December 2004, Issue Brief #22🔁

Caring for Rhode Island's Infants and Toddlers, November 2004, Issue Brief #21 🔁

Access to Dental Care For Children in Rhode Island, October 2004, Issue Brief #20 🔁

Children with Autism in Rhode Island, December 2003, Issue Brief #19.🔁

Improving Outcomes for Children with Special Needs, November 2003, Issue Brief #18.🔁

Health Insurance for Children and Families, March 2003, Issue Brief #17. 🔁

Childhood Lead Poisoning, February 2003, Issue Brief #16.🔁

Children's Mental Health Services in Rhode Island, October 2002, Issue Brief #15.🔁

Child Poverty in Rhode Island, September 2002, Issue Brief #14.🔁

Safe and Affordable Housing for Rhode Island's Children, June, 2001 (updated June 2002), Issue Brief #13.🔁

School-Based Health Centers In Rhode Island, May 2001 (updated May 2002), Issue Brief #12.🔁

Access to Dental Care for Children in Rhode Island, January 2001 (updated May 2002), Issue Brief #11.🔁

Appendix E
Simmons: Keep Slave History Alive

Source: *Education,* Providence Journal {March 26, 2011]
Title: *Simmons: Keep Slave History Alive*
Author: Paul Davis, Journal Staff Writer
Brown University president speaks at United Nations event remembering victims of slavery.

Nations, and universities, must never forget that millions of Africans endured inhuman treatment during the transatlantic slave trade, Brown University President Ruth Simmons said at a United Nations event Friday.

Seated at a table with U.N. Secretary-General Ban Kimoon and other dignitaries, Simmons talked about the importance of keeping that dark history alive.

Before nations can fully embrace the principles of fairness and equality, she said, they must acknowledge the "heinous" crimes against 30 million Africans who were killed or sold into slavery during a 400-year history that marked the rise of global capitalism.

In the interests of commerce, "nations permitted the systematic destruction" of just not lands and families but languages, religions and histories, she said.

Simmons, the first African-American president of an Ivy League university, was the keynote speaker on the last day of a weeklong event centering on the U.N.'s International Day of Remembrance of the Victims of Slavery and the Transatlantic Slave Trade.

Eight years ago, she said, Brown probed its own ties to slavery. A committee of professors and students learned that Brown's first building in Providence was built, in part, by slaves, and that some of the college's officers and supporters – along with students and faculty – owned slaves.

In response, the college is rewriting its history and plans to place a slavery memorial on campus, she said. Officials have also started a center for the study of slavery and the slave trade. And the university is helping students in Providence's public schools, she said.

"These small steps are by no means intended to make amends for this history," said Simmons, a great granddaughter of slaves. Rather, the efforts are a constant reminder" that the university must seek justice as it goes forward.

U.N. officials hope the events will give voices and faces to those who suffered and help world leaders deal with other forms of contemporary bondage, from forced or early marriages to the trafficking in children.

The **transatlantic** slave trade, the largest long-distance forced movement of innocent people in history, uprooted 25 to 30 million Africans, according to UNESCO estimates. They were shackled, dragged off to the Americas and Caribbean and forced to endure unspeakable misery, as did their descendants for hundreds of years.

In the American colonies, Rhode Island merchants and captains accounted for more than half the U.S. slave trade. They made more than 1000 voyages to Africa and forced more than 100,000 men, women and children into slavery.

"There are those who say that slavery is an issue that is past, and we don't need to rehash a debate on the topic," said Jamaica's U.N. ambassador, Raymond O. White.

But, he said, we cannot ignore the lingering legacies of the slave trade in many parts of the world today, "a legacy of hatred, prejudice and racial discrimination."

"We feel that the stories need to be told because the lessons from our past inform the present, and will most certainly influence the future."

Friday's discussion included performances by African drummers and singers.

More than 60 years ago, U.N. delegates declared their support for a universal declaration on human rights, said Iceland's U.N. ambassador, Gunnar Palsson. It says, in part, that "no one shall be held in slavery or serfdom," he said.

"Nevertheless, millions of people worldwide continue to be treated as property," and are sold for sex and forced labor, he said.

Laborers toil in mines, textile mills and in fields. And "women and children are subject to forced sexual labor, violence and abuse, and many of them lose their lives to HIV and AIDS," he said.

"All of our countries are affected; some have become major destinations for victims while others lose many of their citizens to this hideous and lucrative practice."

Appendix F
Decision/Choices Talk to Teens/Young Adults

Source: Author
Title: SUCCESS IS A CHOICE [aka CHOICE & CONSEQUENCES]
The following are notes from some formal/informal discussions with student groups, professional colleagues, my children and grandchildren and, on more than several occasions, *with the children, teens and adults at St. Ann's.* The starting point at any given time was dependent upon the situation and those present at that time. However, when the discussion was in a seminar setting I would always open the discussion with "Who wants to be successful?" Of course, the response was always a positive and a unanimous one! I would also ask the attendees just what they had in their minds about the definition of 'success'; the responses were always varied, sometimes surprising and very interesting. Without addressing the merits or realities of their view of 'success', I advocated that "Each of you can really be whatever you wish to be!" and that it is a healthy exercise to look beyond the present, think about your dreams, look into your hearts and passions as you lift your individual visions and self-expectations to the 'mountain top'. Keep that vision in mind all the days of your life which, as history has amply told us, will inevitably encounter times of trial and tribulation. I emphasized that others who have come before had overcome those situational disadvantages, e.g., the family arena, school, the work place, the social arena, etc. and climbed the mountain of success. The climb, unfortunately, isn't a one-way trip upward; it has its ups and downs. Climbing takes *effort*, i.e., the ability and perseverance to keep on trying when you slip and fall; keep your mind on your goal and what it will feel like to achieve that goal. The view from the mountain top is so much more than that along the way.

Despite the wide spectrum of these definitions, there is a common thread, actually a series of 'dots' that when connected inevitably lead each of us to that mountain top labeled 'success'. Conversely, when you stop trying, there is little hope for success. There are so many things that we cannot control in our journey of life but there is one factor that each of us controls, i.e., no one else, and that factor is *E-F-F-O-R-T!*

Each of us here today will have a path through life that is a direct result of the *choices* that each of us make: the choice to study [or not to study], the choice to be a good person, i.e., giving life to the 'golden rule' [or not to], the choice to help those that are in need [or not to help], the choice to make something of our lives [or not to], the choice to shape our lives as we can [or not to]......but, most importantly, the choice to never quit and the choice to persevere especially when things get difficult or disappointing. Each of us are where we are today- and where we will be in the days and years to come-because of the choices that we have made and those that we will make. With reference to the parenthesized 'not to' statements above: let each of us be crystal clear that standing on the proverbial 'sideline', not getting involved, looking the other way, yielding to the conveniences of life, following the path of least resistance and all those other maneuvers that are enabling factors for *not making a good choice* is in itself 'your choice'. *Simply put, 'success' does not happen by accident and, so sadly so, neither does 'failure'; both outcomes are direct results of one's choices.*

Perhaps it's time to address the definition of a good choice. *The* unique criteria that defines your choice as 'good' or 'not so good' are the results- aka consequences-of your choice. Of course, in our younger years, each of us seem to learn that only via hindsight; aka 'when it's too late', in the case of undesired or negative consequences. The point here is that it is certainly a wise strategy or 'rule of life' to think about the possible consequences of your choice-to-be *before* the choice is made.

Let's look at a few examples of the choice of effort and perseverance: take Michael Jordan of the Chicago Bulls. He was dropped from his high school basketball team. He had a choice to either stop trying and give up that particular path to 'success'... or try harder...well, we all know what choice Michael Jordan made. Take Walt Disney [of movies, cartoons and Disney World fame]. He was told in his early years that he lacked imagination and really didn't have any good ideas. He, too, was faced with a choice. Each of us will face the opportunity-and it is an opportunity-to make choices in our lives, not once but time and time again and again. Think about Winston Churchill, Prime Minister of England during World War II; he actually failed the 6th grade but he chose to persevere. Thomas Edison was a youngster when he was told that he was too stupid to learn anything. History is abundant with success stories that came about because of sheer perseverance in effort time and time again. Inevitably, there will be individuals who will try to discourage an individual from trying harder or "You cannot do this." or "You cannot do that." There are people everywhere who will provide myriad reasons to deter you from your path of success; there rationale is based on their own fears and timid hearts. Again, destiny always provides you with another opportunity to make a choice of [1] listening to the naysayers, doubters and uninformed or [2] listening to yourself, your mind, your heart, your passion and your dream of success, your dream of the mountain top! It is your mindset that guarantees 'success' in every field of endeavor; think 'success'.

Remember Ludwig von Beethoven? Well, his music teacher once said of him "As a composer, you are hopeless." It's a good thing that Beethoven made the choice not to listen!

The following are some one-liner reminders about 'success':

- **Success is <u>your</u> choice.**
- **Where you are today is a result of <u>your</u> past choices.**
- **Where you will be in all <u>your</u> tomorrows will be a result of <u>your</u> choices today and in the future.**
- **<u>Your</u> choices create a path-<u>your</u> path throughout life.**
- **Everyone wants/wishes to be successful.**
- **"I want to be successful." = "Talking the talk."**
- **"I choose to be successful and doing whatever it takes and however long it takes to be successful. = "Walking the walk."**
- **Fast forward technique: Today, any day, think of what you would like to claim at the end of the day, at the end of an academic year, at the end of a project,....... at the end of your life. Don't become a member of the *shoulda- woulda-coulda club*.**
- **Success is really looking back and knowing that you really did <u>your</u> best and that you did provide <u>your</u> best effort.**
- **We must believe in ourselves and somewhere along the road life, we will meet someone who sees greatness in us, expects it from us and lets us know that our effort is the golden key to success. In the same spirit, then, be an advocate for someone who needs support and encouragement along their road of life.**

Appendix G
Rules of Life [aka 'Keys of Life']

Source: Author
Title: Some Rules of Life [aka 'Keys of Life]
Elsewhere in these writings I have referred to certain principles, practices, procedures and protocols that, collectively, could be called 'rules' or 'keys of life'; as you all know and have experienced [often with respectful patience] the many talks, speeches, seminars, stories et al that I have shared with you. Sometimes they may have been humorous, serious, informative and even entertaining and, at other times, you may have thought "Why is Grandpa talking about this or that?" Well, here's your answer: during my lifetime I was fortunate enough to have the opportunity to identify, understand **_and_** apply those 'rules' that proved to be assets/resources for me and for others; certainly as a Dad and a Grandpa but also in other and varied arenas of teaching, mentoring, tutoring and learning, For example, I paid sufficient attention to the academic material that would enable individuals to finish a course, a certification, an undergraduate degree or an advanced degree but I gave equal emphasis to those 'rules' that would complement their academic abilities when taking up residence in the real world of responsibility, professions, trades, families and relationships. I remember one of my favorite classroom tactics was to display a large set of keys; I would identify one key after another that I said I used to open this door or that door and still another door and so on. I remember asking different students at opportune times [and there were many!], "I have all these keys that were used to get me where I am today! How many keys do **_you_** have?" I called these 'keys of life' when used appropriately and judiciously; the 'keys of life' because they could open doors and gateways

to areas of opportunity, information, horizons and progress that would not normally be available to the individual. Simply put, without these 'keys of life', one's journey is inevitably a difficult one. *It's important to note that the leveraging 'power' or 'strength' of these rules, these 'keys of life', have a synergistic quality. Read on!*

[1]   **EFFORT** - if I had to select a single 'key' it would be this one. Effort is the fuel that moves you forward especially in difficult and challenging situations. Effort-continuous over time-always produces positive results. Too often, the communications media highlights the achievement of an individual, e.g., take the athlete who wins the 100 meter or 400 meter event at, say, the Olympics. The winner raises his arms in victory, wraps himself/herself in their national flag, the bands play and the crowds cheer-a great and moving event that lasts for seconds or minutes. What you don't get a sense of is the *effort* that made this victory possible. The winner, to be sure, incurred losses and setbacks along the way [a long way usually measured in years]. In **Grandpa's Treasure Chest** there is a book entitled *The Road To Success Is Paved With Failures* by Rick Pitino [basketball coach at Providence College, the Boston Celtics, the Universities of Kentucky and Louisville]. Everyone is an expert at handling success but it is *effort* that enables the individual to get through, over and beyond a failure or setback; and the decision to provide that *effort* is really and solely an individual choice [a topic addressed within this book]. *Effort does not depend upon the environment, other individuals, the weather, the alignment of the planets, etc., the choice to provide effort comes from within your mind and heart.* Different people talk about control, the lack of control within their lives, etc. but the ability to make a choice is really the ultimate form of control for the individual-simply put, we are always in control when we can make choices. As Calvin Coolidge-another 'old-timer' and President of the United States from 1923 to 1929 said "Persistence and determination [aka **effort**] alone are

omnipotent. The slogan "Press On" has solved and always will solve the problems of the human race.

[2]   **EDUCATION** – has always been the 'key' that opens many doors; it certainly was the key for Uncle Gus and I that opened the door to professional careers. The genesis for our 'taste', our 'hunger', our 'drive' for an education was our parents' emphasis that-in their times, i.e., the early years of the 20th century-education [which neither really had] was the means of living a meaningful and higher quality life. They not only stressed the formal education in the academic sense but also a worldly education outside of the classrooms; *in fact, some of these rules/'keys of life' provided here can be traced back to their influence upon our lives.* They also and always reminded us that education via learning is a lifelong process; when teaching at a college or university, I discovered that the 'instructor' learns in equal measure with the 'students'. Can you imagine the power of *effort + education*?

[3]   **DAD'S TOP FIVE 'WORDS OF WISDOM'** – I would be remiss in my responsibility if I don't mention those 'words of wisdom' that my daughters had printed on a bookmark marking my 70th birthday: **1. "Step up to the plate", 2. "Take the high road", 3. "Be accountable", "Keep up the good work" and 5. "Make good choices".** Each of them-and many others [students, mentorees, etc]-have heard these words mentioned on special occasions; these words are individually addressed [some several times] within this book.

[4]   **FAIRNESS** – be willing to give to others whatever you take/receive from others; just a simple version of the golden rule: 'Do unto others what you would have others do unto you.' Do you remember the cries of "That's not fair!" that each of you, me,... everybody has uttered in our childhood years? Well this is the adult mature version!

[5] **CHOICE** – be aware of 'choice'; in every situation the individual *always* has a choice; and every choice has a consequence; a neat strategy for making a 'good choice' and, therefore, resultant 'good consequences', is to 'fast forward' your mind to visualize the consequences of candidate choices. Usually, it becomes crystal clear as to those consequences that we would prefer, embrace and for which we would claim responsibility.

[6] **COMMON SENSE** – in the analytical and engineering world, I was always amazed at the absence of 'common sense' in many programs and projects. Educated, intelligent people would easily get lost, so to speak, in the complexities, the verbiage and the irrelevant when attempting to forge a solution to a particular problem. A close second to '**effort**' as the most important key of all is '**common sense**'. Don't lose sight of the forest because of the trees!

[7] **UNDERSTAND 'PROCESS'** – sometimes an event takes place that is difficult to understand and to deal with-call this event a 'snapshot'. In reality it is a single 'snapshot' within a series of 'snapshots'. The series of 'snapshots' provides a more meaningful context in which to understand the 'process' that is taking place before your very eyes; but you only see a single 'snapshot and you inevitably respond to that single snapshot [which is only one piece of the puzzle]. Recognizing that a 'process' is taking place enables the individual to look backward in time and understand the series of snapshots that led to this single event or snapshot. This recognition also enables the individual to look ahead in time in order to visualize what will most likely happen in the future. Knowing the history of a single snapshot and projecting likely events to follow places you in a more informed position about the relevance, meaning and importance of the original single snapshot. Better information certainly leads to more informed decisions to guide/shape your reaction.

[8] **POWER OF PRAYER** – I believe in the power of prayer: not in a magical sense but in a sense of awareness that there is a more meaningful resource beyond luck, good fortune and magic. The best way in which I can explain the power of prayer is to say "When people stop praying, coincidences will stop occurring."Hmmmmm! There is another section in this book that could have been called *Amazing Grace 101* but it is entitled **Introduction to Amazing Grace**.

[9] **DREAM, DARE, DO** – don't be afraid to be an idealist and a believer in dreams; good and great things have their beginning in dreams founded on good principles; having dreams has an intangible product even when the dreams are not realized ["at this time and place"]; having dreams also means that we will always have *hope*. Dreams are realized when that special window of opportunity opens and you're ready for it. Someone once said that luck happens when preparedness meets opportunity [hmmmmm!]. Have your dreams! Dare to reach for them! Do the very best that you can! One of my favorite quotations was taken from the eulogy for Robert F. Kennedy given by Ted Kennedy in 1968. Speaking about Robert F. Kennedy: "Some see things as they are and ask Why?; my brother saw things as they could be and asked Why not? As further validation, refer to the section on **Step Up To The Plate!** and especially the lyrics of the Impossible Dream. In the face of adversity, don't relinquish your dream; following the death of his brother, John F. Kennedy, and the death of Dr. Martin Luther King, Jr., Robert F. Kennedy reminded us that *"For all those whose cares have been our concern, the work goes on, the cause endures, the hope still lives, and the dream shall never die."*

One of the most moving 'dream speeches was that given by Dr. Martin Luther King, Jr. on the steps of the Lincoln Memorial in Washington, DC on august 28, 1963. That time was a time of social change and awakening in America; it was the time of the civil rights movement. This '**I have A**

Dream Speech' can be found elsewhere in these writings. It's very interesting to note that 24 years [April 9, 1939] earlier-also on the steps of the Lincoln Memorial-Marian Andersen joined one of the earliest calls for 'equality for all' and used the song 'God Bless America' to emphasize her 'dream', her hopes for and belief in America. Recently, there was a documentary, **'Eyes on the Prize'**; it's the story that may be fading, like the images of old film stock, from the country's consciousness. **'Eyes on the Prize'** is a most powerful reminder we have of how broad the struggle was, how many people of great courage-from very small children to very old men and women-signed on to it, how many of them suffered and often died, and what all of us owe to all of them. Black Americans are far better off in almost every respect than they were in the mid-1960s, thanks in large part to the successes of the civil rights movement. But racism and discrimination persist and there are still substantial disparities between blacks and whites on most indicators of social and economic well-being. There is also much to be done about the self-inflicted wounds that have hindered the progress of many blacks. [Author's note: James T. Patterson's *Freedom Is Not Enough* recommended reading for a comprehensive understanding of the history of most African-American families. This is an exemplary excerpt from his book: "That Wilson [William Julius Wilson] went out of his way to praise Moynihan's interpretation attested to his belief that many black leaders as well as many whites on the left had been guilty of posturing when they condemned Moynihan for blaming the victim." True then; perhaps, still true!]

However, **'Eyes on the Prize is a demonstration that even the greatest challenges can be overcome. It's a national treasure, important for all the reasons that history is important!**

[10] **BEWARE OF THE NAYSAYERS** – you will inevitably run into the naysayers and doubters of the world-and

they are a sad bunch for they live their lives without the excitement, promise and greatness of dreams and what those dreams sometimes produce. In the academic arena, other students may ask "Why are you always studying?". In the family arena, someone may ask "Why do you waste your time doing that [where 'that' is a good deed]?". In the communities where you will have residence and some of those residents will question the reason that you are active in outreach and community service. A convenient response to new ideas and progress is to find reasons why a new idea will not work. They will spread their 'negative sunshine' around with statements like "We tried that before and it didn't work.", "We don't have the time [or money] to do that.", It'll take too much of my time.", "It's too difficult.", "It's too cold.", "it's too hot.",.......too this or too that! One's response to such statements could be shaped from the sections on **It's O.K. To Be Assertive, Step Up To The Plate, etc.** Another response based on faith and courage is to remember that anything is possible-even that which appears to be impossible to some-simply put: set your goals [aka: dream, dare and do!] and don't listen to those reasons why not to do it. Again, you always have a choice: listen to your own heart and mind and not the naysayers and doubters!

[11] **BE ACCOUNTABLE** – this is a word/phrase that you will hear often and usually from individuals who want others to be accountable and not necessarily themselves. No one is perfect and we all make mistakes, errors, misjudgments that, I am sure, we all know that we 'goofed' and wish that we hadn't. However, some of these individuals simply refuse [actually they choose to refuse] to be accountable for their actions; they find a myriad ways to attribute the blame to others, to coincidences, etc. Simply put, these individuals are absolutely irresponsible-not for making an error et al but refusing to take ownership of the outcome of that error. Such refusal allows the doer of the deed, so to speak, to do nothing about compensating for the effects of the error-

this is such an easier path for the irresponsible parties-it is the path of least resistance-later we will talk about the 'high road vs. the low road'. Responsible individuals always take the' high road' [rarely is it the path of least resistance whereas irresponsible individuals take up residence on the 'low road']. *Being accountable is to quickly, publicly and completely take responsibility for the outcomes of errors, mistakes and misjudgments!* In a way, this is really a way of saying "I'm sorry." Especially to those who were affected by your errors, mistakes, etc. Being 'accountable' and 'taking responsibility' are more than words and a nice-sounding sound byte; they are **'actions'**. Strategies for accountability are to be identified and defined prior to a process, e.g., penalties for breaking civil and criminal laws are predetermined; another way of saying the same thing in a general sense is that *accountability must be enforceable in order to have meaning, relevance and effectiveness.*

[12] **STORIES HAVE AT LEAST TWO SIDES** – how many times have we heard the sad story of something that was said or done from our peers, friends and associates and, then, responded with sympathy, understanding and empathy for a peer, a friend or an associate? Then, as time goes by, we sense some contradictions about what really may have been said or done and doubt and uncertainty set in about the truth of the situation. We then don't really know who or what to believe; if we had then reacted to the original 'story', we may have found ourselves in an embarrassing situation. From experience in the family, community, academic and professional arenas, I frequently had to broker a peace between two parties [two associates, two family members, a faculty member and a student, etc.] who each had their 'story'. I came to understand that the initial story is simply one's [preferred] version of the truth and the second story from the other person is simply that person's [preferred] version of the truth. These two versions were always different-sometimes radically different

and even so unrelated that it seemed that two mutually exclusive events had taken place. Initially-as the broker/peacemaker-I consumed large amounts of time, travel, patience and frustration talking to one person and then the second one. My quickly-developed strategy to resolve the issue was to have both parties in my office at the same time; each would be given an opportunity to tell their version without interruption. Just the setting encouraged each of the two to move away from their respective, preferred versions and closer to the 'truth'. Most conflicts were resolved in minutes and to everyone's satisfaction. I stress three points: [1] there are **always** two sides to every story [and three should there be three individuals involved], [2] one's credibility is inversely proportional to the distance between one's [preferred] version and what one really knows as the 'truth' and [3] always hear both sides of the story regardless of how good, how believable or how rational that one side of the story seems to be.

[13] **THE HIDDEN AGENDA** – in the communication process between two [or more] individuals, there are often misunderstandings and such about what was really said by one or the other. There is a growing trend in the world today [2008] to [1] say what you think the other person wants to hear, [2] put a 'slant' or 'spin' on your message, [3] say something that is simply not what you really believe, [4] put forth words that are irrelevant and constitute 'noise' [aka 'babble'], [5] issue a statement that has little credibility or foundation and [6] use the communication process as a tool for deception and/or devious manipulation of either an individual or a situation. *So beware of the 'hidden agenda'.*

[14] **LOOK FOR THE 'INCONSISTENCY'** - an effective strategy for arriving at the 'truth' of a specific situation whether it be at the personal, family, business or professional level is to be aware of the inconsistencies between what is said, written and done. History is abundant with examples

of inconsistencies in situations that generate confusion, fear and even bewilderment. An inconsistency, i.e., a contradiction is really a 'red light' that something is awry; an inconsistency is a lie in camouflage! The basic form of inconsistency reveals itself in personal relationships in which one of the individuals **says** 'one thing' but always ***does*** another. Of course, the classic example is the confusion that results when "he says he loves me." But "why does he abuse [in one way or another] me?.Now that's an inconsistency; the result is often a need to hear the "I love you!" at the awful expense of accepting the abuse. The abuse could be emotional, mental, psychological and/ or physical. Recognizing an inconsistency is a gateway to reality and its truth.

[15] **DON'T FORGET THE GREEN LIGHTS** – when we are driving in traffic [and especially when we are in a hurry!] we are always perturbed by 'catching' a red traffic light-we wait that incredibly long time of 20 or 30 seconds and we're on our way again. Sometimes we may even curse the red light [and that never helps]. Let me ask the following question: "As you drive from point A to point B in a reasonable amount of time, do you ever acknowledge [and even give thanks] for those green traffic lights along the way?" Probably not! Life is also a journey during which we encounter delays, detours, etc. and we get disturbed, perturbed and agitated because of them; but how many times are we aware of those individuals and situations that have made our journey of life free of bumps, delays, detours et al? What's your answer? The irony and the beauty of the green lights of life is that those individuals and situations that enable and facilitate your 'drive' through life do so quietly, anonymously and willingly. The next two rules are derivatives of this rule; the next two rules will address *'balance'* and then *'pay it forward'*.

[16] **BALANCE** – recognizing and acknowledging both the green lights and the red lights allows us to bring a balanced

perspective to the driving in traffic situation; such balance enables us not to overreact to either extreme of any situation in life, e.g., study time vs. recreation time, spending time with your family and friends, celebrating a victory or grieving over a defeat, eating healthy foods and the other stuff, stepping into a situation to help or standing back and give someone else the opportunity to 'figure things out for themselves, physical exercise as a healthy regimen as opposed to an obsession or some delusional perspective of one's health via poor eating habits, bulk/strength via steroids, etc., etc, etc. Where you locate yourself within the spectrum between two extremes is a *choice* that you can make where the criterion could be: "What's really good and healthy [physical, mental and emotional] for me?"

[17] **'PASS IT ON'** [aka **'PAY IT FORWARD'**] - when we do recognize, acknowledge [...and appreciate...] those individuals who have in some way made our journey a bit smoother, a bit more pleasant, more enriched, happier, more meaningful, ... there is usually a feeling or urge to 'pay the individuals back' for what they have done for you; a natural human response, to be sure. It is important to note that these generous and giving individuals really don't expect 'payback' but rather prefer and hope that instead of 'paying it back' that you 'pay it forward [as they did]' to other people-young, older or in-between- who may need a little advocacy, encouragement and push along their life's journey. *What a wonderful philosophy: help others in need as others have helped me. It's more than a philosophy-it's also a principle and a practice.*

[18] **POWER AND MONEY** – never be surprised or shocked at what people will do to acquire and retain power and/ or money! Such individuals will brush aside principles, responsibilities, morals, ethics, a sense of 'right' and 'wrong' for power and/or money. Their actions, inevitably, render damage onto others who can least handle it. Power and money are resources that can be used in a way based on

293

principles and a sense of responsibility, morals and ethics. *It is said that power/money will make the blind see!*

[19] **DON'T FORGET THE GAME** – there are the 'pep' rallies of life, i.e., a gathering of people who are excited and emotionally charged by the prospect of their participation in some worthwhile [even noble] cause. The air is full of words of 'can do', bravado, 'bring it on', a PA system that blares out the theme from 'Rocky', etc. Once the pep rally is over and things quiet down, the game must still be played [aka the work must still get done]. It is at this point that some of the loudest, most excited and most emotional individuals of the pep rally simple fade away and forget to show up for the game or the work that must still be done. These 'cheerleaders'-although proficient at what they do-sometimes do not understand that there is life after the pep rally and confuse the pep rally for the game itself. *Beware of these 'cheerleaders' who relish the excitement, the rush and the high feelings of the pep rally who don't show up for the game/work.*

[20] **DON'T LIE; IT'S SIMPLY NOT WORTH IT**-lying: it always 'appears' to be an easy and attractive option to telling the truth, facing reality, being accountable and/ or the consequences of one's past action. *But there are options and all are there for your choosing!* First, you can actually tell the truth [even as you see it through your personal prism]; secondly, you can opt for lying with all of the above 'apparent' advantages [which always disappear like smoke in the wind]-this option to lie is also known as 'postponing the inevitable'; thirdly, you can always take the position that 'you prefer not to talk about it now, but perhaps later'. The third option encourages you not to lie [always and inevitably, a good strategy!] and it really gives you time to get the truth straightened out in your mind. The third option also allows you to preserve your integrity which-as we all come to appreciate-is priceless and extremely difficult to regain once lost or compromised. The

second disadvantage [1] carries the burden and associated 'risk' of not remembering the truth as you perceived it and presented it and [2] the fear that the truth will show itself.

[21] **UNDERSTAND 'RISK'** – whatever the cause, whatever the endeavor, whatever the challenge, whatever the promise, whatever the expectation, whatever the most favorable odds, whatever the super-high probability of success, there is always the element of *risk*. Since nothing is perfect, i.e., there are no guarantees or 100% probabilities of 'success', one must recognize that the difference-albeit a microscopic difference-between a very high [but not 100%] probability of success is a measurement of *risk. However, of far greater importance and relevance is that the time of occurrence of risk, however small, is unpredictable!* The acknowledgement of *risk* enables alternative strategies to be developed for various real-world scenarios where *risk* may unexpectedly raise its ugly head. Having some reasonable plans of action in the face of *risk* will always be better than the "What do we do now?" strategy.

[22] **IF IT ISN'T BROKEN, DON'T FIX IT** – sounds like an obvious rule but there are those individuals who will always try to suggest/invoke/recommend ways of doing something in an alternative manner. Whether it's a personal trait, an obsession or a matter of not knowing when to be quiet, these individuals seem to be blind to the fact that "it works and works well". So-o-o-o-o, don't waste your time fixing something that isn't broken and don't let other people waste your time either.

[23] **LEAD, FOLLOW OR GET OUT OF THE WAY** – another obvious rule! There will be countless situations in your family, personal, professional and organizational lives where there is a 'job to be done'. There are three ways to be a productive participant: [1] *lead,* [2] *follow* or [3] *get out of the way.* You can only choose one of the options;

when you try to do more than one, you become an active participant in a process known as 'confusion'.

[24] **REMEMBER MIDNIGHT** – each of you will have good days and those challenging days that seem to last forever, i.e., "Will this day ever end?". I've had more than my share but I do remember one early morning driving to my office and thinking about all those tasks that needed to be done and having to deal with some difficult people in order to get them done. It certainly looked like a very lo-n-n-n-n-n-g day was ahead of me. I was driving by a community bulletin board that would display items like 'Have a good day!' or "There's a sun shining behind those clouds!" but the very best was: **"At midnight, this day will be over!"** Wow, I said, it's so very true that time always moves and in a few hours I will be driving by this bulletin board again but I'll be going home.

[25] **RECOGNIZE OPPORTUNITY**- it is said that 'luck' is when opportunity meets preparedness. Education-academic and experiential, the development of a positive mindset, the awareness of your 'practice' of life based a healthy philosophy of life and principles of living that life- are examples of 'preparedness'. But what of 'opportunity'? Sometimes 'opportunity' is quite obvious but, most of the time, it simply isn't obvious and hardly so in times of trial and tribulation. Our minds and our eyes are too busy with the tasks, duties and responsibilities of life or the negative impact of a sad/tragic event.

The Chinese alphabet has more than 5000 characters [as compared to our 26 letters of the alphabet]; additional words can be created within the Chinese alphabet by combining several individual characters. John F. Kennedy said: "When written in Chinese, the word crisis is composed of two characters. One represents danger and the other represents opportunity." So keep your eyes, hearts and minds open!

[26] **MORE ON OPPORTUNITY** – to those who have

developed a healthy philosophy and principles of life and who have practice both, you will inherently have the 'gift' of a sense of the unfairness of life and the imperfections of individuals [and that includes everyone]. Of course, our first reaction to unfairness and human imperfections may be disappointment and even anger because "neither are right". However, beyond our initial reaction lies the valley of opportunity to rise above the inevitable unfairness and human imperfection and maybe, just maybe, to do something about it, e.g., 'stepping up to the plate'. Hmmmm!

[27] **LEADERSHIP** – remember the words of **21. LEAD, FOLLOW OR GET OUT OF THE WAY?** Let me address the more challenging of these three options: leadership. In many situations, there is a need for 'leadership', a need for someone to be a hero by 'stepping up to the plate', a need to seize the opportunity at hand. The word 'leadership' is a much-used term but "Just what is leadership?". Leadership is an ability held by few. We often fail to recognize it when it's in our presence. Leaders are articulate, decisive, charismatic and [are you ready?] accountable. Leaders see the world as it should be, rather than as it is. They have a vision that is neither too narrow or too broad, but attainable. Leaders work tirelessly to achieve the vision they believe will make a difference. They are passionate about their ideas, but more passionate about the people around them. They are selfless individuals who want those around them to excel. We generally see them as our friends. They work in the background of change. They listen [with their hearts, minds and souls], process and act to do what's right, rather than what's most expedient. Another way of defining leadership: leadership is having [1] a **vision**, i.e., a goal, [2] a **strategy**, i.e., a methodology of those steps necessary and sufficient to attain that vision and [3] an ability to motivate/inspire/equip others to follow you there.

[28] **EVERYBODY'S IMPORTANT** – every single person in

the world is important because they are a human being with feelings. Remember, as Vaughn Avedisian always said, "No one is spared; everybody gets something with which to cope." Simply put, some plates are fuller than others! As we journey through life we encounter a spectrum of people: people that are great to be with, people that are always spreading sunshine, people who are 'gloom and doom' individuals, people who are comfortable in life, people who are deprived, disenfranchised and/or disadvantaged in life and, as a result, are always struggling simply to survive, people who . . . . . etc. As we engage these people-especially those who struggle, e.g., the poor, the disadvantaged, the mental and physically ill, those who are challenged, those who are in need, ... etc., let us remember that each and everyone is important and so very much deserving of whatever we can do for them.

[29] **CHOOSE YOUR HILLS CAREFULLY** - two components of decision making are [1] emotion and [2] intelligence; in Kahlil's Gibran's *The Prophet* [in Grandpa's treasure Chest], one of his many writings about life is one called ***Reason and Passion***; he states that both are omnipresent but, in the final analysis, reason should outweigh passion. There will be times in each of your lives when you are emotionally driven and want to 'draw a line in the sand' meaning that you won't take another step aside or back. You may want to throttle your passion and engage your intelligence before you choose to make a stand on some particular issue; a helpful strategy is to pause, fast forward your mind to possible outcomes and their relevance and importance before 'you choose the hill on which to die' [figuratively, of course]. More often than not, your intelligence will guide you to choose another hill on another day.

[30] **WHAT'S REALLY GOING ON HERE?** – this is strongly related to 27. 'Choose Your Hills Carefully. There is a four-step process that can guide you through a potentially confrontational process with another individual; it follows:

[1]   Ask yourself: "what's really going on here? Sometimes the spoken words don't really convey the intended 'message'; identify the specific issue. [task of intelligence]

[2]   What am I feeling? [task of emotions]

[3]   What do I need? [task of honesty and assertiveness]

[4]   What I need you to do for me. [task of a rational request]

[31]   **MOVING ON** – there will be times in your life when your inner self [aka your sixth sense, your common sense, your 'gut' feeling] will be telling you that it's time to 'move on'. It may be a challenging relationship that you really wish would work but deep down this voice, this inner voice is telling you that it takes two to make a friendship, a relationship, a marriage, a contract, an agreement et al work. Whatever the situation, there is a point after which all your efforts, your resources, your creativity simply aren't enough to 'fix' the situation. When this point has been reached and frustration, disappointment, even anger and those other entities that detract from **your quality** of life become your way of life, it's o.k. 'to pick up your sandals, shake off the sand in them' and 'move on'. Life is simply too precious a gift to waste on a situation or an individual that will remain unchanged following your departure. In other words, understand when and where you can make a difference and when and where it just isn't going to happen.

[32]   **REQUEST VS. GOING ON THE OFFENSE** – this section is addressed to a very common situation within the management process. Specifically, it is a strategy for equipping/persuading/encouraging individuals to assist and support you in your duties, tasks and responsibilities. It is a strategy to engage your peers, your supervisors and those who are within your own circle of supervision. It is especially effective with those who are not cooperative and even adversarial. Rather than start your conversation

with "You . . . . . " [which immediately puts the individual on the 'defense'] try opening the communication process with "I really need your guidance, your help, the benefit of your expertise and experience, . . . " [which immediately empowers the individual to be helpful because you are then perceived as 'needy' and the individual as the only one who can fulfill that 'need'.

[33] **RIGHTS VS. RESPONSIBILITIES** – it is quite acceptable to understand your entitlement to rights, e.g., the Bill of Rights, your rights as a member of a particular community, as a member of a family, as a student, etc., etc., etc. However, bear in mind that each 'right' that you willingly claim, embrace or expect, there is an imbedded 'responsibility' associated with each 'right'. Pay attention to each 'right' because they inherently enhance your overall quality of life but also pay equal attention to the imbedded responsibility. It is absolutely mind-boggling to me that individuals are always aware of their 'rights' but not the associated 'responsibilities'; in my interactions with these individuals [youth, students, peers, neighbors, etc.] they not only are surprised that about the responsibilities but often are reluctant to accept them and give them life.

[34] **BE WHO YOU ARE** - Now this may sound very obvious, very simplistic and a point that, perhaps, doesn't qualify as a 'rule' or 'key of life'; well, let's see how it plays out. First, **Be Who You Are**, only applies to the individual that is inherently a 'good' person; you know, one who is respectful of himself/herself and of others, responsible, rational, etc. It is not applicable to those individuals who simply don't fit into the first category-I call them the 'jerks' of life: there are more earthy and descriptive terms but common sense tells me to leave this to your imagination. I believe that every individual intends to be a good person, contribute to society, be that person that his/her mother would be proud of and, basically, one that wouldn't be embarrassed if his/her actions would be printed in the morning paper

[and on the front page]. However, as we journey along the road of life, we are inevitably challenged, encouraged and persuaded to be someone other than who we really are. There will be peer pressure-*throughout your life*- to be one of the gang, group or clique who have their own agenda and well-being in mind and, usually, not yours. You will have as many opportunities to '*be who you are*' as there will be challenges to your own set of values, ethics and morals. Certainly, not an easy or pleasant assignment, but one for which you will be a better individual should you choose to complete it successfully or a diminished and regretful person should you choose to be someone other than who you really are. This 'rule' or 'key of life' is equally valid in the personal arena, the academic arena, the professional arena, the financial arena, the family arena and unbelievably true for the arenas of friendship and personal relationships. You're welcome and encouraged to revisit this particular 'rule' [and others] in the years to follow.

One more thing: when '*You are who you are.*' [aka 'asserting yourself', i.e., your entire being, your values, your individuality] you really make life easier for yourself and others around you. Practically speaking, you don't have to get entrapped in the inevitable spin, deception [intended or not] and those 'games of life' that exist between individuals. Often we are perplexed and puzzled by the contradiction between one's words and one's action: the words can be part of the 'game' but the actions clearly reveal the real person. When there is consistency between 'words' and 'actions', you can rest assured that that person is not playing games. Rather that type of person is credible, reliable and just great to be with. A representative example is in that social arena involving teenagers and young adults where the guys are trying to be who they believe/perceive the ladies are looking for; conversely, the ladies are trying to be who they believe/ perceive the guys are looking for. The games become so prevalent that it's like one giant stage façade. Of course, time reveals each of the real identities and the impact of the 'games of life'. This example is directly applicable to other arenas: family, community, business, corporate, ………...!

[35] **GOLDEN RULES FOR LIVING [by Miriam Hamilton Keare]**

a. If you open it [the right] close it [the responsibility].

b. If you turn it on, turn it off.

c. If you unlock it, lock it up.

d. If you break it, admit it.

e. If you can't fix it, call in someone who can.

f. If you value it, take care of it.

g. If you make a mess, clean it up.

h. If you move it, put it back.

i. If it belongs to someone else, get permission to use it.

j. If you borrow it, return it.

k. If you don't know how to operate it, leave it alone.

l. If it's none of your business, don't ask questions.

Grandpa's note: these rules may be mostly applicable to the younger set but experience and history tell us that they are usually applicable to the adult and older set, e.g., Grandpa!

[36] **MAKE A DIFFERENCE** - it's a common feeling amongst many to think that they are not capable of affecting a situation, making a difference, that they are powerless, that 'one person simply cannot make a difference in this challenging world'. Some of this human reluctance, self-doubt and feeling of powerlessness probably comes from the enormity of the many needs out in the local, national and global communities. I have heard people say that no one should go to bed-anywhere in the world-hungry but 'How can we feed everyone?" Rather than focus on the enormity

and apparent impossibility of fulfilling a particular need for all, keep your heart and mind on that one person [or two or more or . . .]; if there a hundred people who needed a coat against the cold weather and your mind said "What good will one coat do? Simply ask that person to whom you gave the coat. You remember the story of the man walking with his friend along the beach and taking the effort and time to throw a starfish [amongst hundreds stranded in the beach sand] back into the ocean. His friend asked "What good is that? Do you really believe you're making a difference?" The man picked up another starfish to throw back into the ocean and responded to his friend: "Ask the one that I just returned to the ocean! *Every single individual-regardless of personal circumstances-can make a difference in the lives of others as well as in their own lives.* Some years ago, Father Theodore Hesburgh of Notre Dame heard about a student there who twice a day would stand outside a dining hall and ask for contributions for the hungry people of the world. He would stand there in the sun, rain and snow and hail. Well, this young man, Al Sondej, collected $25,000.00 in two years. Did this one individual make a difference? Ask those recipients of that food purchased with that $25,000.00 who live in third world countries and some equivalent areas here in the United States. Father Hesburgh himself feels this kind of action is enormously powerful, but only when 'linked' directly and immediately to the need. "People have to know that the good they are giving up is going to someone in need."

In our continuing outreach efforts with the children of the South Bronx [a third world equivalent area], our success there was made possible by the donations, advocacy and participation of hundreds of parishioners and friends of St. John's Episcopal Church. A key to their enthusiastic response to support the outreach efforts was, as Father Hesburgh stated, we provided feedback about the enormous impact of the overall outreach efforts in the lives of the children. We even had some of the children come to St. John's to provide a personal witness to the difference we made in their lives. One parent, in response to a parishioner's question "What is life like in the South Bronx?" His response, after thinking about his answer, was "It's like being in a dark room, you don't know where you are going, you don't know what to do and there's no one there to show you! You have showed us another side of life that is possible for many and already a reality for some!" **Grandpa's note:** "Now go and make a difference!"

Appendix H

ST. John's Experiential Outreach Model at St. John's

Source: Author
Title: EXPERIENTIAL OUTREACH MODEL AT ST. JOHN'S CHURCH

INTRODUCTION

It is important to understand that this outreach model is [1] *spiritually driven* and [2] *experiential*. During the early years of this particular ministry at St. Ann's in the South Bronx, the needs were so great in number, scope and depth that ministry resources were readily addressed to those needs that seemed to be most outstanding. However, as this collaborative ministry and the relationship of two communities matured, there came a very fundamental need to document the content, essence and dynamics of the spectrum of ministry activities. First, the Outreach Team at St. John's had always thought and *practiced* that 'feedback' was an integral part of the ministry, i.e., an acknowledgement and accountability of the increasingly greater parishioners' support of the ministry. Secondly, the growth and success of the ministry strongly suggested that the documentation of the ministry functions and interactive dynamics would not only maintain the level of order required for overall ministry efficiency and effectiveness but also provide a sort of roadmap for future ministry endeavors. Time would prove that this model would become a roadmap both for forthcoming outreach and community services at St. John's and for similar efforts well beyond the St. John's community.

It is a *spiritually driven* model because its fuel is derived from the energy of one's expression of *faith in action*, i.e., 'doing the work that God has given us to do' and an *understanding* that 'Whatsoever you do for the least of your brethren, you do for Me.' It is also an *experiential* model because it is based on experience in and observations of the real world rather than theory.

Functional Outreach Model

The Outreach model fits perfectly into the Christian hierarchy; in fact, it is a natural derivative of this hierarchy. This spiritual lineage has God as its natural genesis and then Jesus Christ as both His spiritual and earthly representative; the words of Christ as put forth in the New Testament given rise to myriad commitments within the Christian community. At St. John's, it gave rise to the following mission statement: *'The mission of St. John's Church is to be a community of Christians committed to the care, nourishment and spiritual growth of all.'*

The functional Outreach model is shown in Figure H-1 and has as its starting point the **ST. JOHN'S MISSION STATEMENT**. However, the reader could note that the last word of this mission statement in Figure H-1 is underlined; this became a necessary part of the response of the Outreach team to questions like 'Why the South Bronx?', 'Why this?', 'Why that?' The initial spiritual mandate handed down Of course, the Outreach team mindset wanted to not only underline 'all' but also add 'No exceptions!' to the mission statement.

The output of St. John's mission statement is directly consistent with [1] **PARISH GOAL #3** and [2] the spectrum of ministries within the St. John's community. St. John's has five standing parish goals and the third is *"Demonstrate God's love by supporting spiritual growth of parishioners through expanded outreach programs."* The growth of the ministry at St. Ann's was an emphatic realization of this goal especially when one considers the number of parishioners-and the collateral age spectrum-who actively participate in the ministry in one way or another.

The output of the third parish goal is also a parallel input, along with the Church's mission statement, to the many on-going ministries at St. John's. Although this book focuses upon the efforts of the Outreach team at St. Ann's, the spectrum of outreach and community service efforts at St. John's does include a litany of 'quiet' and unheralded personal and family ministries as well as those that are more well known within St. John's and within the greater community beyond St. John's. This dynamic is shown in figure H-1 via the inclusion of **COMMUNITY NEEDS** which are interactively linked with the totality of efforts by the **OUTREACH MINISTRY**.

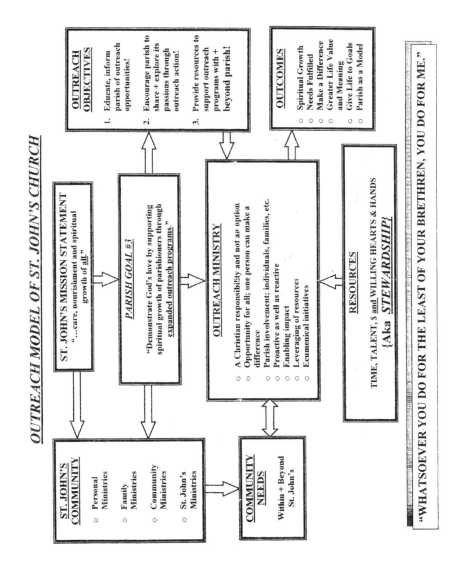

OUTREACH MODEL OF ST. JOHN'S CHURCH

ST. JOHN'S MISSION STATEMENT
"....care, nourishment and spiritual growth of all."

PARISH GOAL #3
"Demonstrate God's love by supporting spiritual growth of parishioners through expanded outreach programs."

OUTREACH OBJECTIVES
1. Educate, inform parish of outreach opportunities!
2. Encourage parish to share + explore its passions through outreach action!
3. Provide resources to support outreach programs with + beyond parish!

OUTREACH MINISTRY
o A Christian responsibility and not an option
o Opportunity for all; one person can make a difference
o Parish involvement; individuals, families, etc.
o Proactive as well as reactive
o Enabling impact
o Leveraging of resources
o Ecumenical initiatives

OUTCOMES
o Spiritual Growth Needs Fulfilled
o Make a Difference
o Greater Life Value and Meaning
o Give Life to Goals
o Parish as a Model

ST. JOHN'S COMMUNITY
o Personal Ministries
o Family Ministries
o Community Ministries
o St. John's Ministries

COMMUNITY NEEDS
Within + Beyond St. John's

RESOURCES
TIME, TALENT, $ and WILLING HEARTS & HANDS
{Aka *STEWARDSHIP*}

"WHATSOEVER YOU DO FOR THE LEAST OF YOUR BRETHREN, YOU DO FOR ME."

Looking at the functional model of Figure H-1, it is time to look at the derivatives of **PARISH GOAL #3**, i.e., the **OUTREACH OBJECTIVES** and, then, the **OUTREACH MINISTRY** itself. The Outreach Objectives are a direct reflection of Parish Goal #3.

In order to achieve that particular goal, it is incumbent upon the ministry to:

[1]   Educate and inform the parishioners of outreach opportunities.

[2]   Encourage and enable the parishioners to share and leverage their individual and collective gifts and passions through faith in action-outreach action.

[3]   Provide resources, i.e., time, talent and treasure, to support those outreach ministries both within and beyond the parish.

The **OUTREACH MINISTRY** is best characterized by the synergistic sum of its components which are:

[1]   Ministry, i.e., helping those in need-wherever they may be-is no longer a option of convenience but rather a humanitarian responsibility-regardless of its inconvenience.

[2]   This responsibility can be viewed through the lens of opportunity. In an article, entitled *Trying to Change the World, written* more than a few years ago by Georgie Anne Geyer, a columnist of the Chicago Daily News, Notre Dame's Father Theodore Hesburgh has commented on the humanitarian efforts of a single student. His comments address both the power of goodness of a single individual and the 'despair' of this goodness being able to move this recalcitrant and self-satisfied and increasingly authoritarian world..... unless, of course, *there are enough of them.*

[3] Parish-wide involvement including individuals, families, friends and, yes, even strangers.

[4] Being reactive not only to well-recognized needs within any community but also a proactive awareness of those needs that are not so obvious.

[5] An enabling impact that creates a 'ripple factor' for additional ministries. This characteristic manifested itself quite frequently within the ministry at St. Ann's especially amongst the younger set who subsequently created their own follow-on ministries based upon the inspiring influence of their experience at St. Ann's.

[6] The synergistic integration and leveraging of the spectrum of **RESOURCES** of time, talent and treasure and, most importantly, willing hearts and hands.

[7] The development of ecumenical initiatives and ministries, e.g., *Beyond our Walls,* the organization in Barrington, RI that marshaled the resources of the ten Barrington faith communities. *Beyond our Walls* started its annual day of community service with fifteen projects and [about] two hundred volunteers. In 2011, its day of community service included more than fifty projects and [about] seven hundred volunteers.

Finally, the **OUTCOMES** do include a marked spiritual growth and maturity amongst the participants and, somewhat unexpectedly, amongst the observers. There is a fulfillment of individual, family and community needs and, in the process, the participants do acquire [1] the satisfaction of making a difference in the lives of others and [2] some measure of insight into the added meaningfulness of their lives.

Additionally, it transforms the words of mission statements and goals into a reality. It is this reality that becomes a credible foundation for the *Outreach Model of St. John's Church* to becoming a roadmap for other parishes and organizations, e.g., that Church in Texas that had representatives at the 2006 CEEP Conference.

Another Perspective

A time-based view of the functional outreach model is provided in order to better understand the *before, during and after* activities of a single ministry event.

BEFORE

[1] Explore the spiritual basis for the ministry: prayer, service to others, moral and spiritual mandate of service, the golden rule, etc.

[2] Explore the belief that the life of Jesus Christ was indeed a life of outreach for those with the greater need.

[3] Awareness of service to others as an obligation rather than an option.

[4] Identify individual passions, ministry skills and leadership roles.

[5] Address the realities of parish goals and mission statement.

[6] Potential for ecumenical opportunities.

DURING

[7] Needs vs. gifts using the Gift Workshop model.

[8] Identify the spectrum of specific needs [aka 'there's always something for everyone'].

[9] Address related current outreach efforts; identify candidate *improvements and/or extensions.*

[10] Mobilize required resources [volunteers, their skills, their gifts, their passions, funding, commitments of time and participation]

[11] Portray the entire parish as the 'Outreach team'.

[12] Identify parish, team, family, organization, individual projects.

[13] Address site visits and liaison with the needs community to determine how the ministry effort can best be helpful.

[14] Spread the word via forums, service announcements, articles in church and local papers.

AFTER

[15] Provide feedback to parishioners.

[16] Stress the principle that *'Givers become receivers and receivers become givers.'*

[17] Provide the answer to *'Did we, i.e., the entire parish,*

really make a difference?'

[18] Provide the experienced spiritual growth by the participants using the 'In their own words!' concept.

[19] Reflect the life that has been given to parish goals.

[20] Maintain the momentum!

Example of the functional model

A very representative example of the implementation of the outreach model of St. John's used at St. Ann's is provided in Appendix K. It is entitled *Amazing Grace-Based Outreach: Modeling Shared ministry*. It is the forum presentation made at the 2006 annual meeting of the *Consortium of*

Endowed Episcopal Parishes [CEEP]. This workshop addressed the genesis, development and progress of the Outreach Ministry Team of St. John's, Barrington, RI at St. Ann's in the South Bronx.

Outreach at St. John's in 2012

The 2012 Outreach activities, as in the past, include those 'quiet' and very effective efforts that are carried on by individuals, families and groups within the parish and community families. The 2012 activities [as found in the *Parish Guide, 2011-2012, St. John's Episcopal Church]* also include those inevitable efforts for which planning is not feasible, i.e., needs that simply surface during the year. However, the 2012 outreach efforts include a 'menu' of core activities-some with a history and usually some new initiatives. They follow with a brief description:

St. John's Open Hands Garden-grows and provides fresh produce to community food and feeding programs that service those in need.

Mobile Loaves and Fishes-partnering with other local faith groups that prepare complete meals, organize clothing and, then, accompanying the loaded lunch truck to areas where homeless folks gather and to low-income housing projects.

John's Mobile Meals-this ministry is a mini-version of *Meals-On-Wheels;* meals are prepared on Saturdays and delivered to folks within the community who lack the mobility to provide their own meals.

TAP-IN {Touch A Person In Need}-founded some years ago by St. John's parishioners, this special ministry collects and distributes food, clothing, transportation and other needed goods and services to those in need. In 2011, TAP-IN serviced more than 10,000 clients.

St. John's Giving Tree-a Christmas tradition that has 'tags' rather than bulbs on the church Christmas tree; each tag has the name, age, gender and specific need of children and some adults. The parishioners select one or more tags, purchase the needed 'gift'; the gifts are then distributed to those families.

George Hunt H.E.LP. Center-Collects men's clothing for an inner-city drop-in center for the homeless established and named for former Bishop George Hunt.

B.O.W. {Beyond Our Walls}-this organization membership includes all the faith groups in Barrington. The genesis of B.O.W. is a direct result of an initiative by the Outreach team at St. John's. B.O.W. sponsors two annual events: The Great Day of Services and Project HOPE. Both events are major community service endeavors.

ENCORE – The St. John's Consignment Shop- This operation has been active and very successful for 40 years. All of the funds raised go directly to E.C.W. and its impressive litany of outreach and community service projects and some that are national and global.

E.C.W. – Episcopal Church Women—this very quiet and unheralded – but eminently successful - ministry has been a model of faith, generosity and philanthropy. In addition to the spectrum of recipients of grants from E.C. W., St. John's itself has received extremely generous funding for a variety of needs within the parish.

Appendix I
Speak to Us of Giving by Kahlil Gibran

Source: 'Speak to Us of Giving', pp 19-22, from The Prophet, Alfred A. Knopf, 1984.

Then said a rich man, Speak to us of Giving.

And he answered:

You give but little when you give of your possessions.

It is when you give of yourself that you truly give.

For what are your possessions but things you keep and guard for fear you may need them tomorrow?

And tomorrow, what shall tomorrow bring to the overprudent dog burying bones in the trackless sand as he follows the pilgrims to the holy city?

And what is fear of need but need itself?

Is not dread of thirst when your well is full, the thirst that is unquenchable?

There are those who give little of the much which the have-and then give it for recognition and their hidden desire makes their gifts unwholesome.

And there are those who have little and give it all.

These are the believers in life and the bounty of life, and their coffer is never empty.

There are those who give with joy, and that joy is their reward.

And there are those who give with pain, and that pain is their baptism.

And there are those who give and know not pain in giving, nor do they seek joy, nor give with mindfulness of virtue;

They give as in yonder valley the myrtle breathes its fragrance into space.

Through the hands of such as these God speaks, and from behind their eyes He smiles upon the earth.

It is well to give when asked, but it is better to give unasked, through understanding;

And to the open-handed the search for one who shall receive is joy greater than giving.

And is there aught you would withhold? All you have shall some day be given.

Therefore give now, that the season of giving may be yours and not your inheritors.

You often say, "I would give, but only to the deserving."

The trees in your orchard say not so, nor the flocks in your pasture.

They give that they may live, for to withhold is to perish.

Surely he who is worthy to receive his days and nights, is worthy of all else from you.

And he who has deserved to drink from the ocean of life deserves to fill his cup from your little stream.

And what desert greater shall there be, than that which lies in the courage and the confidence, nay the charity, of receiving?

And who are you that men should rend their bosom and unveil their pride, that you may see their worth naked and their pride unabashed? See first that you yourself deserve to be a giver, and an instrument of giving.

For in truth it is life that gives unto life-while you, who deem yourself a giver, are but a witness.

And you receivers-and you are all receivers-assume no weight of gratitude, lest you lay a yoke upon yourself and upon him who gives.

Rather rise together with the giver on his gifts as on wings;

For to be overmindful of your debt, is to doubt his generosity who has the freehearted earth for mother, and God for father.

Appendix J
History of St. Ann's Episcopal Church

Source: http://stannsb.discovery.org/welcome2.htm
Title: St. Ann's Episcopal Church-The First Church in the Bronx-Welcomes You!

St. Ann's Episcopal Church occupies a spacious close along St. Ann's Avenue opposite the center of 140th Street in New York's South Bronx. Founded over a century and a half ago by members of the Morris family, the landmark church and close is the resting place for such notables as Louis Morris and Gouvernor Morris. The church takes its name from Ann Morris – among other things, a descendant of Pocahontas. The church house excellent examples of late 19th century stained glass.

But St. Ann's is more than a museum; it is a vital center of community activity. Mott Haven – St. Ann's neighborhood – is the heart of the poorest congressional district in the United States. St. Ann's addresses the urgent needs of its neighbors with food and such assistance as it can give. St. Ann's has developed a dramatically successful after-school for elementary school children, featured in the available literature and on Oprah. And sometimes, it is just sheer relief from urban pressures that St. Ann's trees and grass afford, along with the only swings in the neighborhood and a really good jungle-gym, that is the best thing of all.

Source: St. Ann's Episcopal Church
Title: A BRIEF HISTORY OF ST. ANN'S CHURCH [1952]

St. Ann's of Morrisania ["The Church of the Patriots"]is an ivy covered building of simple English design located at East 140th Street & St. Ann's Avenue in New York City, occupying property consisting of two city

316

blocks, part of the original farm of Jonas Bronck. This property, now a Churchyard, has been in use as a burial place for 128 years and the Church edifice, on a grassy hillock in the midst of the same, has been a House of Worship for 111 years.

The Church was erected in 1841 by Gouvernor Morris, the son of the honorable Gouvenor Morris and Anne Carey Randolph of Virginia. It was dedicated in honor of blessed St. Ann and Anne Carey Randolph of Virginia and consecrated on the 28th day of June, 1841 by the Rev. Benjamin Tredwell Onderdonk, D.D., Bishop of the Diocese of New York. By the same venerated prelate its cornerstone had been laid with appropriate ceremonies in the previous October.

On the 17th of July, 1841, a Vestry was formed and incorporated by the style of St. Ann's Church of Morrisania. The Church, with its adjoining grounds was munificently conveyed to them as a donation by its Founder, Gouvernor Morris, Esq. in a deed securing the holy and beautiful house, which God had moved him to erect, to the service of the blessed Lord Jesus Christ and of His Holy Catholic Church in America.

On opening the first Parish register the above historical notice was inserted by the hand of the first Rector of St. Ann's with the Prayer of God's Blessing on the thousands which shall be born again at Morrisania in Holy baptism.

Though the Church of St. Ann's of Morrisania is but 111 years old, the American history of the land on which it stands and of the family whom it commemorates, who owned the land by Royal Letters from King William the Third, dates back over 250 years.

St. Ann's, the first building devoted to Divine Worship in Morrisania, has become one of the large Episcopal Parishes in the Bronx. It is a Shrine where lie buried Founding Fathers of our Country. In the Crypt of St. Ann's Church lie buried Lewis Morris, "Signer' of the Declaration of Independence, Mary Walton Morris, "Mother of Patriots" after whom Walton High School in the Bronx* is named. Also, Anne Carey Randolph, seventh in line from the Princess Pocahontas, Judge Lewis Morris, first Governor of the state of New Jersey, and first native born Chief Justice of the State of New York, Judge Robert Hunter Morris of Pennsylvania, 1754.

In the peaceful precincts of St. Ann's is the tomb of Honorable Gouvernor Morris "Penman" of the Constitution of the United States, Washington's Minister to Paris during the French Revolution, with the distinction of being the only foreign diplomat at his post during the historical event.

*The following two references provide graphical descriptions of the early Bronx:

[1]   The Bronx In The Innocent Years, 1890-1925, Lloyd Ultan
       and Gary Hermalyn, The Bronx County Historical Society,
       1991.

[2]   The Beautiful Bronx, 1920-1950, Lloyd Ultan, written in
       collaboration with The Bronx Historical Society, Harmony
       Books, 1979.

Appendix K

Consortium of Endowed Episcopal Parishes,
Power Point Presentation [2006]

Source: Annual Conference 2006], Consortium of Endowed Episcopal Parishes at Alexandria, VA
Title: *Amazing Grace-Based Outreach: 'Modeling Shared Ministry'*
Authors: The Reverend Martha Overall, St. Ann's Episcopal Church
Liz Crawley, Jan Malcolm, Al Colella, St. John's Episcopal Church

WINDOW #1

AMAZING GRACE-BASED OUTREACH
"MODELING SHARED MINISTRY"

The Reverend Martha Overall: St. Ann's Church; Liz Crawley, Jan Malcom and Al Colella, St. John's Church

WINDOW #2

WORKSHOP GOALS

- **DESCRIBE GENESIS, DEVELOPMENT, IMPACT OF ST. ANN'S/ST. JOHN'S RELATIONSHIP**
- **PROVIDE A REALITY-BASED EXPERIENTIAL MINISTRY MODEL**
- **'LESSONS LEARNED' – PARISH APPLICATIONS**
- **PROVIDE A FORUM FOR INTERACTION**

WINDOW #3

WORKSHOP AGENDA

- *OUTREACH MODEL AT ST. JOHN'S*
- GENESIS OF ST. ANN'S/ST. JOHN'S COLLABORATION
- SOME KEY ACCOMPLISHMENTS
- 'GIVERS AND RECEIVERS'
- MOTHER MARTHA'S PERSPECTIVE
- BIRTH OF ADDITIONAL MINISTRIES
- SOME REALITIES OF OUTREACH
- CANDIDATE MINISTRY IDEAS & DEVELOPMENT
- POST-WORKSHOP AVAILABILITY & MEETINGS

WINDOW #4

OUTREACH MODEL AT ST. JOHN'S
FUNCTIONAL MODEL IS PROVIDED IN APPENDIX H

WINDOW #5

GENESIS OF ST. ANN'S/ST. JOHN'S COLLABORATION

- *AWARENESS OF INNER CITY SITUATION*
- *AWARENESS OF MOTHER MARTHA AT ST. ANN'S*
- *AWARENESS OF THE NEEDS AT ST. ANN'S*
- *CALL TO ACTION*
- 9/11 AND GROUND ZERO
- SUMMER CAMPERSHIPS IN RHODE ISLAND
- GROWTH, TEAM, PARISH INVOLVEMENT

WINDOW #6

SOME KEY ACCOMPLISHMENTS OVER THE YEARS

- SCHOOL SUPPLIES
- LIBRARY
- COMPUTER LABS
- MISSION TRIPS
- SUMMER CAMPERSHIPS
- SLEEPOVERS IN BARRINGTON, RHODE ISLAND
- CHRISTMAS CARDS
- COOKOUTS AT ST. ANN'S
- FREEZER & REFRIGERATOR STORY
- THE MIRACLE OF THE BACKPACKS
- LOADED VANS AND CARS
- FIELD TRIPS BEYOND THE SOUTH BRONX
- 'AMAZING' OR 'AMAZING GRACE'

WINDOW #7

'GIVERS BECOME RECEIVERS AND RECEIVERS BECOME GIVERS'

WINDOW #8

THE *KEY* ACCOMPLISHMENTS

- RAISE THE HOPES, VISIONS AND SELF-EXPECTATIONS OF THE CHILDREN
- RELATIONSHIPS
- OUTCOMES ACHIEVED
- *ENABLE/ENCOUREAGE/EMPOWER/GROWTH*

WINDOW #9

"IN HER OWN WORDS"
The Reverend Martha Overall
St. Ann's Episcopal Church, Bronx NY

Al Colella

WINDOW #10

BIRTH OF ADDITIONAL MINISTRIES

- "B.O.W.", BEYOND OUR WALLS
- ST. MATTHEW'S, BOGALUSA, LA
- GROWTH OF MINISTRY NETWORK
- COMMUNITY MINISTRIES

WINDOW #11

SOME REALITIES OF OUTREACH I

Before:
- SPIRITUAL FOUNDATION
- CHRIST'S LIFE IS A LIFE OF OUTREACH
- OUTREACH IS NOT AN OPTION
- LEADERSHIP + PASSION
- LINKAGE TO PARISH GOALS
- ECUMENICAL POTENTIAL & POSSIBILITIES

WINDOW # 12

SOME REALITIES OF OUTREACH II

During:
- GIFTS MODEL: NEEDS, ABILITIES AND PASSIONS
- NEEDS SPECTRUM: AKA 'THERE'S SOMETHING FOR EVERYONE
- IDENTIFY SPECIFIC NEEDS
- IDENTIFY REQUIRED RESOURCES
- THE PARISH AS THE OUTREACH TEAM
- BUILDING RELATIONSHIPS: INDIVIDUAL, FAMILY, TEAM, PARISH
- SITE VISITS; LIAISON
- MAINTAIN FOCUS UPON THE NEEDS
- MINISTRY ANNOUNCEMENTS. FORUMS, ARTICLES, POSTERS

322

WINDOW #13

SOME REALITIES OF OUTREACH III

After:

- FEEDBACK TO PARISHIONERS: RESULTS, 'THANK YOU'
- LESSONS LEARNED
- ADDITIONAL MINISTRIES
- UNEXPECTED BENEFITS, OUTCOMES
- SPIRITUAL GROWTH
- ADDS TO PARISH LIFE & FELLOWSHIP
- AS GIVERS, "YOU HAVE MADE A DIFFERENCE"
- AS RECEIVERS: MEANINGFULNESS WITHIN YOUR LIVES
- MAINTAIN MOMENTUM: LOOK TO THE FUTURE

WINDOW #14

CANDIDATE MINISTRY IDEAS & DEVELOPMENT

- 5 PERSON INTER/INTRA PARISH TEAMS
- IDENTIFY OUTREACH 'AREAS OF INTEREST'
- IDENTIFY & DESCRIBE A SPECIFIC NEED
- EMBRACE A 'CAN DO' MINDSET
- LEVERAGE EXPERIENCE AND 'LESSONS LEARNED'
- MOTHER MARTHA, LIZ, JAN AND AL WILL FACILITIATE POST-WORKSHOPS MEETINGS AND DISCUSSIONS
- OBSERVATION AND COMMENTARY ABOUT THE UTILITY AND VALUE OF THE OUTREACH MODEL

22783455R00182

Made in the USA
Lexington, KY
18 May 2013